GLOBALIZATION AND THE POSTCOLONIAL WORLD

Globalization and the Postcolonial World

The New Political Economy of Development

Ankie Hoogvelt

The Johns Hopkins University Press
Baltimore, Maryland

Printed in Hong Kong on paper suitable for recycling and made from fully managed and sustained forest resource.

06 05 04 03 02 01 00 99 98 97   5   4   3   2   1

The Johns Hopkins University Press
2715 North Charles Street
Baltimore, Maryland 21218-4319

Library of Congress Cataloging-in-Publication Data
Hoogvelt, Ankie M. M.
    Globalization and the postcolonial world : the new political economy of development / Ankie Hoogvelt.
        p.   cm.
    Includes bibliographical references and index.
    ISBN 0-8018-5644-2 (hc : alk. paper). — ISBN 0-8018-5645-0 (pbk. : alk. paper)
        1. Developing countries—Foreign economic relations.
    2. Developing countries—Dependency on foreign countries.
    3. International economic relations.   4. Capitalism—Developing countries.   5. Competition, International.   I. Title.
    HF1413.H66   1997
    337—dc21   96-49958
                                                                             CIP

A catalog record for this book is available from the British Library.

Contents

List of Figures and Tables

Figures

Tables

Preface

My intention when I embarked on writing this book was to provide an account and assessment of recent trends in world political economy and the development prospects of the Third World within it. It would serve as a successor volume to my 1982 book *The Third World in Global Development*. Changing realities, however, have proved a hard taskmaster. Development Studies no longer exists as a body of knowledge with a coherent identity, or even coherent identities, as in competing schools of theory or paradigms. It no longer has pretensions of being or becoming a full-blown academic discipline but rather is gradually being replaced by, or is merging into, other subjects. In the words of one of its pioneers, Dudley Seers, 'Development Studies is over the hill or downright dead'.[1]

The idea of a Third World never proved an entirely satisfactory analytical category for understanding the economic, social and political conditions of the countries of Africa, Latin America and Asia. For much of the period following the Second World War, however, it was a very useful way of summarising the common experiences and attitudes of the countries of these regions. The demise of the concept today has effectively mirrored the dissolution of the Third World itself, as some regions of the Third World have shamed the pundits of doom by becoming the dynamic growth centres of the world economy (East Asia), and others have declined to the point of extinction, snuffing out all belief in progress. As Wolfgang Sachs writes: 'The idea of development was once a towering monument inspiring international enthusiasm. Today, the structure is falling apart and in danger of total collapse'.[2]

In the early 1980s Development Studies became stranded in what was widely referred to as 'the Impasse'. Work in the field of development studies fragmented into a diverse range of intellectual pursuits without any sense of common direction or purpose. *First*, it fragmented into area studies, in which the success of the East Asian

x

'developmental' states offered a promising focus for theoretical renewal albeit rather more for the field of comparative political economy than for development studies itself. *Second*, there were meta-theoretical critiques of those theoretical constructs that had long constituted the toolbox of development theory. Dependency, exploitation, unequal exchange, mode of production, modernisation, rationalisation, progress – all these came under the deconstructing axe of postmodernists, post-marxists and post-structuralists alike. *Third*, much work on development issues became subsumed in the field of international political economy literature, focusing in particular on issues of debt, poverty and peripheralisation, perceived as the downside of a quickening process of globalisation of the world economy. *Fourth*, a strong surge of interest in gender relations provided a welcome relief from the tedium of class relations that had dominated much of the development agenda previously. *Fifth*, in engaging with Environmental Studies, some development literature came to focus on poverty in the poor world as even more damaging to 'our' ozone layer than the pursuit of wealth in the rich world.

This, certainly, is not an exhaustive list, but it serves to show how Development Studies has been scattered by the winds of change over a wide terrain of intellectual enquiry, making the task of synthesis *a priori* impossible. What then should be the purpose of writing a general introductory text on the subject? And if one did find such purpose, how would it help organise the sequencing of chapters in a manner that will ensure that at least some of the new agendas are incorporated in a coherent way?

It seems to me that a chief purpose should be to understand the processes of crisis and transformation of the world economy that constitute the winds of change that are now blowing development studies into different directions. Without such understanding we will lose sight of the *continuity in change* of the historical process. Today there are over 1.2 billion people in the world living in absolute poverty and misery, and their number is growing, increasingly enveloping those who previously formed part of the rich, First World, and of the semi-developed Second World.[3] Furthermore, the gap between the richest and poorest quinquile of the world's population is twice as big today than it was 30 years ago.[4] On the other hand, it is also the case that some countries, notably in East Asia, have grown, and are still growing, very fast indeed and that they have managed to translate that growth into improved standards of living for the masses of the population. However, the rising fortunes of new regions or groups of countries in the world economy, and the decline of others, should not blind us to the way that wealth and poverty are connected. I remain convinced that poverty and wealth-creation are but two sides of the same historical process, even if that historical process itself undergoes fundamental changes in the manner in which it is organised. But when the understanding and interpretation of wealth and poverty themselves become fragmented, divorced from one another as they are today, there is a danger that rather than working to eradicate poverty we shall end up, in true postmodern style, celebrating it as a form of 'difference'.

While there is continuity in the fact that wealth and poverty creation are connected, it is nevertheless one of the main organising themes of the book that at the present time we are experiencing a complete, radical break, a *qualitative* change, in the historical development of capitalism. The world economic crisis which began in the 1970s has led, not just to a restructuring of the world economy, but to a major transformation of the way in which production and distribution is organised. There is a new political economy in the making. But, in contrast to the past, this new political economy is not a political economy that first developed and became organised within one specific territorial space and next expanded outward; rather it is a new political economy that is global from the very beginning. This has consequences for our understanding of the locational distribution of wealth and poverty, of development and underdevelopment. The familiar pyramid of the core–periphery hierarchy is no longer a geographic but a social division of the world economy. The designation 'postcolonial' world in preference to 'Third World' serves to articulate at once the shift from national origin to subject-position in the global political economy and a movement beyond a specific period in history, that of colonialism and Third World nationalist struggles.

Outline of the Book

As the subtitle suggests, the book is about the *new political economy of development*. These very words beg at least two questions: one, that there is an understood and generally accepted meaning of the term 'political economy', and two, that there is an old version of it, now distinct from and discarded by different interpretations. As we shall see in the introduction to Part I, there is no such thing as a unified methodology or theory of political economy. What there is is a set of questions about the relationship between power and wealth, between politics and economics, between states and markets. Depending on how this relationship has been understood and conceptualised, different theories of world order have held sway for a considerable time, namely realism, institutionalism and Marxism/structuralism. Their common ground was the state/market interaction as the embodiment of politics and economics in the modern world. And a central question became how to grasp the conflicting logic of an evolving and progressively integrating world market, on the one hand, with the continuing compartmentalisation of the world political order into sovereign nation-states on the other.

Within the Marxist structuralist tradition the evolving international state/market nexus was analysed in terms of the *dialectical* development of capitalism in historical periods. Capitalism's inherent contradictions were said to be worked out in different phases of expansion, punctuated by crises, in which state and interstate relations were time and again rearranged as political structures that held in place the exploitative economic relationship between core and peripheral economies. In Chapters 1, 2 and 3, we look back on this tradition from the vantage-point of Robert Cox's critical theory of historical structures. Thus each phase of capitalist expansion is described in turn and we review the theories that emerged whether as hegemonic, legitimating, ideology or as counter-hegemonic critique, within each evolving phase. In this way the *historical specificity* of theories of imperialism, of modernisation and dependency, of post-imperialism and world system, and of the New International Division of Labour, will become clarified.

Part II begins, in Chapter 4, with a statistical portrait of the dialectical development of capitalism over the past two hundred years. We discover that world trade and capital flows, while at first expanding to embrace ever more areas of the world, gradually turned into a process of implosion when capital relations became intensified within the core while selectively withdrawing from the periphery. Meanwhile this process resulted in cumulatively growing differences in income between rich and poor nations.

The historically generated structure of deepening inequality provides the backdrop for our understanding of the present crisis and transformation debate to which we turn in subsequent chapters. By the 1970s, capitalism had reached the limits of its own expansion and this became the crucible of fundamental change. This change is becoming visible in an information-technology driven new political economy that characterises the production process and its global, though not world-wide, embrace. In Chapter 5 we discuss the changes in economic production and industrial organisation which are today widely referred to as flexible production. Using the theory and the research agenda of the Regulation School, we note that there is a new techno-economic paradigm that gives structural direction to the process of social transformation but which requires an appropriate mode of regulation before a new regime of accumulation can be achieved. I shall argue that the structural properties of the new techno-economic paradigm point towards a mode of regulation which is likely to be global from the outset.

Chapters 6 and 7 discuss the global aspects of the process of transformation. Pertinently, in contributing to a theory of globalisation, I privilege the *sociology* of globalisation over the *economics* of globalisation. I argue that the reconstitution of the world into a single social space today drives the economics of globalisation even though the preceding period of economic internationalisation has itself created the conditions for the emergence of this single social space. The contemporary process of globalisation signals a 'higher' level of intensifying economic, financial, cultural and social cross-border networks than before. It is accompanied by processes of disintegration, as old structures of political power and social and economic organisation are being eroded, and new ones are slowly being formed. Here is the locus of the current crisis and transformation experience. Ever larger segments of the world population, both inside the advanced countries, but more numerous still inside the Third World, are being expelled from the emerging 'thickening' network of human social and economic interaction. Rather than being an *expansive* process, the present process of globalisation appears to be an *imploding* or *shrinking* one.

Part III of the book addresses the implications of globalisation for the postcolonial world. The term postcolonial is a very recent arrival to development literature. It is a term of complex origins which we shall explore in the introduction to the final part of the book. For now, it suffices to note that the concept has merits simply because it groups together all formerly colonial societies despite differences in their relation to the global capitalist system, while at the same time offering a point of entry for the study of those differences. This point of entry is the 'aftermath' of the colonial relation and the manner in which this becomes reconstituted *and* contested in the process of the present transformation of the global political economy. Thus we may study the postcolonial condition as a state of being that is the combined outcome of external pressures (globalisation, the post-cold war order, and so forth) and locally and historically specific characteristics and struggles arising out of the (neo)colonial relation.

I consider four types of postcolonial 'conditions' or 'situations' or 'social formations', each exemplified in one of four regions of the world, though not necessarily exclusive to it. Neither are these four exhaustive of all social formations in the postcolonial world. There are plenty of postcolonial conditions which we do not discuss in this book, for example India, China and South Africa. We shall examine in turn the following regions and conditions: Sub-Saharan Africa – exclusion and anarchy (Chapter 8); the Middle East – Islamic revolt and anti-developmentalism (Chapter 9); East Asia – State-led developmentalism and regionalisation (Chapter 10); and Latin America – Democracy, civil society and postdevelopment (Chapter 11).

To write about so many different parts of the world is an audacious undertaking. It would not have come to pass had it not been for the inspiration and help, direct and indirect, that has been given to me by my research and graduate students who after all are a pretty international bunch. They have taught me many things I didn't know and brought to my attention literatures that I had never read. Where appropriate I have referred to their theses in the normal way through references in the text. Any errors or flaws however are all mine. Here I want to thank them, Masae Yuasa, Rongyan Qi, Lucy Walker, Gillian Koh, Rachel Tibbett, Dong Sook Gills, Fithri Othman, Anne Holgate Lowe, Mark Christian and many others, for pushing me all the time to keep up with them. In so doing they have turned teaching into a real learning experience and a delightful vocation!

It astonishes me that in these times of intensified workloads, and ever more oppressive working conditions in universities, one can still find colleagues willing to sit down and wholly selflessly go through some half-baked manuscript, make meticulous comments and constructive criticisms and tune their minds to somebody else's intellectual problems. I am deeply grateful to my colleagues Tony Payne, Lena Dominelli, Dave Phillips and Nick Stevenson, who each have gone through all or various bits of earlier drafts and made helpful comments and encouraging suggestions as I went along. Naturally they are relieved of any responsibility for the contents, even though without them I might not have completed the task.

If I mention her last it is not because of her contribution being least, but because hers happened to come at the very end of all the other work: scrubbing the text clean and making it presentable to the publisher. Marg Walker has given the manuscript the precision and care that it was in danger of losing when I hurried towards the deadline. I thank her for her support and patience.

ANKIE HOOGVELT

PART I
HISTORICAL STRUCTURES

Introduction

The term 'political economy' has a long history. It was first coined by a French writer, Montchrétien de Watteville, in 1615, when he used it to describe 'the science of wealth acquisition common to the State as well as the Family'.[1]

Writing in the early period of the great transition from small primordial communities to national social formations, de Watteville's invention of the concept proved to be an expression of extraordinary vision. For it not only presaged the emergence of economics as a scientific discipline in the nineteenth century, but it also reflected this discipline's enduring preoccupation with *national territorial* accumulation.

By 'national territorial accumulation' we understand a process of continuous self-expansion of capital within the territorial boundedness of the nation-state. Another expression for it would be 'economic growth of the nation'. But economic growth of a nation may conceivably be achieved (at least temporarily) through a sudden growth of income, say, from natural resources like oil, or rent income, or from financial investments in other parts of the world and so on. 'National accumulation' is a term preferred by Marxists which tries to encapsulate the growth of productive capacity and technological advance within a national territorial context. 'National economic development' is the nearest non-Marxist synonym.

Strangely enough in the mercantilist period in which de Watteville was writing and which lasted until Adam Smith's formal establishment of political economy in the nineteenth century, the term 'political economy' was not much used. Mercantilism, however, was a system of political economy *par excellence*.

Mercantilism is best described as the striving after political power through economic means. In the seventeenth and eighteenth centuries the emergence of strong national states, each competing with the other, formed the backdrop of mercantilist policies designed to foster economic growth and so raise revenue – if necessary for the waging of war. The economy was put to the service of the polity. In

3

the circumstances of the time, it meant the encouragement of trade and manufacture, the pursuit of protectionist policies, and the stimulation of export trade rather than the improvement of land. International trade was seen to be a zero-sum game. The mercantilists thought of wealth in competitive terms, as something taken by one nation from another, an inherently differential gain like winning a race. The words of Thomas Mun, writing in 1664, summed up the attitude towards foreign trade: 'The ordinary means therefore to encrease our wealth and treasure is by Forraign Trade, wherein wee must observe this rule; to sell more to strangers yearly than we consume of theirs in value'.[2] By the same token a nation must try to produce at home, instead of buying abroad.

Many writers, particularly those standing in a Marxist tradition (the so-called 'world system' writers – for example Immanuel Wallerstein[3]), also believe that capitalism is a negative-sum game, and that the rise of some nations is always accompanied by the fall of others. But it is also a view that is today shared by some conservative, nationalist elements in those advanced countries like the USA who see power and economic wealth slipping away from their nation and passing into the hands of Japanese or European nations.

If for the seventeenth and eighteenth century mercantilist writers and policy-makers the economy was intended to serve the power and glory of the (nation) state, with the writing of Adam Smith in the nineteenth century this picture was entirely reversed. He wrote in *An Inquiry into the Nature and Causes of the Wealth of Nations* (1776):

> Political economy, considered as a branch of the science of a statesman or legislator, proposes two distinct objects: first, to provide a plentiful revenue or subsistence for the people . . . and secondly, to supply the state . . . with a revenue sufficient for the public services.[4]

For Adam Smith the 'wealth' of a nation was different from that which it had been for the mercantilists. For Smith wealth consisted of real goods and services (not just the ability to maintain a large army), and a nation was rich or poor according to its annual production *in proportion to its population*. It is interesting that the world community has maintained this definition of wealth up to this day. This is evidenced in the universal use of the term gross domestic product (GDP) *per capita*. Also, for Smith, the nation was coextensive with all its people, not just the upper classes or the body politic as had been the case with the mercantilists. The actors in the drama of political economy were households and firms.

But the biggest difference, the great watershed between mercantilist and Smith's and subsequent (classical) economist thought, lay in that the mercantilists concentrated on the *transfer of wealth* from the nation to the rulers to enable them to wage war with the nation's enemies. In contrast Smith, and classical economists after him, concentrated on the *production* of wealth. In Adam Smith's work, economics became the science of statecraft. It was the task of the policy-makers and legislators to ensure the optimum conditions for production. But this was also the very point where Adam Smith became the founder of *liberal economics*, the view namely which preferred markets to politics and which emphasised the invisible hand of the market as the best regulator of the economy. In a politically uncontrolled economy, Smith argued, the efforts of each to better himself would lead to that distribution of capital, labour, and land which maximised their respective returns by maximising the value of the output to the public. In a celebrated phrase Smith said 'Each intends only his own gain', but in the end 'promotes that of society' although this 'was no part of his intention'.[5]

The subsequent development of liberal economics or, as it increasingly came to be known, neo-classical economics, as the study of production, distribution and consumption of wealth, was marked by an ever stronger emphasis on its *scientific* character, almost as if economic processes were taking place independent of human will. This led to some ambiguity and confusion over the continued prefix 'political' in the words 'political economy'. Neo-classical economists, unsurprisingly, preferred to drop the prefix 'political' altogether. Consequently, nowadays, when we look up the definition of political economy in a dictionary we often find a simple statement saying that it is economics as it *used* to be called in the days of the classical economists. When writers within this liberal tradition still sometimes use the words political economy, it is to indicate a much more narrow field of enquiry, namely the study of economic policy and the linkages between economic and political factors in public policy.

Karl Marx, and Marxist tradition ever since, have used the term 'political economy' in an altogether different sense. After all, Karl Marx wrote a *critique* of political economy. While he accepted much of Smith's and Ricardo's basic premises, in particular that labour is the source of all value, he questioned the alleged positive aspects of the functioning of capitalism (or the free market economy). He used historical materialism to demonstrate the historicity of capitalism. Marx developed a theory of class struggle and he wanted to demonstrate that the individual pursuit of self-interest leads *not* to enhanced public/collective good, but to recurring crises and the eventual breakdown of capitalism.

What is important for our purposes is that Marx's generic concept of political economy was more general and *not* coincidental with the nation-state. Marx referred to the way social relations and power relations (which is another way of saying class relations) affect and organise the economy and, in turn, are organised by it. For Marx, in the historical evolution of human society these social or class relations have not always been contained within the boundaries of the nation-state. When a chief in a primitive society can command respect and tribute from the people (including a substantial amount of their production), then that is political economy for Marx. Or when a feudal lord has domain over land which means his tenant farmers have to pay him ground rent to use the land, then that is political economy too. In capitalist societies, the fact that an entrepreneur can hire free labour and make a profit out of the difference between what he pays his workers in wages and that which the products fetch in the market, that too is political economy. Marx tried to show that there have been different political economies which he called *modes of production* in different historical periods, and that the political economy that Smith and Ricardo were writing about was just one of a sequence of five historical modes of production (primitive – slave – feudal – capitalist – communist).[6] The Marxist study of political economy involves a study of the *historical* laws of motion that govern the evolution of this sequence of modes of production and, at the time of Marx's writing, more in particular from capitalist to communist.

International Political Economy

These three different conceptualisations or models of political economy came to undergird the different perspectives on what the study of international political economy is all about, namely:

1. Realism;
2. Institutionalism/pluralism; and
3. Structuralism.

But whatever the perspective on the relationship between politics and economics, it was shaped and cast in cement by the historical experience of the nation-state. Statism came to prevail in international theory, even in the Marxist structuralist perspective. International society was generally conceived of as a society of states. The dominant motif of all three theories of international political economy became the need to explain the paradox between an economy that was clearly internationalising amidst a world political system that was continuing to be compartmentalised into separate nation-states.[7] And thus they elaborated their existing conceptual schemata to cover this historical contingency rather than to start afresh and invent new models.

Realism

The realist position is inspired by a mercantilist conception of political economy. It gives primacy to the body politic, conceives of the nation-state as actor, and imagines the world as a competition of units (nation-states) in an anarchic international arena dominated by the struggle for power among states.[8] In analogy with what Hobbes had to say about 'man eats man' (*homo homini lupus*), so the realist sees the world as a jungle of nation-states all out to further their own interests. The realist perspective focuses on interstate competition, and on the use of *power* by nations in interfering in international markets on behalf of their own states. Based on their analysis of continual interstate competition, the realist comes up with a normative theory of international *order and stability* rooted in conceptions of *hegemony* and *balance of power* (for example American postwar hegemony; and the balance of power between the US-dominated and the USSR-dominated blocs).

Institutionalism or Pluralism

The second position is that of the pluralist or institutionalist perspective. This perspective is more in tune with Adam Smith's classical liberal economics. It recognises the increasing economic interdependence between states, and sees this as grounded in what is regarded as the all-round growth-maximising and beneficial operations of the now world-wide free market system. It argues that increasing economic interdependence forces states to develop and pursue policies of rational self-interest which lead to greater economic cooperation between them rather than to conflict. Cooperation becomes necessary and institutionalised in intergovernmental regimes of governance and coordination. Thus, for example, the institutionalists argue that the postwar stable world-order owed not so much to American hegemony and a balance of power between the USA and USSR, but rather to development of viable international institutions, such as United Nations organisations, international treaties, regional blocs and so on. The perspective is sometimes referred to as 'pluralist' because it believes that cooperation can take place without the supremacy of any one nation, but rather on the basis of a plurality of coordinated and interlocking interests between nations: a plural world order. The international political economy is seen to consist of the emergence, at an accelerating pace, of international institutions for the management of the internationalised economy.[9]

Structuralism

A third perspective on international political economy is the structuralist perspective. This derives from a Marxist notion of political economy as described above. Structuralists basically apply the Marxist study of capitalist political economy to international relations. That is to say, the study of the relations between states is derived from, and subsidiary to, the concern with the development of capitalism on a global scale. It is argued that capitalism is a mode of production that has become trans-societal and which today spans practically all nations of the world. But although structuralists thus begin with a conception of the totality of the world system, they next look at states as constitutive units which have a structural relationship predetermined by the world capitalist economy. It is called 'structuralist' because it challenges the assumption that national societies constitute 'independent' units whose development can be understood without taking into account the *systemic* ways in which these societies are linked to one another in the context of an ever-expanding network of material (economic) exchanges. In the view of the structuralists, it is the deep logic of the capitalist mode of production itself which yields the nodal positions (for example of core, periphery and semi-periphery) within the global structure which nations occupy. These intersocietal and trans-societal networks of material exchanges are either termed *world-systems* as in Wallerstein's theory, or *global social formations* as in Amin's terminology,[10] or *global formations* as in Chase-Dunn's work.[11]

What is especially confusing about the three competing perspectives is that they may pair up, two against one, depending on the analytical question posed. For example, both realists and Marxists tend to regard the outcome of international economic relations as a redistributive, non-sum game. The gain of some nations is always at the expense of others. This contrasts with the liberals, who have a more optimistic view of the outcome of international economic relations: they see it as a positive-sum game in which eventually all participants will be better-off, even if the distribution of gains is not equal. On the other hand, liberals and Marxists in their turn line up together when it comes to giving primacy to the economy in shaping the body politic, in contrast to the realists who see the relationship the other way around. But when it comes to offering an explanation of social change, both realists and liberals have nothing to present: theirs is a theory of *stasis* and *equilibrium*, while here it is the Marxists who are alone in developing a theory of social change.[12]

This incompatibility of conceptual frameworks has led over time to sterile inter-paradigmatic debates, and eventually to a polarisation of the field of international relations into separate subfields. Neo-realists focused on strategic studies, American foreign policy and the cold war; neo-institutionalists looked at international organisations, multinational companies and the developing international economy; neo-Marxists on the core–periphery hierarchy in the world economy. However, in the 1970s a powerful wind of intellectual change began to blow across the fields of *all* social sciences and eventually swept across the study of international political economy too.

Postmodernist knowledge theory began to break the hold of progressivist thinking over liberal and Marxist traditions; it opened up the space for human agency in structuralist analyses and thus made them less deterministic, and at the same time it made scholars more self-aware about the relationship between truth and power, that is the rules of 'knowledge' that are never far from the social context in which they operate. The outcome was a critical social theory that proliferated as an 'agenda of dissent' in the field of international political economy.[13] Soon that agenda would yield the beginnings of new theoretical approaches. For example, in the trailblazing work of Robert Cox we find critical social theory applied to the problem of world order and historical transformation. Cox has managed to synthesize and transcend the neo-realist and neo-Marxist approaches, re-integrate the separate subfields of international economic relations and strategic studies, and overcome the structure/agency dichotomy. Indeed, for a growing number of scholars in the field Robert Cox has become the founding father of a *new* international political economy.[14]

The Critical Theory of Robert Cox: Historical Structure

Robert Cox's[15] main contribution lies in the development of a *methodology* for the study of historical change in international political economy. He begins by critiquing conventional international relations theory, neo-realism and neo-Marxism alike, (1) for being altogether too obsessed with the relations between *states*, (2) for failing to develop conceptual apparatuses that may account for the many trans-societal linkages that are growing up today, and (3) for not being critically aware of their own historical roots. He next grapples with two problems. One is that of world order: what is it and how can it be described? The second is that of historical change, by which he means transformative change in the organisation of human affairs. Put the two together and the problematic is: how do world orders change?

What is interesting about Cox's theory is that he answers this question by a process of reversal: the question of change has to be understood from the vantage point of comprehending what makes for stability. At this point Cox makes his most important contribution to the study of international political economy: he injects Gramsci's notion of hegemony into the study of world order. Antonio Gramsci[16] had originally developed the notion of hegemony as a 'fit' between power, ideas and institutions to explain the stability of capitalist class relations and *national* social order. Cox now uses Gramsci's concept of hegemony to explain a stable *world* order, rather than – as in conventional international relations theories – single state dominance or bipolar state balance of power or some such.

Cox deploys the concept of 'historical structure' to examine how and why the fit comes about, and why and how it comes apart. He defines a historical structure as 'a particular configuration between ideas, institutions and material forces'. It is no more than a framework of action which constitutes the context of habits, pressures, expectations and constraints within which actions take place, but which does not determine actions in any direct, mechanical way. 'Individuals may move with the pressures or resist and oppose them, but they cannot ignore them. To the extent that they do successfully resist a prevailing historical structure, they buttress their actions with an alternative, emerging configuration of forces: a rival structure.'[17] Thus, we notice that the concept of historical structure is far less deterministic than most Marxist accounts of history, and that it leaves open the possibility that history can develop in a variety of directions. The task of the critical social scientist is to uncover 'plausible' alternative futures, instead of remaining trapped in some transhistorical essentialism in which either the present is forever (as for example in Fukuyama's End of History scenario) or the future is a foregone conclusion, as in orthodox historical materialism.

On the question of what is the *source* of historical change, Cox argues that historical materialism unlike structural or (neo)Marxism does in fact have a lot to offer to a theory of historical change. He submits that it is the foremost source of 'critical theory' for two reasons: *firstly* because it focuses on the principle of the *dialectic* as a source of transformative changes between grand, epochal, systems of human socio-economic organisation (modes of production) – the principle of the dialectic refers to the search for contradictions in social life as the mainspring of social change. And, *second*, because it identifies changes in social forces shaped by production relations as a prime mover in these transformations. However, historical materialism has failed in three respects: *first*, in the lack of awareness of its own historical boundedness; *second*, in the pre-Gramscian conception of a unidirectional connection between economic structure on the one hand and institutions and ideas on the other; and *third*, in the altogether too abstract and deterministic presentation of an unfolding history in which the progressive transformation of modes of production through the dialectic is a foregone teleological conclusion. Instead, Cox recognises that ideas which have become institutionalised may hang on long after the material forces that gave rise to them have been transformed, and well after the hegemonic power that institutionalised and universalised them has demised, and while rivalling social forces, growing out of changed material conditions, struggle for ideological and institutional ascendancy.

Thus, in line with most other contemporary postmodernist, poststructuralist thinking, Cox wants to break with the determinism of historical theory. He sees history as open-ended, and he wants us to realize that not only human structures and action but also *theory itself is part of a historical structure*, and therefore constitutes part of the problematic that we are researching. This is the kernel of Cox's meta-theoretical concept of critical theory. 'Critical theory is conscious of its own relativity but through this consciousness can achieve a broader time perspective and become less relative. . .',[18] that is it is less bound at its historical origin. It knows that the task of theorising can never be finished in an enclosed system but must continually begin anew, beginning *not* with abstract conceptions but with a description of historical experience, ferreting out the emerging contradictions between changing material conditions and associated social forces on the one hand, and the vested interests or overhangs from past institutions and ideologies on the other.

Historical Structure and Stage Theory

I have introduced the reader to Cox's work not with the pretense of doing justice to the innovative richness of this leading theorist, but because I want to borrow his concept of 'historical structure' to look back over the history of the relations between rich and poor countries both materially, and in respect of how these relations were time and again institutionalised and theorised, and how they changed.

Writers standing in the structural Marxist tradition have tended to analyse the history of those relations in terms of a dialectical development of the capitalist world system in distinctive historical *stages*. Capitalism's inherent contradictions (the driving force of the dynamics of change) were thought to be worked out in different phases of expansion, punctuated by crises, in which state and interstate relations were time and again re-arranged as political structures that held in place a continuing exploitative economic relationship between 'core' and 'peripheral' areas. In each of the expansive phases of capitalism, the peripheral areas of the world were assigned a particular *function* at the service of the essential needs of accumulation at the centre, or core, of the system. Each phase of expansion, however, resulted in cumulative differences in productive capacity and income between core and periphery, leading to recurring crises of disequilibrium after which the relationship needed to be re-jigged.

Thus (and very sketchily), in historical succession, the periphery is said to have served: first (in the mercantile period) as a source of primitive accumulation, financing the industrial revolution in the core; next, in the colonial period, it served as supplier of raw materials and foodstuffs; and, subsequently, in the neo-colonial period, it graduated to become modernising developmental states, providing the export markets for late industrialism's producer goods.

In Chapters 1, 2 and 3, I describe the dialectic unfolding of the relations between core and periphery from within this stage-theoretical perspective. However, I propose that we borrow Cox's concept of 'historical structure' to distance ourselves from the determinism that is implied in this perspective. Thus, rather than viewing these stages as inevitable steps in some unfolding, progressive logic of capitalist history, let us theorise them as periods in which there was, each time, a 'fit' between material conditions, institutions and ideology including the reflections and 'theories' of the time. It was the 'fit' that created a momentary stability in the process of international capital accumulation (and which allows us to identify them as stages), until structural contradictions engendered by new developments in material production *or* by rivalling ideologies forced a process of crisis and change. When material, institutional and ideological elements once more fell into place, there came about a next phase of relatively stable international capital accumulation.

1

The History of Capitalist Expansion

There is considerable agreement among economic historians that capitalism as a mode of organising social and economic life not only began in one miniscule little corner of the globe, namely north-west Europe, but from its very beginnings, while it was itself still in the process of being formed in the fifteenth and sixteenth centuries, involved outward expansion gradually encompassing ever-larger areas of the globe in a network of material exchanges. This network of material exchanges over time developed into a world market for goods and services, or an international division of labour. By the end of the nineteenth century the project of a single capitalist world economy had been completed in the sense that the grid of exchange relationships now covered practically all geographical areas of the world.

The nineteenth century in particular stands out as the prime time of the development of an international division of labour. It is estimated that in each of the decades of that century world trade grew about 11 times faster than world production, and that by 1913, on the eve of the First World War, some 33 per cent of world production was trading across national frontiers.[1] What is even more significant for the theme of this book is the fact that in those days the geographical areas of the world, since designated as the Third World, namely South America, Africa and Asia excluding Japan, participated fully, if not on equal terms, in this international market. In 1913 the Third World captured about 50 per cent of world trade compared with about 22 per cent today.[2]

Following Immanuel Wallerstein,[3] we call this international division of labour a *capitalist* world economy because its defining
criterion was: production of goods and services for sale in a market
in which the object is to realise the maximum profit. In a capitalist
market it is the seemingly neutral forces of supply and demand that
determine the price of a product and thereby signal to the producers
whether they should expand production, cut back on output, or
change production techniques and cut their cost structure and so on.
In other words, through the medium of Adam Smith's celebrated
invisible hand, which already by the end of the nineteenth century
had become a *global* invisible hand, human activities were pretty
well coordinated across national frontiers.

The Political Nature of the Capitalist World Economy

There should be no illusion that this coordination came about
spontaneously or peacefully, or that it dealt a fair hand to all the
players. Indeed the merit and lasting achievement of the Marxist
tradition has been to show that at all times, and at all levels, the
'invisible' hand was guided and steered by politics and power, and
that it always, and indeed cumulatively so, ended up in concentration of wealth and prosperity for some people in some places, while
causing abject misery, poverty and appalling subjugation for a
majority of people in most other places.

Marx's great theoretical contribution was to show how the formal
equality of the market could produce socially structured inequality.
Wallerstein adds to this the insight that commodity production
regularly takes place in an arena that is importantly structured by
power relations between states. Within the historically developing
international division of labour, it was the first capitalist developers,
the 'core' states, who gained the historical upper hand, and thus
were able to protect and assist, with gunboat diplomacy and other
forms of political coercion, their own capitalists in imposing world
market relations and shaping these to their advantage. Wallerstein
has shown how the interstate system is in fact the political system of
the world capitalist economy, and how the core–periphery hierarchy
and the exploitation of the periphery by the core are in fact
necessary to the reproduction of capitalism as a system.[4]

The Dialectical Development of Capitalism as a World System

What concerns us next is how this relationship has unfolded in a *dialectical* manner. What do we mean by dialectics? Simply put, it is the study of systemic *contradictions*. An analysis which follows the dialectical method searches for inherent tendencies within a system which create and bring forth their own conflicts until such a system can no longer maintain and reproduce itself without far-reaching structural adjustments. In the case of the capitalist mode of production, or socio-economic system, the question of adjustment or transformation has occupied an immense space in Marxist literature, to which we shall refer at a later stage in this book. For practical purposes it is sufficient to note at this point that so far the world capitalist system has shown amazing resilience in adapting to changing circumstances brought on by its very own laws of motion. We shall concentrate first on how it has managed to do this so far.

A Periodisation of Capitalist Development and Expansion

A number of writers who focus on the world-system have proposed a *periodisation* of capitalist development in which both the characteristics of core capital *and* its relationship to the peripheral areas vary. These variations themselves are seen as a dialectical outcome of the contradictions engendered in each (previous) period of interaction. Neo-Marxist writers, such as Samir Amin,[5] Andre Gunder Frank,[6] Ernest Mandel,[7] Albert Szymanski[8] and Harry Magdoff,[9] commonly identify a mercantilist pre-competitive stage (1500–1800), a competitive capitalist stage (1800–80), a monopoly/imperialist stage (1880–1960), and some even a late monopoly capitalist/imperialist stage (beginning with the crisis of 1968).[10]

In each of the periods, the periphery performs specific functions at the service of the essential needs of accumulation at the centre. But these essential needs change precisely as a result of the successful outcome of the service. And because the dialectical interaction between core and periphery yields increasingly disparate levels of developments in core and periphery within each period, the core and periphery, as it were, drift further apart, each time leading to a point of crisis in the relationship which is then overcome by altering its formal structure, and the method of surplus extraction by the core from the periphery.

In this, and in the next two chapters, I shall distinguish four periods (very roughly and ignoring wide geographical variations) as follows:

- 1500–1800 mercantile phase; transfer of economic surplus through looting and plundering, disguised as trade;
- 1800–1950 colonial period; transfer of economic surplus through 'unequal terms of trade' by virtue of a colonially-imposed international division of labour;
- 1950–70 neo-colonial period; transfer of economic surplus through 'developmentalism' and technological rents;
- 1970– post-imperialism; transfer of economic surplus through debt peonage.

The Mercantile Phase of European Expansion

During the mercantile phase of European expansion, from about 1500 to 1800, European merchants scoured the coasts of Africa and Asia, and the lands of South America in search of gold, spices, slaves and the conquest of existing trade routes. Paul Baran, in his famous work *The Political Economy of Growth*,[11] has drawn attention to the way this trading relationship was no more than a disguised form of looting and plundering, in which the Europeans were able to transfer the *economic surplus* of pre-industrial overseas communities back to Europe where it helped pay for the industrial revolution. Economic surplus is investible surplus: it is that part of production that is not consumed by a community but is piled up in hoarded wealth. But this form of development was a two-way street: at the same time that the overseas lands were indirectly helping to pay for Europe's technological and industrial advance, the loss of their economic surplus removed the opportunity for economic advancement in the territories where the West traded, and so arrested their further internal development. Not only was their internal development halted, their confrontation with the West actually had a *regressive* effect on the level of societal evolution which they had already reached, as for instance Walter Rodney has detailed in his book *How Europe Underdeveloped Africa*.[12]

The resulting disparity of societal advance – economic, political and social – at some stage turned into a bottleneck for the further advance of the West.[13] After 1800, Europe had decisively embarked upon a path of mass industrialisation and it was looking for market outlets, as well as secure supplies of raw materials and foodstuffs, on a scale and requiring a degree of predictability and regularity that simply defied the arbitrary looting and plunder of the mercantile arrangement. As Magdoff comments, 'But there was a limit to the profitability of the first wave of expansion: the wealth obtained by plunder of hoards amassed over years can only be taken once.'[14] After 1875, outright territorial annexation was moreover frequently forced upon reluctant European statesmen and public opinion by the ever more frantic rivalry between the European nations.

The Colonial Phase of European Expansion

Direct political control and administration of the overseas territories was often a convenient method for organising the production systems and laying the infrastructure in the ancillary economies at that time. Between 1800 and 1878, actual European rule including former colonies in North and South America increased from 35 to 67 per cent of the earth's land surface; another 18 per cent was added in the new wave of annexations between 1875 and 1914.[15]

The period of formal colonialism, especially between 1875 and 1914, witnessed an extraordinary and globe-girding internationalisation of capital. A handful of countries in Europe together with the US were responsible for 85 per cent of all international lending, totalling, by 1913, 44 billion dollars.[16] About one-half of this international lending went to the continents of Asia, Africa and South America. There it found its way into the building of railways, port installations, mines and factories. Capital accumulation and savings in the core of the world system was channelled to the periphery through the financial intermediation of international portfolio lending and, to a lesser extent, direct investments by emerging multinational companies. In the periphery it converted into fixed investments laying the foundations for future wealth creation.

In a glowing tribute to the Victorian attitudes towards capitalist expansion, Alex Cairncross has described the monumental quality of the effort involved:

The forty or fifty years before 1914 were clearly an exceptional period in economic history. It was symptomatic of the period that western Europe had invested abroad almost as much as the entire national wealth of Great Britain, the leading industrial country, and a good deal more than the value of the capital physically located in Great Britain. It was also symptomatic that Britain herself had invested abroad as much as her entire industrial and commercial capital, excluding land, and that one-tenth of her national income came to her as interest on foreign investments. These conditions can hardly recur.[17]

It was thus in this period that the periphery was brought into an *expanding* and intensifying network of economic exchanges with the core. It was incorporated in a vigorous geographical extension of capitalism that was quite the opposite of the 'imploding globalisation' that we are witnessing today and from which most of the areas of the Third World are excluded.

In contrast to more recent historical narratives, which as we shall see below tend to play down the commercial interests involved, the colonial period itself did not lack advocates and crusaders who robustly identified the economic need for colonies and who legitimised this need to the public back home with the promise of jobs and trade, as well as with noble sentiments of civilisation and universal progress.

Not only was the need for such colonies argued in economic terms, it was indeed often expressed as a vital national interest. This was especially so after 1875 when national rivalries between European states reached a frantic crescendo in the 'scramble for Africa'. As Thornton has argued, the ideology of imperialism involved a legitimate attitude towards the world that was shaped by nationalistic and patriotic sentiments. For example, Chamberlain and his school drew attention to the vulnerability of an England that did not command a world position. In their speeches and writings they argued that half the population of Britain would starve if England was ever reduced to Little England, if ever the British Empire narrowed down to a 'mere' United Kingdom dimension.[18]

Colonialism was seen by many not only as a form of survival but as the sole policy of survival. Cecil Rhodes argued the same point in even stronger terms. Great Britain's world position depended, he said, upon her trade, and if her people did not take over and open up those areas of the world that were at present in the grip of barbarism, they would be shut off from the world's trade, since other nations would do the job for them. 'I would annexe the planets if I could', he exclaimed.[19]

The policy of territorial annexations was thus justified and defended to the taxpayers at home because it would create trade and jobs at home and make the nation big and strong in the rivalry with other nations.

In this conception of imperialism as economic necessity, colonies were regarded as national property, as estates that must be developed using the most up-to-date methods. This brought with it a missionary zeal to civilise the colonised people and to bring their culture, their way of life, into the twentieth century so that they would be able to participate in modern commerce and industry. Thus, civilisation and commercialisation went hand in hand and were generally seen as positive benefits for the colonised peoples. This indeed was the 'White Man's Burden', in Rudyard Kipling's celebrated phrase. As Benjamin Kidd, an English sociologist at the turn of the century, wrote:

> The task of governing from a distance the inferior races of mankind will be one of great difficulty. One that will tax every resource of intellect and character. But it is one that must be faced and overcome if the civilised world is not to abandon all hope of its continuing economic conquest of the natural resources of the globe.[20]

The imperialists thus saw it as part of their mission to disseminate law, order, justice, education, peace and prosperity. Even Bernard Shaw could argue that if the Chinese were incapable of establishing conditions in their own country which would promote peaceful commerce and civilised life, it was the duty of the Europan powers to establish such conditions for them.[21]

Such a view of the territorial conquest of the colonial period owes more to the notion that political rivalry, or economic and social inadequacy in the *periphery*, stimulated the drive to colonial annexation rather than any 'necessary' causative link with the development of monopoly capital in the *core* countries.[22] The latter was the stubborn view of the classical Marxist theories of imperialism as developed by Lenin, Bukharin and Hilferding.[23] However, a proper analysis of the dialectically unfolding relationship between core and periphery of the developing world capitalist system will give equal credit to both sets of reasons. For, just as the periphery had *under*developed as a result of its mercantile relations with the core (requiring 'civilisation through commerce' in Bismarck's celebrated phrase), so the core of the capitalist system had itself developed to a higher stage of capitalist development in which the conditions for further accumulation of capital called for a dramatic change of production relations, whether between capital and labour at home (this was the preferred solution of the social reformers in the core economies) or in a new wave and pattern of imperialist expansion abroad. The inevitability of this expansion was the key point of the Marxist critics of capitalist imperialism.

Marxist Theories of Capitalist Imperialism

The classical Marxist theories of imperialism began with an analysis of the workings of capitalism in the core countries. Interestingly, a first foundation of these theories was laid by a liberal, J. A. Hobson, in 1905.[24] While his analysis may be said to have been Marxist, since he used the dialectic method of tracing the contradictions of contemporary capitalism, his solution and policy prescription were liberal and reformist. Hobson wanted to end imperialism by changing production relations at home.

Hobson argued that capitalist societies tend to save money and to invest these savings as capital in order to produce more goods in the future. Accumulation of capital is crucial if society is to progress, because otherwise production will be static. Also it is the drive behind the capitalist entrepreneur's profit motivation, because only if he invests his profits in more and better equipment can he save on the costs of production and thereby successfully compete with his rivals. But capital accumulation ultimately depends on the general level of profits remaining above the point at which capitalists would prefer to consume their savings rather than to invest them. This then leads to the vital question whether profit rates in capitalist societies will tend to rise or decline over a period of time.

It is in the answer to this question that we find the roots of theories of capitalist imperialism, as developed by Hobson and also by many Marxist writers. They believed that the normal tendency of the rate of profit in industrialised countries is to decline over a long period. The *rate* of profit is thought to decline because the very process of capital accumulation itself increases the amount of fixed capital per worker and increases productivity. The result is the tendency of the system of accumulation to produce ever more goods with fewer income-earning workers, leading to periodic crises of *over-production* and *under-consumption*.

Hobson concentrated exclusively on the over-production and under-consumptionist aspect of the tendency of the rate of profit to decline. For Hobson, the link between under-consumption at home and imperialism was that capitalist entrepreneurs would, in consequence, find fewer outlets for their capital at home and instead would channel it into overseas investments. For Hobson, imperialism did *not* serve the nation of small producers and workers and taxpayers, in the way liberal apologists of imperialism often argued. It merely served the interests of a small ruling class, the financiers, who would usurp the taxpayers' money into overseas investments, as well as into the provision of ships, guns, military equipment, railways and so on.

In this way, Hobson turned the arguments of the liberal apologists of imperialism completely on their heads. According to Hobson, investments in weak and backward countries required political control as an insurance, and the financiers and cliques of stockbrokers in the city knew how to lobby politicians into backing them. Hobson attributed the exodus of capital to *lack of investment at home* and his remedy therefore was to improve living standards at home. In other words: *social reform*. This remained the favourite prescription of liberals for decades to come. But the impossibility of social reform under capitalism became one of the leading tenets of Marxist theories of imperialism.

Marxist writers did not disagree with Hobson's position. However, they saw it as a kind of minimum statement, not the whole story, and they decried the conclusions as 'reformist': as if capitalism would allow itself to be reformed and mend its ways!

Classical Marxist theorists of imperialism, such as Lenin, Hilferding and Bukharin, instead argued a 'necessity of imperialism' thesis.[25] In positing this thesis, these authors took their clues from Marx's own writings on the laws of motion of capitalism, even though Marx himself contributed very little to a proper theory of imperialism. These laws of motion predicted the centralisation and concentration of capital arising out of the contradictions of competitive capitalism, and leading to a stage of *monopoly capitalism*. When they were writing in the early part of this century, it appeared to them that this condition of monopoly capitalism had fully arrived. Moreover, it had arrived under the compelling force of 'finance capital', which referred not to money or financial capital but to the 'merging of banking and industrial capital'. And thus, in their theory of imperialism, they came to describe the phenomenon as a necessary policy of this, the 'highest' stage of capitalism.

Classical Marxist writers were also influenced by the turbulent years of the second decade of this century in which two puzzlingly contrasting phenomena dominated the scene. On the one hand there was the intensifying *nationalist* rivalry between the capitalist countries which boiled over into the First World War, and on the other there was the phenomenal growth, not just of a world market for commodities freely exchanged across borders, but of the *internationalisation of production* itself when giant firms from metropolitan countries began to vertically integrate mine-to-market production chains across the globe, when international trusts and cartels appeared to set world market prices and allocate spheres of investments and distribution outlets, and when shares began to be traded across frontiers and international loans became the order of the day. As Bukharin pointed out, all these were examples of an international organisation of the world economy which attested to a 'thickening' network of global economic and social relations supplanting the anarchy of the world market.[26]

This puzzling paradox of nationalism and internationalisation was explained with reference to Marx's theory of the laws of motion of capitalism. For Lenin, Hilferding and Bukharin, the monopoly stage of capitalism is definitive of imperialism. It was, in their view, imperialism that staved off the collapse of capitalism. How did that stage come about?

Marx had already referred to two laws of motion of capitalism whereby it would inevitably and unavoidably develop from the competitive stage to the monopoly stage. These two laws were those referring to the processes of concentration and centralisation. *Concentration* refers to the enlargement of an individual enterprise's capital out of its own accumulated profits, while *centralisation* refers to the process whereby, under competition, individual capitalist enterprises again and again lose their independence and are brought under the centralised control of one big firm. Centralisation refers, in other words, to cartelisation, mergers and take-overs. This process of concentration and centralisation goes hand in hand with the rise of what Hilferding called *finance-capital* (or bank capital transformed into and controlling industrial capital).

How does the interwovenness of industrial and financial capital, and their increasing concentration and centralisation, affect imperialism, that is the export of capital and the territorial annexation of colonies that accompanied it?

Hilferding argued that the problem with cartels was that being so powerful they lobbied their governments to go against the principles of free trade (characteristic of the previous, competitive epoch) and demanded *protective tariffs*: once they had the whole domestic market for themselves they wanted to keep it from intrusion by other cartels of other nations. Thus the competition between nations intensified. This, Hilferding was absolutely right about at the time. The hallmark of the inter-war period was protectionism and an increasingly souring trade relationship between nations.

Cartels, however, are also associated with an increase in the price of products: monopolistic prices are higher than would pertain under competitive conditions. The point then is reached, and this is crucial, where it no longer makes sense to produce more of the same product, or to produce the product at lower cost for the home market, because the market is controlled anyway, so why bother – the results would be to drive the monopoly price down. So what to do with the profits? Markets must be found abroad! But the opportunity for expansion abroad is limited. It is not possible to go into neighbouring advanced and cartelised countries because they have their own protective tariffs. So markets further afield must be sought, conquering overseas territories (colonies) and erecting tariffs around these too.

Both Hilferding and Lenin recognised the other reasons which Marxist critiques of capitalist imperialism have brought to bear on the explanation for capital exports, namely the need for secure supplies of raw materials and foodstuffs to feed into the smoke-stack industries of the centre capitalist countries. But their main emphasis was on monopolies, protection, tariffs and on the manner in which *protection hinders the export of goods while promoting the export of capital.*

And, thus, the principal feature that classical Marxist writers identified in imperialism is that it hinges on this very dangerous paradox: namely of internationalisation of capital on the one hand, and on the other of intensified nationalist struggles between advanced nations for the remaining bits of the globe, leading to for example 'the scramble for Africa', and eventually to imperialist wars.

Critiques of Marxist Theories of Imperialism

In the inter-war period, theories of 'capitalist' imperialism became widely influential. The word 'imperialism' became a term of abuse, and its causal link with the recurring crises of modern capitalism was sufficiently widely understood to make for a growing chorus for social reforms and redistribution which had become an electoral platform of social democratic movements in the core countries.

It is therefore somewhat paradoxical to find that in the *post*-war period which spelt the end of formal colonialism, the balance of scholarly opinion has swung the other way. There has of late been considerable soul-searching over the question why European influence converted into *formal* empire when it did; whether it was political and strategic factors that pushed otherwise (and by many accounts) unenthusiastic European statesmen and parliaments into territorial annexations, or whether it was economic factors that provided the causal connection.

As Kiernan[27] has reported, modern historical scholarship, with few exceptions, has come down on the side of 'politics' as the real villain. Sectional economic interests indeed might have been served on occasion by the imposition of direct political control, but rarely, so it is argued, did territorial conquest serve, or was it directly inspired by, vital national economic interests. More often than not the decision to occupy foreign lands came as an *ad hoc* response to local problems, such as when existing treaties or alliances with local fiefs were threatened either by indigenous rebellions or by European rivals.

Sometimes territories were captured not because of their economic value, but because they had strategic importance as gateways to other areas where economic or security interests *were* dominant (for example the Suez and Panama Canals). On other occasions there was a diplomatic use for colonies, such as when a threat to territories regarded by one power as a special interest could be made a bargaining point in negotiations over quite a different matter.[28] Finally political rivalry at home could tempt nations into colonial adventures to regain a sense of glory and grandeur or to give employment and experience to its soldiers.[29]

And not only had capitalism nothing to do with the historical accident that was imperialism, neither did it benefit from it! Economic historians have eagerly seized on the 'evidence': trade with the colonial dependencies was generally only a small fraction of all British and French foreign trade; noncolonial powers had the advantage of having easy access to markets of colonies of other states; direct investment in raw materials (mines and plantations) was only about 10 per cent of all foreign investment in the periphery, and the share of colonial raw materials in the raw material market as a whole was relatively slight. Terms of trade were not particularly favourable to Europe during the high tide of imperialism; non-imperialist states found little difficulty in attaining a high level of growth, foreign trade, and foreign investments, and so on.[30]

However, this is taking a petty-foggingly narrow view of the historical process, as if the profits from imperialism could be expected to be cashed in at the very same moment that the investments were made! It makes more sense to see the formal period as one of preparatory construction, of laying the foundations of future wealth creation and surplus extraction. Almost three-quarters of all British capital investments were in railways, canals, electricity and other social overheads, and together with the 'mere' 10 per cent that went into mines and plantations they would not reap their full harvest until after the end of formal empire.[31]

It is in the continuing structural connections, both physical, as for example in the measurement of the gauge of railways which determines future procurement of rail coaches, *and* in terms of production relations as in the continued metropolitan ownership and control of mineral production and exports of cash crops, *and* in the cultural and social nurturing of local élites, that we must see the 'economic' importance of the period of formal colonialism. Indeed, the importance of formal colonialism lay in the legacy of the international division of labour, of resource bondage and the westernisation of the peripheral élites.

As for the Marxist contention of the causal link between the overripeness of capitalism, capital exports and the new imperialism after 1875, here too the weight of academic opinion is fully against the recognition of any such link. The grave of the Marxist theory of imperialism has been dug jointly by liberals and those standing in the Marxist tradition themselves!

For example, Bill Warren in his powerful critique of Lenin[32] points out, as others had done before him (notably Schumpeter[33]), that the actual record of the export of capital in the period of 1880–1914, however formidable, does not tally with Lenin's descriptions of monopoly capital doing the exporting of capital, nor with the idea of main rivalling imperialist countries doing the exporting, nor indeed with the notion that capital exports went primarily to the colonies.

First, many of the chief participants in the great imperialist wars which were to break out after 1914, namely Russia, USA, Italy, Germany and Japan, contributed an insignificant proportion of capital exports (especially capital exports to the Third World) at least during the period that Lenin describes; *second*, the bulk, that is 60 per cent of capital exports from Britain, went to the New World, 40 per cent went to what is now called the Third World, but a much smaller proportion of this again went to the actual colonial territories; and, *third*, most damaging of all to Lenin's theory is that before 1914, 90 per cent of all investments were *portfolio investments* rather than direct investments. Says Bill Warren:

> the empirical evidence does not support the contention that monopolization was the causal link between the 'overripeness' of capitalism, capital exports and the new imperialism. The partition of the world among the imperialist powers had been largely completed before the end of the nineteenth century, by which time one-fifth of the land surface of the globe and one-tenth of the world's population were under the direct control of European powers. By 1900, some 90 per cent of Africa had been subjected to Europe and most of that part of Asia that was ever to be directly colonized. But as Lenin himself recognized, the domination of the major economies by industrial combinations took hold no earlier than the first decade of the twentieth century. Even this is too early for Britain which had by far the largest empire and exported the greatest volume of capital. Indeed, at the

end of the nineteenth century the greatest imperial powers, Britain and France, possessed the least and most recently concentrated industrial structures of all the major powers: both countries achieved their imperial status well before an oligopolistic and centralised industrial structure took root.[34]

If modern scholarship, including contemporary Marxist scholarship, denies any 'necessary' causative link between the logic of capitalist development and the period of formal colonialism, this is not to say that there was no *historical* connection between the two. Alain Lipietz resolves the difference rather neatly when he argues that we can remain faithful to a theory of the historical dialectic while abandoning the notion of any necessary unfolding of a capitalist logic in a *specific direction:*

In capitalism, there are general contradictions, and if imperialism can resolve them, even temporarily, then it is legitimate to say that imperialism developed by resolving the general contradictions to the benefit of specific national capitalism. Imperialism was not specifically created to resolve these contradictions, but it continued to exist; it developed because, in fact, it resolved them. It could disappear, be modified, or hold on by habit if other solutions were found to these contradictions, or if other contradictions developed. Only in that sense can it be said that things being what they are and history having its habits, that imperialism's function is to resolve these contradictions.[35]

In the next chapter we shall see how the formal phase of imperialism developed its own contradictions to which other solutions were found, not in any predetermined fashion, but rather as a contingent outcome of the historical process.

2

Neo-colonialism, Modernisation and Dependency

Neither independence nor neo-colonialism 'fell from the sky'. They did not just happen by chance, nor as the fruit of some new insight. Rather, they were the outcome of profound historical pressures and struggles. These pressures and struggles themselves, paradoxically, were engendered by the very success of colonialism as a hegemonic organisation of international production relations which had permitted vast accumulation of wealth and progress to occur in the nations of western Europe. It is the very success of this pattern of global accumulation that brought forth its own contradictions, pressures for change and adaptation which needed to be made if the continuity of global accumulation was to be safeguarded.

We may class these successess and the pressures that they created into three groups:

1. Pressures arising from the developing material capabilities at the level of the global economy;
2. Domestic political struggles relating to the organisation of production relations within the colonial countries; and
3. Geo-political conflicts, relating to the interstate system and world order.

Global Economic Pressures

The imposition of the international division of labour under formal colonialism had the indirect effect of laying the foundations for continued economic control and domination over colonial resources even in the absence of direct political overlordship and administration. Prime agricultural land had been passed into the possession of foreign plantation owners or had otherwise been directed towards the large-scale production of export crops. Long-term concessions for mineral exploration and exploitation had been granted and mines had been established as wholly-owned subsidiaries of metropolitan firms. Capitalist markets and market institutions had been set up, and the import/export trade was firmly in the hands of such metropolitan multi-commodity traders as Unilever, John Holt or the Compagnie Française de L'Afrique Occidentale, to name but a few.

In other words, once the most important productive sectors of the colonial countries had been 'slotted' into the system of world capitalism and its institutions, control over these economic resources could be relied upon to continue at 'arm's length' even without direct political suzerainty. The period of colonialism had prepared and firmed up those institutions necessary for the 'historical structure' of international capitalism in the neo-colonial period. The most important of these institutions was undoubtedly the sanctity of private property abroad, which a good deal of international law and much consensus on the part of the international community had learnt to protect. It permitted the emergence of neo-colonialism as the survival and continuation of the colonial system in spite of formal recognition of political independence in emerging countries. Instead they became 'the victims of an indirect and subtle form of domination by political, economic, social, military or technical forces. . .', as in the official declaration of the Third All-African People's Conference held in Cairo in 1961.[1] While neo-colonialism was recognized to have many political manifestations (for example puppet governments, foreign military bases, balkanisation) it was the continuing 'resource-bondage' which became the main plank both of Third World solidarity and Third World demands for global reforms in the 1950s and 1960s.

If economic resource bondage merely allowed and enabled the dissolution of the formal colonial form, there were other pressures created under colonialism which positively encouraged it. The internationally imposed division of labour had relegated the colonial areas to the status of producers and exporters of primary, unprocessed commodities, who traded these for the manufactured consumer goods from the metropolitan countries. The terms of the exchange were unfavourable to the primary producers. They were unfavourable both from a point of view of long-term price development, and from the point of view of wildly gyrating price fluctuations,[2] the reasons for which I shall discuss below in relation to dependency theory. The critical point to make here is that the 'unequal trade' charge became yet another constitutive element in the ideology of neo-colonialism, a rallying cry which united the Third World around a set of demands for global reforms, and which fed into a self-reliant developmentalist ideology in which import-substitutive industrialisation featured most prominently.

What may only be appreciated in hindsight is that those very pressures and those very aspirations of the newly-emerging nations were structurally in keeping with the level of development of the productive forces in the advanced countries, and that, therefore, both the process of de-colonisation and the ideologies of 'modernisation' and 'development' (which the colonially nurtured westernised élite sported with great enthusiasm), amounted to a historically necessary re-constitution of international relations of production.

Already in the 1950s, in the turbulent years of independence, the leading branches of industry in the metropolitan countries had shifted from the production of consumer goods to the production of producer goods. No longer did it make sense to see the colonial areas primarily as market outlets for consumer items such as textiles, matches and cigarettes. Instead they now needed to become upgraded to being market outlets for spinning and weaving tools, matchmaking machines and cigarette production lines. The springing up of many small independent national units adopting a 'development and modernisation ideology' feverishly wishing to catch up with the West and seeking western patent solutions to basic human needs, all dovetailed neatly with the level of industrialisation achieved by then in the metropolitan countries.

And thus, while colonial profits continued to be made in the resources sector, a new form of surplus extraction entered in the neo-colonial period and eventually became the dominant form, namely *technological rents*.[3] These are the super profits that monopolist sellers of machines and equipment goods and of 'patented' technology can harvest in the absence of competitive markets for their products. The technological backwardness of the modernising countries created this monopoly. They had to invite foreign direct investors, multinational companies, to help them produce locally what had previously been imported.

Domestic Tensions

A second set of contradictions heralding the decline of colonialism as a formal arrangement of international relations expressed itself at the political and social levels *inside* the colonial countries. The system of European colonial rule had involved selective co-option and careful nurturing of a class 'who may be interpreters between us and the millions whom we govern . . . a class of persons Indian in blood and colour but English in tastes, in opinions, in morals and intellect', as one Governor of India had put it none too delicately.[4] This class needed to be educated and ultimately it was being educated to rule. For it was not only taught to read and write in English, or French, or Dutch, but in the process it was also taught how to think in the best European critical traditions. Inevitably this class discovered the contradictions between that which the great European thinkers had had to say about those fundamentals of European society and culture: equality, liberty and brotherhood, and the hypocritical, oppressive, racist institutions of European colonialism under which they were made to suffer. They drew inspiration from western political writings on democracy, nationhood and socialism.

The awakening spirit of nationalism and independence created a momentary alliance between this western educated class, these 'evolués' as the French patronisingly called them, and the masses of peasants and urban poor from whom colonial society had so carefully separated them. The independence struggle even brought together the disparate ethnic groups which the colonial powers with their talent to 'divide and rule' had thus far managed to keep in a state of mutual animosity and suspicion. But this alliance proved temporary and fragile, for such was the pitfall of nationalist consciousness, in Frantz Fanon's famous description, that no sooner had the politics of take-over been exhausted than the national bourgeoisie lapsed into extreme political lethargy, motivated only by private greed and vanity.[5] With no historic mission to fulfil, the national bourgeoisie had nowhere to go and so didn't bother to try and take the people with them. As a class secure in the financial, political and military backing of its neo-colonial paymasters, the national bourgoisie turned its back on the people and became a 'comprador' bourgeoisie instead.

Geo-political Relations

Already in the period leading up to the Second World War, the economy of the US, a late starter compared with the western European economies, had caught up and had reached a level of industrial development comparable with, and overtaking that of, the first developers. It too had now reached a stage where the continued growth of its economy depended on foreign expansion, on overseas market outlets for manufactures, on access to raw materials re-sources, and on investment opportunities around the world.

While the US had already practically secured its dominance over Latin America since the promulgation of the Monroe doctrine of 1823, it was still frustrated by the continuing presence of British, French and Dutch colonialism elsewhere, in Asia and Africa. In respect of these territories, America championed the cause of a non-discriminating international economic system the so-called 'Open Door' policy, expressing hostility to great power spheres of influence and supporting the calls for self-determination and national sover-eignty of the colonially oppressed.

The Second World War was a watershed. There were winners and losers. There were some winners who lost all except the victory and there were some losers who eventually gained all except the victory. But there was really only one country which came out victorious in every respect, and that country was the US.

In exchange for sacrificing American lives in the cause of its European allies, the US demanded a price. That price was a new international economic order under US hegemony. Already in the early stages of the war, the American Council of Foreign Relations had drawn up a memorandum to this effect. The memorandum described the policy needs of the US in 'a world in which it proposes to hold unquestioned power'. It outlined the component parts of an integrated policy to achieve military and economic supremacy for the United States within the non-German world, including the western hemisphere. This US-led, non-German world was to be called the Grand Area. Decolonisation and the guaranteeing of markets and access to raw materials was an essential turnpike around which the plan revolved.[6]

Before the dust had settled on the Second World War, much of the Grand Area plan had been accomplished. The dying days of the war saw the coming together of all victorious nations in a remarkably swift agreement on the need to manage the world economy through effective international institutions and principles under the acknowledged leadership of the US (for example the Bretton Woods institutions of the International Monetary Fund (IMF) and the World Bank, 1944, and the General Agreement on Tariffs and Trade (GATT, 1947)). Barely a couple of years later, tight political and military alliances were woven around the 'free world' economy (NATO) while the cold war with the one group of nations not prepared to play ball within the Grand Area became the legitimising force behind the Truman Doctrine (1947) in which the US formally announced its intentions to act as a global policeman, 'defending free people anywhere in the world who were threatened by armed minorities or by outside pressures'.[7]

The Bretton Woods institutions, together with the Truman Doctrine, constituted the system of informal imperialism under the *Pax Americana* which was the hallmark of the neo-colonial period and which lasted until about 1970. But it was the very informality and indirectedness of the system that gave it an aura of invisibility and that made it so difficult for people to see through.

Of course, when indirect tactics of 'informal' imperialism failed, the US on many occasions resorted to direct and military intervention to secure a stable investment climate and keep the lifelines of resources and markets open to the 'free world'. Between 1945 and 1970, the US in fact intervened militarily in Greece, Korea, Lebanon, Dominican Republic, Grenada and, of course, Vietnam. It was further involved in the destabilisation of regimes in Turkey, Iran, Guatemala, Cambodia, South Korea, Lebanon, Laos, Cuba, Dominican Republic, El Salvador, Chile, Ghana, Zaire and Mali.

Since the dominant features of neo-colonialism – resource bondage, technological dependency and subjection to informal imperialism – were features commonly shared by the new nations of Africa and Asia, and by the 'semi-colonies' of Latin America, the neo-colonial period was also the period which fostered and defined the solidarity of all of the Third World in its political and ideological stance against the First World-dominated world order.

Modernisation Theory

In the same way that the colonial period had thrown up its own theories of imperialism, of the apologetic *and* of the critical variety, so too did the neo-colonial period encourage the development of a body of knowledge historically specific to its own time. On the one hand there were the 'modernisation theories' which uncritically accepted the structure of the relationships between rich and poor countries that had evolved during the preceding epochs of capitalist expansion. They wrote a kind of 'How to develop' manual for less-developed countries. On the other hand, there were the dependency theories which critiqued the modernisation theories and, by bringing the structure of unequal relationships between rich and poor countries back into the picture, demonstrated that modernisation theories served to mask the continuing imperialist nature of those relationships.

Modernisation theories were problem-solving and policy-oriented theories of social change and economic development. David Harrison[8] records how President Truman in his inaugural address of 1949 announced the Point Four Programme of Development Aid. It then became the policy of the US to aid the efforts of the peoples of economically underdeveloped areas to develop their resources and improve their living conditions. This policy was not put forward as altruism – it took place against the backdrop of the cold war and the political independence and liberation of less-developed countries from colonialism which the US favoured. There was an understanding on the part of policy-makers in the US of the need to keep the Third World out of communist hands.

Economic and technological aid was at first a means. But it was soon realised that the transplantation of capital and technology to the Third World would not bear fruit unless it was accompanied by wider and *consistent* social, cultural and political changes. Early theories of the modernisation school were often advanced by economists who had been hired by the US as practical advisers; people on aid missions. It was they who observed how cultural diffusion and the introduction of technology from the outside were frustrated by the negative role that traditional culture played in 'blocking' development. They were the first to call for 'comprehensive social and economic change'. These were continuing and recurring themes, as was the threat of Soviet influence, if development, that is, the American way of life, were to fail.[9]

It was not until the late 1950s that sociologists got involved in what became for their discipline an extremely profitable bandwagon. One of the very early sociological contributions was a collection of essays by F. Hoselitz in 1957.[10] Where the contributions of the economists had been piecemeal – not going beyond such observations as it not being possible to introduce an agricultural tractor into a community that has communal rights to land and knows no property rights, or that kinship obligations stood in the way of appointing people by merit and so on – the sociologists set about the task of developing a comprehensive all-encompassing theory of *all* the processes and structural changes required to transform non-industrial into industrial societies.

These modernisation theories were in turn embedded in abstract, formal theories of societal evolution. The circumstance that these models of societal evolution had themselves been scripted from the historical experience of the development of the West did not prevent them from becoming normative and prescriptive. For they turned the abstracted, generalised history of European development into necessary *logic*. The formal western models had described the interactive processes through which undeveloped societies of all periods were thought to become developed. They theorised the compatibility or 'correspondence' between certain advanced economic institutions (money, markets, occupational specialisation, profit maximisation) on the one hand, and certain 'modern' political, cultural and social forms on the other, thereby turning the latter into necessary prerequisites or 'logical requirements' for the former. For example, modernisation studies would examine the processes of secularisation consequent upon the introduction of cash crops into traditional peasant communities, or the effect of industrialisation on the nuclearisation of family systems, or the need for multi-party democracy to support the division of labour. When traditional institutions or values did not fit, they were considered 'dysfunctional' to the process of development and regarded as 'problems' which comprehensive socio-economic planning could be designed to correct. Progress became a matter of ordered social reform.[11]

By highlighting the complementarity between compatible institutions and values, modernisation theorists came, in practice if not always in intent, to advocate the convergence of less-developed societies to the western model. But they also helped to strengthen the illusion of independence and of the sovereignty of the national developmental state, since they were ensconced in a theoretical framework which accorded integrity to 'society' as a self-regulating 'social whole' within which social and political institutions, cultural values as well as economic organisations, were comprehended as constituent parts.

This was a key assumption with which dependency theory took issue. Rather than perceive societies as ever so many independent units, *their* unit of analysis was capitalism as a world system that spans across nations and places them at different positions according to their structural place in an historically developed international division of labour.

Dependency Theory

Although dependency theory, like modernisation theory, emerged in the postwar period, it had intellectual roots that stretched into the past. Classical theories of imperialism (Hilferding, Bukharin, Lenin, Luxemburg) had also addressed relations of domination and subjection between nations. But the classical Marxist theories of imperialism had in the main focused on the question of what it was about the capitalist system that drove it to extend itself beyond its own borders and to expand geographically in an ever-widening circumference. And precisely because classical theories of imperialism were really only interested in the *causes* of imperialism, they did not bother overmuch with the study of the *effects* of imperialism overseas. They generally took it for granted that export of capital was the same as export of capitalist relations of production, and that therefore capitalism overseas would everywhere work up the same social tensions and class conflicts (between bourgeoisie and proletariat) that the home variety was already doing at home.

One exception amongst classical Marxists was Leon Trotsky who had already, in the 1920s, formulated the unicity of the world system in his Law of Combined and Uneven Development.[12] Trotsky argued that, with the development of capitalism as a world system due to the internationalisation of capital, world history becomes a contradictory but concrete totality. In this totality countries develop at an uneven pace in relation to one another, and even inside the backward nations themselves advanced and primitive features of economy and society co-exist. This constitutes a unique historical situation which is ripe for socialist revolution. This more complex view of history enabled Trotsky to transcend the evolutionist conception of history as a succession of rigidly pre-determined stages which was the received Soviet interpretation of Marx's theory of history, just as it was the liberal western model of social evolution.

The original version of the dependency and underdevelopment theory as outlined first by Paul Baran[13] and next more popularly and grandly by Andre Gunder Frank,[14] T. dos Santos[15] and others, was akin to this Trotskyist line of thought. But the impetus for the postwar dependency perspective was the felt need to critique bourgeois modernisation theory. Dependency theory concentrated on locating the cause of backwardness of Third World countries (initially more especially Latin America), within the dynamic and contradictory growth of the world capitalist system. Underdevelopment as distinct from *un*development – it was claimed – is not due to some original state of affairs as modernisation theory had argued but rather the result of the same world historical process in which the now developed capitalist countries became developed. Thus, from the very beginning, the dependency approach has been a world system approach, explicitly rejecting the concept of the unified state as actor and the notion of the global system as a collection of nation-states.

The essence of the dependency theory is the contention that as a result of penetration by colonial capital a distorted structure of economy and society had been created in the colonial countries which would reproduce overall economic stagnation and extreme pauperisation of the masses for all time.

A distorted structure of economy implied two things:

1. The *subordination* of the economy to the structure of advanced capitalist countries. This had involved a re-organisation of the economy in such a way that it only produced primary goods for the industrial West, and the prevention (under colonialism) of local industrialisation. Moreover, the production structure was limited in scope and diversity. As late as 1970, about ten years after the last move to formal independence, a UN report

observed that at that time almost 90 per cent of the export earnings of the developing countries derived from primary products; that almost one-half of these countries earned more than 50 per cent of their export receipts from a single primary commodity; and that as many as three-quarters of them earned more than 60 per cent from three primary products.[16]

2. *External orientation* which meant an extreme dependency on overseas markets, both for capital and technology sourcing and for production outlets. External dependency was often exacerbated by extreme concentration of the dependency upon few rather than many metropolitan countries (in the main as a result of continuing linkages with the colonial mother country). There were a number of empirical indicators which were said to reflect such external concentration: trade partner concentration; aid donor concentration; export product specialisation and military trade partner concentration.[17]

By a distorted structure of society, dependency theorists also referred to two main features:

1. A *class alliance* between foreign capital and comprador (mercantile and landed élites). Dependency theory argued that the export-orientated primary production structure found its handmaiden in a frozen *internal* class structure dominated by a small landed and mercantile (or comprador) élite, whose economic interests became increasingly intertwined with those of the advanced capitalist states, and whose cultural life styles and tastes were a faithful imitation of the same;
2. The evolution of *extreme patterns of social inequality* which in turn restricts and distorts the domestic market.

Dependency was thought to generate a structure of internal social relations which corresponds to and is created by the way a country is inserted into the structure of international economic relations. This imposed specialisation of production and the continued coincidence of interests between the imperial states and the ex-colonial élites, even after independence, blocked any attempt at industrialisation and internal social transformation (for example a bourgeois revolution). It was this that resulted in overall economic stagnation and pauperisation. At the time of Frank's writings, import-substitutive industrialisation had of course begun on a large scale in Latin America, but it lasted for only a short while in the late 1950s and early 1960s, and it was quite possible to criticise it as a form of industrialisation that was again 'externally dependent' and constricted (because of the internally restricted market) to produce luxury consumer goods. Also it marginalised ever greater numbers of the proletariat who were being thrown out of existing jobs because the path of industrialisation was capital intensive.[18]

So what we have here is a theory that places the cause of continued underdevelopment in the legacy of a distorted structure of economy and society; it is this distorted structure that is referred to as peripheral economy/society.

The peripheral nature of the economy and the society was said to create its own underdeveloping dynamics because it denied 'autocentric' development. Autocentric development refers to a process of development where the whole cycle of production, reproduction of capital, realisation of capital and valorisation of capital, and the relationship between producer goods and consumer goods industries, are all nicely contained within the same territorial economy and society. As indeed it had been the case in the 'core' economies.[19]

What the dependency theorists further argued was that the interaction between the centre countries of the capitalist system and the peripheral countries involved a transfer of value: an expropriation of *economic surplus* by the centre countries from the poor countries, resulting in capital accumulation in the advanced countries, and in stagnation and impoverishment in the poor countries. Development and underdevelopment was a two-way affair – just as development in one part of the world went hand in hand with underdevelopment in another, so underdevelopment in the periphery contributed to further development in the advanced, core, countries. The key mechanism for this dual outcome was unequal exchange.

Dependency theorists argued that the then prevailing international division of labour involved a transfer of value from poor to rich countries because of the *unequal terms of exchange* of the commodities traded. This point had already been made in the late fifties by liberal writers such as Singer and Prebisch, when for the first time a successful challenge to Ricardo's theory of international trade and comparative advantage had been made.[20] That challenge was a real eye-opener and it motivated Third World grass roots movements in the West for decades to come. The eye-opening point was that in the international exchange of primary commodities for manufactures there occurs – over a long time period – a deterioration of the prices for primary products in relation to those of manufactures. This long-term deterioration was said to occur strictly as a result of *market forces* of supply and demand, namely:

1. Income inelasticity of demand for foodstuffs;
2. Substitution of raw materials by industrial products and/or their replacement by synthetics;
3. A declining ratio of raw material inputs to industrial outputs.

The first of these three represents a restriction on long-term demand for foodstuffs in a growing world economy owing to the circumstance that there is a *physiological* limit to the amount of food people are able to consume; hence a declining proportion of rising income is going to be spent on food. This is bad news for the food producers in the long run. The second and the third refer to *technological* progress, which reduces the importance of raw materials in production. But beyond these purely market-force and technology-related reasons, Prebisch had also added another reason for the deteriorating terms of trade, one which begins to move us more directly into the realm of *the political economy* of international trade. Labour emancipation in the advanced countries, he said, pushes up the price of their commodities in relation to those of the poor countries where no such emancipation had taken place. Since, in terms of historical social development, the periphery lags behind the advanced countries by at least 100 years, there is no way one can bridge this gap.

This view was shared by Arghiri Emmanuel (in his *Unequal Exchange*[21]) who said that the differential evolution of wages is a fundamental cause of unequal exchange. Emmanuel attached little importance to demand factors in explaining the worsening terms of trade of poor countries. Indeed he criticised dependency theorists for focusing too much on the particular kinds of commodities traded. Unequal exchange, he said, does not occur between *commodities* traded, but between trading *countries*. Applying Marx's labour theory of value to international exchanges, he argued that:

1. The prices of goods produced in any country are determined mainly by the level of wages in that country;
2. The level of wages reflects historical and social conditions which vary in time and in place;
3. Equalisation of wage costs at the international level is unlikely to occur because of the immobility of the labour factor (in contrast to the mobility of the capital factor).

Thus the argument here is that because advanced countries are more developed, their price of labour reflects the higher standard of living already obtained. Successful class struggles and labour emancipation in the advanced countries have seen to it that what Marx called a 'historical' or 'ethical' wage has replaced the physiological wage still evident in less-developed countries. This then becomes the normal wage, not easily relinquished even in a recession. No matter what poor countries produce, no matter how comparable their levels of productivity, their exports will always be non-equivalent in value compared with the exports of advanced countries.

The emphasis on the shaping and determining nature of the external relations between poor and rich countries led dependency theorists in the neo-colonial period to advocate a radical break with the world capitalist system as the panacea to development for the poor countries. Their influence on the political ideologies of many less-developed countries at that time cannot be underestimated. It helped underpin an already strong populist tradition favouring domestic policies of economic nationalism, of self-reliance and of de-linking. At the international level it was – for a while – responsible for an effective 'Third Worldist' perspective on international trade and international capital flows. In numerous international negotiating forums, organisations and discussions, the Third World countries took a united stand in demanding fundamental changes in the world market system. They wanted better and more secure prices for their traditional exports; they wanted preferential access to domestic markets in the advanced countries for their 'infant' manufacturing industries; they asked for reforms in the international monetary system and for generous aid flows; and they proposed codes of conduct for multinational companies.

By 1974–5, these demands had been solemnly enshrined in a United Nations Charter of Economic Rights and Duties of States, and in a Programme of Action for the Establishment of a New

International Economic Order (NIEO).[22] But already before the ink was dry on the paper of these arrangements, profound changes in the world capitalist system had taken place which made these demands obsolete and which eroded the political unity which had given expression to them.

3

Crisis and Restructuring: The New International Division of Labour

In this part of the book a stage-theoretical approach is adopted to look at the dialectic unfolding of the world capitalist system in distinct periods or stages. In each period a particular structural arrangement between the core and the periphery succeeds for a while in achieving accumulation on a global scale. But time and again these structural arrangements run up against internal contradictions, which are the result of the very success of the structural arrangement. The conundrum of historical progress is that nothing fails like success. The failures create periods of crises and adjustments when the structural arrangement is re-jigged, and the relationship re-emerges in a new form.

The first neo-colonial phase, which we described in the previous chapter, lasted from about 1950–70. It too developed within itself contradictions which eventually required a reshuffling of the economic and geo-political relations between advanced and poor countries. Some authors (for example Samir Amin[1]) have described the post-1970 period as a 'second' neo-colonial period. Others have used the term 'post'-imperialism (for example David Becker[2]) to denote the characteristics of this period.

Which were the constraints and contradictions of the first neo-colonial period that created the crisis of the 1970s and a re-jigging of North–South relations? Again, as before, we can spot these contradictions breaking through on different though connected levels: the level of the development of material capabilities, the domestic or internal institutional level within the core countries and within the

44

peripheral countries, and the level of economic and geo-political relations between them.

Material Capabilities: Global Fordism

The term 'accumulation', in the Marxist tradition, refers to the self-expanding value of capital. Because of competition, the mere preservation of capital is impossible unless it is, in addition, expanded. Stage theory adds to this the notion that every phase of capitalist expansion is characterised by a particular accumulation model, a particular type of propelling industry, and a leading innovation or invention which is introduced in one industry first before spreading to the rest.[3] In a somewhat over-simplified manner one might say that the term 'accumulation model' refers to the dominant way in which capitalists in the leading branches of economic activity 'make their profits'.

The first neo-colonial period saw an enormous expansion of producer goods and consumer durable industries stimulated by the Fordist model of production and social organisation: flow line technology; mass production of consumer durables; improved wages for workers; Keynesian forms of demand management; welfarism.[4] But from the mid-1960s a dramatic fall in profitability was recorded more or less continuously in all advanced capitalist countries throughout the leading branches of industry. What had gone wrong?

The postwar boom had owed much to the ravages of war which had presented a fantastic opportunity to rebuild industrial sectors. The leading technology was the assembly line, and more generally process-technology. The whole point about mass production as a profitable undertaking is that it achieves *economies of scale*. This means that the more that is produced of a standardised product, the more the unit cost of production comes down. More means cheaper. But the downside is, on one hand, that there is a minimum scale required for economic operation, and on the other, that the success of the operation depends crucially on continuous and uninterrupted expansion of market demand for that same product. The mass production system cannot cope flexibly with either cyclical recessions, or with increased competition, or changing market tastes. The result is under-utilisation of fixed capacity, and over-production, resulting in lay-offs, losses and ultimately closure.

For a long time in the postwar period, the rigidities of this system of accumulation had been masked by the postwar reconstruction boom, and by the fact that the national economies of the advanced countries had put in place a supportive regulatory framework especially designed to balance mass production with mass consumption. State intervention in the economy had a Keynesian emphasis on full employment, public sector expenditure, welfare provisions, social democracy and workers' rights, and all these were novel elements in a complex societal arrangement in which socio-economic management stabilised the relationship between production and consumption. In this societal arrangement we should also mention key trade union concessions in which protest over de-skilling and alienation on the shop-floor had been abandoned in exchange for rising wages; a host of credit and fiscal institutions which helped smooth over ups and downs in the business cycle; and even socio-psychological practices of advertising and commodification of culture, all of which helped promote and maintain a 'consumer society'. Fordism was more than a method of production, it became a whole way of life.[5] It is the merit of the Regulation School (see Chapter 5) to have drawn attention to the way in which the conditions of stable economic growth in society depend on the coming together of a distinctive regime of accumulation with a supportive mode of regulation.

The structural contradiction that is shown up by this analysis is that because the postwar boom period had allowed the massive expansion of the welfare state in the core countries, and the confirmation of the social democratic consensus there, it was very difficult to drive down wages or permit unemployment to rise during cyclical recessions. On the other hand, the technical system of production with its vast outlays of fixed capital formation was too rigid to respond flexibly.

It is therefore not surprising that a first response by capitalists in the core countries to the crisis was to try to *export* Fordism to those areas of the periphery where wage levels were very low, and thus could compensate for the loss of profitability. The material opportunity for this 'global' Fordism was created by the de-composition of the production process into simple tasks able to be carried out by unskilled labour (this itself was a key feature of the Fordist system of production generally known as 'Taylorism'), and by technical innovations in three sectors basic to transport and communications.

Revolutionary strides in containerised shipping made geographic dispersal of production facilities possible; improved engineering techniques provided the complex communications network crucial to the speed of operations; and pervasive computer applications permitted the virtually instantaneous data processing vital for maximisation of global profits and market shares.

Hence, industrial relocation to certain selected sites in the Third World, the so-called newly-industrialising economies of south-east Asia, and Brazil and Mexico in Latin America, have been highlighted as a critical feature of this period of reconstruction in global capital accumulation.[6] Multinational companies developed organically integrated circuits of production in different countries with each country partaking in a part of the production process but not producing the whole product. The term the 'New International Division of Labour', as it came to be known, captured the phenomenon of peripheral industrialisation in which a small number of less-developed countries participated in the global dispersal of production facilities by multinational corporations.

The unevenness of industrial progress as between Third World countries in this period, was succinctly put in the UNCTAD annual trade report of 1982: 'fewer than ten newly industrialised developing countries accounted in 1980 for nearly 30 per cent of developing countries' GDP and nearly half of their manufacturing output, even though their share of the population of the underdeveloped countries was no more than 10 per cent'.[7] In the decade of the 1970s, the developing world as a whole increased its share of world manufacturing exports from 7 per cent to 10 per cent, but two-thirds of this originated in just eight newly-industrialising economies.

Neo-colonial Economic Relations

Throughout that first postwar period (until 1970) imperialist profit had been maintained through direct exploitation of raw material resources by multinational capital. Think for example of the very low costs of energy subsidised by the oil-producing countries. Between 1950 and 1970 the average price of crude oil had slowly and continuously *declined* from just over US$4 per barrel to $1.60 (in constant 1974 prices).[8] The loss in terms of trade to the developing world during the neo-colonial period[9] constituted the 'hidden' imperialist profits to the advanced world which subsidised the Fordist way of life and the democratic social contract there. It has been estimated that during this period between 25 and 40 per cent of the cost of labour in the advanced countries constituted the so-called 'social' wage.[10] A good deal of that again came from imperialist profits. A second component of imperialist profits were contributed by the technological rents discussed in Chapter 2.[11]

This pattern of unequal exchange between the rich and poor worlds had been mediated by neo-colonial class alliances between international capital and Third World bourgeoisies. The downside of this however was that these had engendered such extreme inequalities as to block a widening of the market and a deepening of capitalist relations inside the Third World (as indeed the dependency theorists had argued). By corollary, the peripheral Fordist strategy could only help advance the industrial progress of a small number of less-developed countries, whose industrial output as branch plant economies within the global Fordist production structure had secure access to the markets of the developed world.

It was this aspect of the crisis of the 1970s that distinguished it from normal cyclical crises of overproduction and underconsumption. The drive to expand markets could not be undertaken without major global restructuring.

Imperialism, both in the colonial period and in the neo-colonial period had been characterised by a geographical expansion of the capitalist mode on a world scale. Time and again, geographical expansion had permitted capitalism to overcome its problems of narrowing production relations by encroaching and dominating fresh pre-capitalist areas. What characterised the crisis of the 1970s was that there were simply no more 'fresh' pre-capitalist areas available for further geographical expansion. And thus, as Samir Amin for example has argued, the time had come for capitalism to overcome the crisis without resort to a new imperialism. The way to do this was to re-shuffle the cards and revise North–South relations.[12]

Economic Nationalism in the Third World

A third contradiction that grew out of the neo-colonial settlement of the postwar period was an increasingly strident economic nationalism in the Third World countries themselves. There were several contributing causes. First, the postwar settlement had been overwhelmingly state-centric, and this applied to both advanced and less-developed countries. Self-determination and the sovereignty of the national state, however large or small, was the overriding principle of international relations, and the touchstone of the United Nations.

Second, state-centrism also engulfed notions of the economy. The concept of the nation-state in the postwar period carried more than a mere notion of sovereignty: it implied a neo-mercantilist conception of the state as having responsibility for the administration and development of the national economy. It was the universally recognised task of the state to make the nation 'stronger'. This neo-mercantilist conception applied equally to old and new states. The dominance of Keynesianism as macro-economic theory, with its acceptance of state intervention in the economies of the advanced countries, ideologically spilt over into and converged with the developmentalist state notions of the liberal modernisation theories.[13] Less-developed countries were spurred on to take their economic destinies into their own hands.

Third, the impossibility of this task, given the economic dependency and unequal position of these countries in the world economic order, corrupted the very policies of development, including western forms of aid, leading to a deepening chasm between state and civil society within the Third World.

Politically, the easiest option for the national bourgeoisie was to suppress internal revolt by blaming the continuation of imperialist forms of domination of their countries, while masking their own complicity in this domination. As we have seen, dependency theory did much to legitimise this analysis. In the late 1960s and 1970s, these pressures concretised importantly in a wave of nationalisation and indigenisation policies in which foreign-owned companies and assets were taken over by the state or compulsorily sold to indigenous bourgeoisies. The Third Worldist view of international economic relations culminated in the acquiescence by the international community of the right of less-developed countries to own their own resources, but there was a price to pay. Throughout the developing world the takeover of, or domestic participation in, foreign companies required financial compensation to be paid even if the level of compensation was below market value. The financial resources were obtained from international banks eager to find outlets for accumulated euro- and petrodollars. Whereas in 1970 foreign direct investments to the Third World were slightly larger than the flows of such *in*direct investments to them, by 1980 the latter ran a clear lead with a ratio of 3:1.[14]

The consequence of this changed debt–equity ratio was the debt crisis of the 1980s. What was not appreciated at the time was that the changed equity–debt composition of foreign controlled enterprises in the Third World would lead to gross inefficiencies (and deepening indebtedness) because of the institutional separation of financial responsibility from operational control. Interest on loan capital constitutes a contractual obligation that needs to be discharged irrespective of the profitability of the enterprise or project for which the obligation was contracted. At the same time, the reduced equity exposure of the foreign company which continued to run the enterprise under management contract and/or technical or service agreements, obviated the need for foreign management to worry about locally assessable profitability criteria, because dividends (return on equity) were no longer the *raison d'être* of the foreign involvement. From the parent company's point of view, the local affiliate or joint venture became quintessentially a trading partner, from whom it wished to buy cheap and to sell dear. The existence in many developing countries of centralised state financial institutions responsible for the raising of foreign credit, and the channelling of this credit to individual state enterprises, encouraged the malpractice of prejudicing one project's future viability with another project's bad debts: foreign credit raised to finance one project all too easily found its way into another project's arrears payments. By corollary, general taxation was used by the State to finance unprofitable foreign operations.

In summary, the second neo-colonial period generated a new pattern of extraction of economic surplus of poor by rich countries through the instrument of debt. Where 'resource-bondage', and 'technological rents' had characterised the first neo-colonial period, the hallmark of the second neo-colonial or postimperial period is 'debt-peonage'. By the early 1980s, total capital outflows from the Third World to the advanced countries began to exceed the total of capital inflows to them, for the first time since the second world war. By the end of the 1980s total outstanding Third World debt stood at 1 trillion US dollars, or the equivalent of about one-third of the combined GDP of the developing countries.[15]

But this debt-peonage did not affect all of the Third World in equal measure. For a second characteristic of the postimperial period was a restructuring of world economic relations characterised by a new international division of labour when 'the world factory' superseded the 'world market'.[16] Within this new world factory structure certain selected sites in the Third World, now referred to as newly-industrialising economies, began to partake in the charmed circle of more intensively integrated world capitalist production, while other areas of the Third World became increasingly marginalised from it.

Changing Geo-political Relations

A final contradiction of the neo-colonial period which we are discussing resulted in what has been widely referred to as the crisis of US hegemony. By the late-1960s the Bretton Woods-managed world order which had been established under US informal imperial rule began to be challenged both by some western European states, and by the international capital markets in the form of speculation against the dollar which under the system had underpinned world monetary arrangements. Again, both challenges may be attributed to the very success of the system. For, under the Bretton Woods system, the US had succeeded in re-establishing the unity of the world market and this had encouraged a phenomenal transnational expansion of US capital.

By the late-1960s, Pierre Jalée observed, American industry abroad had become the world's third-ranking industrial power, after the United States and the Soviet Union.[17] The transnational expansion of US capital led to an effective overvaluation of the dollar which precipitated its downfall and the collapse of the Bretton Woods-managed system in 1971. Meanwhile, for their part, the European states had recovered their industrial strength and they began to export capital into the US taking advantage of the, by now, overvalued US dollar. The monetary crisis that followed testified to the autonomy of supranational market forces that would in future dominate the policies of all states alike, if not equally.

The downfall of US political control over world finance was matched by the erosion of US military supremacy in the periphery. The two in fact were linked, as Giovanni Arrighi has pointed out.[18]

On the one hand, the weakening of US financial power placed limits on the escalation of the war in Vietnam. The subsequent American retreat from Vietnam marked a turning point for anti-imperialist Third World movements. Between 1974 and 1980, Fred Halliday records that no less than 14 Third World states fell to national liberation forces.[19] The American withdrawal also contributed to the confidence with which the OPEC countries first unilaterally quadrupled the export price of oil, and next maintained their effective cartel in spite of mounting international pressure. They could do so precisely because of the power of stateless money. The more international dollars they earned, the more they could hold the dollar itself to ransom.

There is no doubt that in the 1970s Third World developmentalism reached its apogee. The weaking of US hegemonic power, and the subsequent inter-imperialist rivalry among the advanced capitalist countries, was matched by a more robust encouragement by the Soviets of anti-imperialist revolt in the Third World. The anarchy of the international financial markets added to this the promise of alternative finance for development without political strings attached, and gave the state in the Third World a stronger, more centralised role in allocating resources and guiding the economic destiny of the nation. The intensification and the re-negotiation of transnational economic linkages, both in respect of the new international division of labour and in respect of the nationalisation of the extractive resource sector, was associated with an expansion of the state's role in a range of developing countries while having a dampening effect on the expansion of the state's role in those core countries that were major capital exporters.

As Peter Evans[20] has argued, under certain circumstances transnational capital preferred dealing with a stronger, more bureaucratically capable state apparatus. He suggests that a natural evolution or outcome of both the conflict between host countries and transnational corporations, and the alliances between them, was to enhance the organisational capacities of the state in certain Third World countries, especially when transnational loan capital began to replace direct investment. Foreign loans (invariably underwritten by the state) substantially increase the power of the state *vis-à-vis* the local bourgeoisie. For instance, one of the primary motivations for Korea's exceptional preference for debt in the 1970s was the leverage that it gave the state over local industrialists. The positive correlation, however, applied only to more advanced Third World states in the postwar period.

For this, to be sure, was the lasting outcome of this period of transition: a deep division *between* Third World countries depending on their respective insertion into the world economy, on the relative level of economic advance already obtained, on the nature of state–civil society relations, and on a number of cultural factors that became increasingly important in explaining the variation in economic progress and social advance. It was these differences that began to shape the theoretical agenda of development literature to which we turn next.

Critical Theory: Diversity and Micro-studies

For most writers, the end of the Third World dominated the theoretical agenda in this period; the end, that is to say, of the Third World both as a unitary category of analysis, and of the mechanistic, deterministic interpretation of the historical outcome. Generalising methodologies that had treated the 'Third World as a whole' were replaced by methodologies that homed in on the specific and the unique, and that focused on the diversity of the development experience in different parts of the world. Geographic and cultural factors, long ignored in Marxist discourse, made a robust reappearance as much of the development literature became fragmented into area studies. The retreat from orthodoxy resulted in a renewed interest in anthropological, ethnographic and historiographic work. Many excellent collections of edited readers that were published in the 1980s testify to a preoccupation with nationally and area-specific features of the development process rather than attempting to fit these into general patterns of structural (under)-development derived from experiences in other regions.[21]

They were concerned, for example, with detailed empirical investigations of the role of the state in industrialisation, of the way in which changing production relations in industry were informed by local habits and struggles, of culturally specific gender relations and ethnic relations, of agrarian transformation and differentiation, and of the role of popular culture whether in acquiescence or protest. It was not so much that external factors of global capitalism were ignored, rather there was an understanding (often implicit) that the task of development theory was to uncover the precise interplay between external factors and internal social structures in order to explain the divergence in national historical trajectories.[22]

Some of this literature echoed the post-Marxist, post-structuralist and even postmodernist turn that had begun to take hold of the Marxist debates in the mainstream philosophy and social sciences. It spawned a broad canvas of critical theory which we have briefly referred to in the introduction to this first part of the book. Critical theory emancipated development theorists from overarching philosphies of progress and doom, 'development and underdevelopment', led them to explore systematic variations in development trajectories, and encouraged the study of the locally specific to combine with a celebration of the politically possible. Moving from structure orientation to actor orientation, the baton of development studies generally passed from the economics of development to the politics of development. The pursuit of such politics led, in one direction, to *micro* local action studies, highlighting for example the success of small-scale 'bottom-up' community participation projects of the kind enthusiastically defined, funded and implemented by NGOs. These aimed to facilitate peoples' own development efforts. 'Empowerment through participation' became the clarion call of development *practice*.[23]

Gender and Development

Probably the most challenging of the new directions in development theory has been opened up by feminist scholarship, especially after its forward leap from women's studies to gender studies. It was not till about 1970[24] that women seriously figured in mainstream development literature, and their 'discovery' was flawed on at least two crucial counts.

First, it was generally but mistakenly assumed that because women had demonstrably *not* benefited from the development process, they had been 'excluded' from it and now needed to be brought in. This was a view that was seized upon with some eagerness by the international development community. The UN launched its Decade for Women in 1975 at its first ever World Conference on Women held in Mexico, which followed barely one year after the UN Conference on Population in Bucharest in 1974. The ideological juxtaposition of the Third World population explosion and the backwardness of its women led to the big idea that there was a trade-off between women's productive functions and their reproductive functions, and that raising women's socio-economic status would lower birth rates. The international aid machine revved up to combine family-planning programmes with income-generating projects for women, whether in rural cooperatives or urban slum community centres.[25]

Socialist feminists soon condemned these programmes for obscuring and compounding the nature of global production relations whereby women's productive work in informal, non-organised, non-protected sectors, articulated with the global system of capital accumulation in a double, or even triple chain of super exploitation.[26]

The *second* problem with the 'women in development' (WID) discourse was epistemological, and had to do with the concept of women as a unitary, analytic category. This was blown apart by the postmodern turn in feminist critique. Why assume that women are the same the world over? What do middle-class white women in New York have in common with rural black women growing coffee for exports in Africa, or with the cloth cutters in the garment sweatshops of Asia? Radical feminists have sought an answer in patriarchy, the notion, namely, that even if women are not the same, their subordination by men is universal.

But this still left world sisterhood without a common political agenda. It was an absence camouflaged and compouded by First World racism. As Maria Mies puts it bluntly: 'whereas Western consumer housewives are encouraged to consume more and to breed more whites, the colonial producer "housewives" are encouraged to produce more and cheaper and to stop breeding blacks.'[27]

A gradual change of focus onto broader issues of 'gender' moved the study of 'women in development' on to a less ambitious, but for all that more empowering, plane. Gender studies does not assume that there is a stable, homogeneous category called 'women' with identical interests and desires. It focuses instead on relations between men and women as these are socially constructed.[28] Gender relations vary greatly in different cultural and historical contexts. What is men's work in some places is women's work in another; in some countries women head up households; in others they do not.

Land tenure, inheritance and usufruct rights also vary, as do legal entitlements, state provisions and marital obligations.

This realisation produced an impressive range of detailed, descriptive, empirical work which showed how even well-intended development-assistance programmes targeted on women were often corrupted and deflected from their original aims by 'gender blindness', because of mistaken assumptions about women's roles and involvement in production and reproduction. For example, dairy cooperative projects for women in Andhra Pradesh (India) inadvertently increased women's workloads without giving them access to the fruits of their labour. Men controlled the paid jobs, and the income from the dairy. They (and their sons) consumed most of the milk, while giving many an excuse to stop working altogether![29]

In the course of these detailed, concrete local studies, two major intellectual advances were made. *First*, through the gender orientation in development studies, Third World feminists found their voice. Not only did they have possession of relevant cultural knowledge that western researchers lacked, they also discovered that the emancipatory agendas of western feminists were wholly inappropriate to the needs, day-to-day lives, and struggles of Third World women. Chandra Mohanty, for instance, argues that the former have a singular focus on gender as a basis for equal rights, while the latter's concern with gender is in relation to race and/or class as part of a broader liberation struggle.[30] This difference explains, for example, why an issue like the woman's right to choose, as in abortion rights, is not as clearcut for 'women of colour' whose right to bear children is often mediated by a coercive, racist state and a fertility obsessed international development machine. Momsen and Townsend have found that in fact fertility is the most studied aspect of women's lives in the Third World.[31] In a remorselessly Foucauldian deconstruction of western feminist writing on Third World women (ignorant, poor, uneducated, tradition-bound, victimized and so on), Mohanty shows up and challenges its political effects, namely as being no more than a prop to a western feminist colonialist move.[32] As Aihwa Ong puts it, 'When feminists look overseas, they frequently seek to establish their authority on the backs of non-Western women, determining for them the meanings and goals of their lives.'[33]

A *second*, and related, intellectual advance involved Third World and First World feminists engaging in what Janet Townsend remarks upon as her own conversion to the 'personal as political'. This is the insight that no outsiders can ever set the agenda for oppressed women's practical or strategic gender needs. A socialist-feminist preoccupation with production and distribution is useless when the practical need is for clean latrines. Liberal agendas of gender equality are pointless when the overwhelming strategic need is to avoid alcoholic and violent husbands. All conceptual baggage must be thrown out if researchers are to understand and empower women to take control over their own lives. And for this only listening will do!

'Dependency Associated' Development Theory

The 'passion for the possible' was also articulated in *meso*-level studies of political choice, the object of which was to identify 'room-for-manoeuvre' policy alternatives at the level of state and civil society. These were particularly advocated by Latin American 'second wave' *dependista* writers who laid great store by the perceived breakdown of American global hegemony, the increase in inter-imperialist rivalry, and the new, historically specific, form of foreign capitalist penetration which involved a new alliance between the state and a truly 'transnational' corporate bourgeoisie.[34]

These 'dependent development' writers went furthest in welding a structuralist analysis of the dynamic unfolding of global capitalism, with an interactionist 'voluntarist' conception of domestic responses. They argued that each expansive phase of capitalism creates new forms of economic dependency, new ways in which the Latin American economies are inserted in the world capitalist economy. Therefore each phase brings forth new class contradictions and requires new class alliances. At the precise historical moment when these new class alliances are being formed, there is scope for political action. They argued that what was specific to the Latin American economies (at the turn of the 1980s) was a new dependency created by foreign penetration and control over the industrial producer-goods sector, which increasingly had to rely on an alliance with the state as direct agent of production.

In this process the state apparatus was becoming ever more divorced from civil society, while at the same time the very expansion of industrial-dependent capitalism (at that moment in time) needed the members of the civil society as both producers and consumers. This offered an opportunity for 'defensive alliances' or 'class compromise' (*concertación*) on the part of the various groups of civil society (for example trade unions as well as the bourgeoisie, and the state bureaucratic class) to pursue the objective of social democracy; or 'substantive' democratisation to complement the formal democratisation which had begun with the defeat of the military oligarchies. They pointed to the variety of contemporary regime types in Latin America as empirical evidence of the scope for manoeuvre and the importance of political struggle. In this way the concern with social democracy replaced the concern with revolution in much of Latin American discourse. We shall be looking at this again in Chapter 11.

Postimperialism and World System Theories

The optimism of the 'dependent development' project was strengthened by *macro*-level theories of postimperialism which were themselves an outcome of stage-theoretical thinking about the dynamic trajectory of world capitalism. The concept of postimperialism, clarified by David Becker,[35] refers to a still-nascent phase in the evolution of world capitalism in which relations of dominance and dependency between nations (the defining characteristic of imperialism) are being relegated to secondary importance. Instead, relations of capitalist domination and exploitation are conceptualised in terms of global class relations which transcend national class structures. Transnational enterprises, in this view, are integrating the world economy and in the process they create an international bourgeoisie alongside an exploited international proletariat. Nation-states mediate in the process of exploitation, but no single state is critical to it. The members of the corporate international bourgeoisie are united by mutual interests which transcend those of the states whose passports they happen to carry. They no longer need the imperialist power of their home states to gain access to resources and markets in the peripheral areas of the world. Instead, they negotiate this access by professing to an ideology which separates the political from the economic sphere.

This ideology, which is expressed in the 'doctrine of domicile', holds that there is no innate antagonism between the global economic interests of the TNCs and the national economic aspirations of host *or* home countries. Transnational corporations are believed to transcend both: their subsidiaries are instructed to behave as 'good citizens' in any country where they do business. As good citizens they are thought to be able to observe national laws and regulations and accommodate national economic and social interests. This corporate hegemonic world view reduces the nation-state of the home countries to a degree of irrelevancy while at the same time, paradoxically, opening up domestic, social and economic opportunities that did not previously exist in the colonial and neo-colonial areas.

The global profit orientation of the contemporary transnational firm, coupled with a growing indifference to its national roots, implies a continuous recalculation of optimal production and profit locations. This means that developing host countries, by offering lower wage rates and competitive tax and other concessions, can achieve rapid industrialisation and economic progress under the auspices of transnational capital. To the extent that the corporate national bourgeoisies in developing countries are able to consolidate these advances through informed state action, including improved bargaining with TNCs in the national economic interests, to that extent will the old international division of labour not remain fixed forever. Although world capitalist development is uneven, some peripheral countries can attain metropolitan status, and some present metropoles may decay to peripheral status without contravening the fundamentals of the international order.

Another reinforcement of the dependent development approach was furnished by the American *world system theories* centred around Immanuel Wallerstein and the State University of New York's Braudel Center. The work of the school, which began in the mid-1970s, dominated the structuralist agenda in the 1970s and 1980s spawning a huge literature, theoretical as well as substantively empirical. In basic outline the theory is not much different from Frank and the dependency theory with which it is normally bracketed. It too was holistic and historical, arguing that a capitalist world economy had existed since the sixteenth century, that is since the beginning of European overseas expansion.

In Wallerstein's terminology, the world system is 'a single division of labour, comprising multiple cultural systems, multiple political entities and even different modes of surplus appropriation' (that is feudal, slave mode and wage labour).[36] When such a world system has a common political system, Wallerstein uses the expression, 'world-*empire*' – when it does not, he uses the expression, 'world-*economy*'. The essential feature of the capitalist world economy is production for sale in a market in which the object is to realise the maximum profit. Since its inception in the sixteenth century, the capitalist world economy has 'naturally' developed a hierarchy of occupational tasks yielding different rewards for labour. Over time, exchange has become unequal and has remained unequal as a result of different wage levels operating in different regions and nations. This unequal exchange, however, has been and continues to be reinforced by political interference on the part of strong states on weak ones. In this way capitalism involves not only appropriation of the surplus value by an owner from a labourer, but also appropriation of the whole economy by the 'core' areas. The core–periphery hierarchy and the exploitation of the periphery by the core are necessary to the reproduction of capitalism as a system.

From the beginning, however, the world economy has been stratified into three, not two, layers: core, periphery and semi-periphery. The reasons for the emergence of semi-peripheral nations are both political and economic: politically, semi-peripheral nations are 'go-between' nations, and they perform the same function as do the middle classes within national stratification systems. They form a necessary buffer in a system so based on unequal rewards that sooner or later it would lead to rebellion. Within the world system the go-between nations also assume an economic role: they seek trade with both core and periphery exchanging different kinds of products with each and achieving intermediate wage levels and profit margins. The *dynamic* quality of the world system is that it allows for the upward and downward mobility of nations. This is a function of the cyclical nature of the capitalist mode of production, but is made possible by the very fact of unequal wage levels, coupled with the relative rigidities in national wage levels.

And so it happens that it is during the world economic recessions that most of the relative shifting of positions occurs. It is theoretically not possible for all states to develop simultaneously. The rise of some nations always occurs at the expense of others that decline. Successful strategies of national upward mobility include 'promotion by invitation', 'self-reliance', and 'seizing the chance'. The successful strategy is, however, *un*successful from the point of view of the achieving of national economic independence, and the participation of the masses: marginalisation of the masses is a necessary condition for a country's upward mobility.[37]

Although, clearly, world-system theory ran counter to both the postimperialist view of dynamism created by the transnationalisation of capital, and to the political optimism of the dependent development school, it yet managed to cross-fertilise with those two currents in two fruitful ways. On the one hand, the dynamic quality of the world system which allowed for change of positions within the system suited those post-dependency analysts who tried to make sense of the reversal of fortunes evidently experienced by the newly industrialising countries (NICs) which were upwardly mobile, and some of the core countries (notably Britain) demonstrably in decline by any measure of international statistical comparison. On the other hand, many writers of the world system school began to place increasing stress on the role of the national semi-peripheral state in such cases of ascent (that is, Wallerstein's 'seizing the chance' strategy).

In the end, it was the case of East Asia, rather than Latin America, which clinched the deal and forced a major re-think of the relationship between global capitalism and Third World economic development. It was a re-think that eventually also allowed a certain convergence between neo-Marxist and neo-classical understanding of why some developing countries succeeded in the world economy while others did not. The centrepiece in this new theoretical consensus was the 'developmental state', to which we shall return in Chapter 10.

PART II
GLOBALISATION

Introduction

In Part I of this book we looked at the history of capitalist expansion on a world scale. Using Robert Cox's concept of 'historical structures', we examined the material, institutional and ideological features of sequential stages in core–periphery relations. The ideological features included the intellectual traditions that grew up to explain the historical trajectory, whether as apologists *or* critics. Liberal and (neo)Marxist theories of development[1] were seen as opposing 'paradigms' no less, with all the weight of doctrinal command of emotion and thought that the term since Kuhn has implied. It will therefore come as a surprise that, with the benefit of hindsight, it transpires that more ground was common between them than that which divided them. For they both shared certain fundamental assumptions which we can only now appreciate as 'historically bound at the origin' to borrow Robert Cox's phrase.[2]

The assumption of both of them was that the capitalist system, or the world market system, was inherently *expansive* in character. As such it was forever driven by its own needs to incorporate (or exploit) ever-larger areas of the world. The paradigmatic controversy was over the nature of this expansive process: whether it was exploitative and underdeveloping, or progressive and uplifting. But that the process of expansion was inexorable was not questioned by either perspective. It was thought that the relentless search for raw materials, for cheap labour and for market outlets, time and again would drive capitalism *either* into fresh geographic regions, *or* when these were no longer available, into upgrading existing ones.

In their optimistic interpretation, orthodox Marxists in fact stood closer to the liberal views than did the neo-Marxists, or dependency and world system writers. The liberal tradition was certainly not alone in asserting its belief in the effectiveness of capitalism in raising growth, alleviating poverty and promoting civil liberties everywhere, including the Third World. Echoing Marx's own predictions that capitalism, in spreading through imperialism to the underdeveloped lands, would turn them up and work them over in such a way as to call forth social revolutions, or patterns of democratisation similar to those that had happened in advanced countries, orthodox Marxists such as Bill Warren and, as we have seen, Latin American '*dependista*' writers such as Cardoso and Faletto,[3] assigned a positive role to capitalist imperialism. Incorporation by capitalism in effect resulted, they argued, in *territorial economic development* in which capitalist exploitation under foreign domination merely served as a prelude to internal social struggles and progressive democratisation.

Neo-Marxist writers, on the other hand, for example Paul Baran, A. G. Frank and Samir Amin, have generally held a pessimistic view, namely that incorporation caused internal blockage and distortions, and territorial *under*development. But even for these writers there was still light at the end of the tunnel because of the ultimate prospect of populist anti-capitalist revolutions being 'provoked' by capitalist penetration of the periphery.[4]

Thus the whole edifice of the Marxist tradition, as far as the analysis of development *or* underdevelopment in the periphery is concerned, was built on the assumption of capitalism as an ongoing expanding project, until it would collapse, whether nationally or internationally, under the weight of its own contradictions, after which it would be succeeded by socialism.[5]

The dogmatic belief in the ever-expanding needs of the capitalist system, and the associated 'necessity' of imperialism, was not long ago re-affirmed by Paul Sweezy, himself one of the leading architects of the tradition. Commenting on the process of 'globalisation' during the 1980s, he categorically states in an opening paragraph, 'In the periphery, foreign capital has penetrated more widely and deeply than ever before.'[6]

But do the empirical facts support the argument of continued expansion and incorporation? Is the periphery still 'necessary' for capitalism? Or can the drive to accumulation, which is central to capitalism as an economic system, survive without the periphery? Or, is it the case that in the turmoil of the present crisis a new stage of capitalism is fermenting in the core of the system, one in which the *geographic* core–periphery polarisation is being replaced by a *social* core–periphery polarisation that cuts across territorial boundaries and geographic regions? This is the central theme of this second part of the book.

We shall map out a theory of transformation that defines globalisation as a new social architecture of cross-border human interactions. It breaks down the old international division of labour and the associated hierarchy of rich and poor countries. In this process the integrity of the national territorial state as a more or less coherent political economy is eroded, and the functions of the state become re-organised to adjust domestic economic and social policies to fit the exigencies of the global market and global capitalist accumulation. In this view, domestic peripheralisation in rich and poor countries alike is not merely an unintended outcome but performs a necessary regulatory function. And thus the new global configuration drives a politics of exclusion as contrasted with the politics of incorporation (and 'developmentalism' in the broadest sense) that marked the previous periods of capitalist expansion.

The use of the term 'regulation' reveals the theoretical research agenda of the Regulation School which I adopt in this part of the book. Like Robert Cox's Critical Theory of historical structures, the Regulation School (see Chapters 5 and 6) too is a critical social theory that has been infected by the postmodernist, poststructuralist turn of the 1970s. But while Cox's theory is particularly relevant as a theory of international relations, the Regulation School has more to say about the transformation of production systems, industrial organisation and social institutional complexes that propel the present phase of globalisation. We have to understand the new 'techno-economic' paradigm which emerged during the protracted world economic crisis of the 1970s before we can appreciate the transformation of international political economy that accompanied it.

It has become commonplace to speak of 'crisis and transformation' as one phenomenon. It is a usage that is an indication of a particular view of the world, now widely shared though first articulated by regulation theory, that capitalism, instead of destroying itself in consequence of its systemic internal contradiction, time and again is able to overcome the self-inflicted crises by total renewal.[7] The word 'adjustment' does not cover total renewal, 'transformation' does. Yet crisis and transformation are simultaneous historical processes and may only be separated for analytical purposes. There is no chronological sequence: it is *not* as if the crisis which began in the 1970s *first* gave rise to new production systems and *next* to new social and economic configurations, domestic and

global, that tranformed our way of life. Rather, global transformations were part and parcel of the crisis itself.

In some senses they may even be said to have induced the
crisis. For, as we shall see in Chapter 4, the expansive, incorporatist
phase of capitalism had already shown signs of implosion, when
international economic interactivity and new emerging forms of
international connectivity (for example transnational production
systems) became increasingly concentrated within the core (albeit
a reconstituted core) of the world capitalist system, and previously
incorporated areas and regions were marginalised or expelled from
it. All this began in, and overlapped with, a period that was still
theorised and institutionalised as a period of 'development' of the
'Third World' as a unitary category, objectively related to the 'First
World' in a homogeneously perceived way.

It is, therefore, pertinent that we should start our theorising about
social transformation with a hard look at the long-term empirical
and statistical trends of capitalist expansion and global integration.
The statistical portrait that I sketch in Chapter 4 tells us about the
failure of world capitalism to incorporate the periphery in its
dynamic growth, which in turn set the scene for the period of crisis
and transformation since the 1970s.

4

From Expansion to Implosion

There are three key economic indicators which are conventionally marshalled to attest to the increasing internationalisation of the world economy: world trade figures, in particular the allegedly rising ratio of world trade to output; the growth and spread of foreign direct investments through multinational corporations, again expressed in relation to world output and trade; and the expansion of *all* international capital flows and their pattern of integration. We shall look at each of these, both in regard to their evidentialisation of the general thesis of internationalisation of the world economy, and in regard to the participation of the periphery in this internationalisation.

World Trade: Long-term Trends[1]

The received wisdom of all literature on the postwar period is that world trade has grown very much faster than world production, and that this testifies to 'the increased *internationalization* of activities and of the greater *interconnectedness* which have come to characterise the world economy', to quote but one recent and quite representative textbook on the subject.[2] (Emphasis in original.)

True, world trade *has* grown faster than world output over most of the period since the Second World War, but it is worth going back to the nineteenth century and the early parts of this century in order to assess whether this is something new, different, more of the same, or indeed less of the same as that which happened during previous periods of internationalisation.

69

The standard work to consult here is Nobel prizewinner Simon Kuznets' contribution to the quantitative measurements of world production and trade which was published in 1967, and in which he reviewed, compared and recalculated several longitudinal studies of world production, trade and population over the whole period 1800–1963.[3] What do we learn from Kuznets' figures?

Growth of World Trade in Relation to World Output

The nineteenth century (and more especially the period from 1880–1913) was the peak period of growth of world trade. It was unprecedented and has not been surpassed since. Between 1800–1913, world trade per capita grew 11 times faster than world output, establishing an increasingly more complex network of economic activity which eventually embraced 155 trading areas on all continents.[4] By 1913, on the eve of the First World War, the foreign trade proportion stood at 33 per cent. The foreign trade proportion is measured by the ratio of the volume of world trade (expressed as the sum total of world merchandise exports and imports at current prices) to the volume of world output. This ratio of 33 per cent was up from about 3 per cent in 1800. During, and between, the two world wars that proportion fell to about one-third of its 1913 level, and by 1963, the latest date in Kuznets' time series, it had recovered to about 22 per cent (but note that the figures *after* 1913 exclude the communist bloc). In Table 4.1 we extend Kuznets' figures up to the present, using the UN Yearbook of International Trade Statistics and the UN National Account Statistics (both of which were used by Kuznets for his postwar data). Going by these figures, we note that even today the foreign trade proportion has not yet overtaken its peak level of 1913.

Core and Periphery: Respective Shares of World Trade

Given our interest in the core–periphery structure, it is of still greater relevance to look at the long-term data in respect of the participation of each of these two subgroups, and the evolution of trade between the two.

Kuznets made an admittedly crude distinction between 'developed' and 'underdeveloped' groups of countries. The underdeveloped group covered Africa (excluding the Union of South Africa after 1880), Asia (excluding Japan after 1880, and the Communist

Table 4.1   *The ratio of commodity world trade to world output, 1800–1993*
(per cent)

Year	Kuznets' Figure	UN Yearbook's Figure
1800	3.0	—
1850*	8.9	—
1880*	17.1	—
1913	33.0	—
1953	16.7	—
1958	19.6	24.7
1963	22.2	25.6
1975	—	28.9
1985	—	31.1
1989	—	30.5
1993	—	31.8*

Note: * The figures for 1850 and 1880 are derived from Kuznets' estimate of a growth rate of 7% per capita product per decade during the period, and a growth rate of 33% per capita world trade. Therefore the decennial rate of trade-to-product growth $= (1.33/1.07 - 1) = 24.3\%$.

Sources: S. Kuznets, 'Quantitative Aspects of the Economic Growth of Nations: X-Level and Structure of Foreign trade: Long-term Trends', Table 1 pp. 4–5, in *Economic Development and Cultural Change*, 15 (2) (1967), and footnote to table I, p. 7.

UN Yearbook figures:

Trade statistics: *Yearbook of International Trade Statistics* (New York: UN, 1963); *International Trade Statistics Yearbook* (New York: UN, 1990 and 1993). The trade figure for 1993 is based on *World Development Report*, World Bank, 1995.

Output statistics: *Yearbook of National Statistics* (New York: UN, 1965); *National Accounts Statistics* (New York: UN, 1982 and 1988–9).

countries after 1913), and Latin America; the developed group covered North America (US and Canada), Europe (excluding Communist countries after 1913), Japan, Australia and New Zealand (Oceania after 1913), and the Union of South Africa after 1880.[5]

According to Kuznets the share of world trade contributed by the regions of Africa, Asia and Latin America was a fairly constant 20 per cent of the total throughout during the period up to 1913, increasing by six percentage points during the period 1913–53; the share of the industrial/developed group declined correspondingly from about three-quarters of world trade to just under 70 per cent in 1953. In Table 4.2 we extend Kuznets' estimates with GATT statistics, to cover the period up to 1990. These make the same crude distinction between industrial and non-industrial areas, while recording the 'eastern trading area' as a separate group. The only incongruity between these two data series is that Kuznets has a residual category of 'other Europe' which includes only eastern Europe and the Soviet Union (after 1913), but not China which he has grouped within the 'underdeveloped' category throughout. The GATT data on the other hand, until 1990, have included China in a separate category 'Eastern Trading Area' together with the former Soviet Union and eastern Europe. As China, even today, contributes only 1.6 per cent of world trade, this does not seriously distort the picture we are presenting in Table 4.2.

Table 4.2   *Share of commodity world trade between economic areas, 1800–1990 (per cent)*

Year	Developed Area	Developing Area	Other Europe/Eastern Trading Area*
Kuznets			
1800	65.0	18.0	17.0
1850	69.0	22.0	9.0
1880	63.0	20.0	8.0
1913	74.3	20.0	5.7
1928	68.9	23.3	7.8
1937	69.2	24.5	6.3
1953	68.9	26.3	4.8
GATT			
1953	58.6	31.3	10.1
1962	63.6	24.1	12.3
1973	69.0	18.1	10.1
1985	68.2	20.8	9.1
1990	71.9	20.0	
	Of which Japan:	*Of which the Four Tigers:*	
	10.0	25.0	6.1

Note: The Kuznets data and the GATT data are not completely comparable since Kuznets' figures for the respective shares of trade are based on the arithmetic means of exports and imports, equally weighted, while the GATT statistics use exports only. This probably accounts for the difference in values for the 'overlapping' year of 1953. But the difference is to be expected because in the prewar period the underdeveloped world exported more to the developed world than it imported from it, while in the postwar period these posititons were reversed.

Sources: Kuznets' figures: *ibid.*, Table 2. p. 11.
GATT figures: 1953 & 1962, GATT *International Trade*, 1962. 1973: *International Trade*, 1973. 1985 & 1990: *International Trade*, 1990–1.
*Comprising Eastern Europe and the USSR.

According to these GATT statistics, by 1962 the share of the industrial areas in world trade was 63.6 per cent and that of the non-industrial areas 24.1 per cent. In fact, it is during the immediate postwar period that the share of the non-industrial group reached its peak level of 31.3 per cent (in 1953). Turning to subsequent years, we find a remarkable continuity in the historical long-run despite small periodic fluctuations. For example in 1973 the percentage share of the industrial areas had climbed back up to 69 per cent, and that of the non-industrial group had fallen back to 18.1 per cent. By 1990 it was 71.9 per cent and 20.0 per cent respectively.

Plus ça change, plus ça reste la même chose? So what, if anything, *has* changed? There have been really only three important changes over this whole period of almost 200 years:

Changes in Positions within the Core–Periphery

Japan has come on the scene to take 10 per cent of the industrial group's share of world trade (in 1990); on the other side, within the non-industrial group, just four countries – Singapore, Hong Kong, Taiwan and Korea (the so-called 'Four Tigers' with a total combined population of just under 72 million) have taken hold of over a quarter of the non-industrial group's share of world trade.[6] If we therefore re-classify these four Asian Tigers to be in the 'industrial group', the share of that group in world trade rises to 76.5 per cent while that of the non-industrial group declines to 16.5 per cent in 1990.

Shifts in Inter-group and Intra-group Trade

There have been significant shifts in inter-group trade. According to Kuznets, in 1876–80 inter-group trade (that is between the industrial and non-industrial groups) accounted for 46 per cent of world trade, while intra-industrial group trade accounted for 45 per cent and intra-non-industrial group trade for only 4 per cent. He observes that this tripartite division remained relatively constant over the whole period, with the respective shares by 1961–3 standing at 44 per cent, 48 per cent and 8 per cent respectively.[7] Looking at the GATT trade statistics, we notice – as before – a brief surge in the Third World's relative participation in world trade during the immediate postwar period. In 1953, for example, intra-industrial

Table 4.3 *Inter- and intra-group trade, 1876–1990 (per cent)*

Source	Year	Inter-Groups	Intra-Industrial	Intra-Non-Industrial	Total
Kuznets	1876–80	51.0	45.0	4.0	100.0
	1961–63	44.0	48.0	8.0	100.0
	1953	43.2	37.1	8.0	88.3
	1962	34.2	44.1	5.8	84.1
*GATT**	1973	25.6	51.7	3.5	80.8
	1985	28.9	49.4	5.9	84.2
	1990	26.6	55.4	5.7	87.7

Note:
*For the GATT figures, the total adds up to less than 100%, the balance being made up by trade with and within the 'Eastern Trading Area'.
Sources: Kuznets' figures: *ibid*, Table 5, p. 27.
GATT figures: 1953 & 1962, GATT *International Trade*, 1962, Table 2 p.7.
1973: *International Trade*, 1973, Table 2, p. 3. 1985 & 1990: *International Trade*, 1990–91, Table A2.

group trade had dropped to 37.1 per cent, while inter-group trade had remained stable at 43.2 per cent. Since the early 1960s, however, there has been a slow but steady increase in the intra-industrial group trade, until – by 1990 – it had reached 55 per cent of world trade, while the inter-group trade on the other hand consistently declined to stand at 27 per cent of world trade in 1990 (see Table 4.3).

Proportions of World Population Involved

By far the most revealing statistic is the proportion of world population involved in the respective world trade shares. In the period before 1880, the population of the 'industrial' or 'core' group of countries included north America and western Europe only. Their combined population rose from about 118 million in 1800 to almost 303 million in 1900. That of the 'Rest of the World' rose from 783 million to 1319 million, giving the 'industrial' group a rising share of the world population from 13 per cent in 1800 to 18.7 per cent in 1900. By 1990, even with the inclusion of Japan as belonging to the core, that proportion is just 15.8 per cent (see Table 4.4).[8] And, even if we were to add the population (72 million) of the four Asian Tigers to the core group, the combined population of the 'core participants', at 17.1 per cent, remains well below the historical bench mark.

Table 4.4 *The world population among groups of countries, 1800–1990 (millions and per cent)*

Year	(a) Core Countries		(b) Rest of World		World Total
1800	118.15	13.1	783.35	86.9	901.50
1850	183.20	15.2	1019.05	84.8	1202.25
1900	302.75	18.7	1319.00	81.3	1621.75
1950	471.50	18.8	2037.50	81.2	2509.00
1990	838.40	15.8	4418.60	84.2	5295.00

(a) includes North America and Western Europe 1800–1950; 1990 data also include Japan.
(b) includes Eastern Europe and Soviet Union; Japan before 1990.
Sources: 1800–1950s data: C. McEvedy and R. Jones, *Atlas of World Population*, London: Penguin, 1978. 1990s data: UN, *Demographic Year-book*, 1992.

The conclusion to be drawn from these figures is that the record of world trade can neither be summoned to testify to 'the increasing interconnectedness which characterises our world economy', nor to evidence of 'the deepening and widening penetration by the core of the periphery'. Rather, it stands as evidence of a modestly thickening network of economic exchanges within the core, a significant redistribution of trade participation within the core, the graduation of a small number of peripheral nations with a comparatively small population base to 'core' status, but above all to a declining economic interaction between core and periphery, both relative to aggregate world trade and relative to total populations participating in the thickening network.[9]

Foreign Direct Investment (FDI) and the Growth of Multinational Enterprises

Even if world trade is *not*, surely foreign direct investment *is* 'the most important manifestation of transnationalisation'?[10] Or is it? The subject of the impressive growth of the multinational enterprise in the postwar period has generally left commentators in search of superlatives: phenomenal, explosive, dramatic, and amounting to a 'complete transformation of the world economy',[11] are descriptions without which no textbook is complete.

Again it is worth peeping back in history to see whether we are indeed confronted here with a truly new phenomenon, or a continuation of past trends. To be sure, in the immediate postwar period, between 1950–70, international direct investments grew at a rate just a little faster than that of the average GDP of the developed market economies (whence nearly all the direct investment flows came from), but it doesn't follow that this presents a significant departure from the prewar situation.

In awe of the 'enormous' size and steadily growing importance of multinational corporations (MNCs) in world economic activities, a UN group of experts in 1973 came to the trend-setting conclusion that *international production* had surpassed *international trade* as the main vehicle of international economic exchange. It was estimated that international production had reached approximately $330 billion in 1971, while the total exports of all market economies was just a little smaller, at $310 billion.[12] The authors defined international production as 'production subject to foreign control and decision', and based the measurement of it on an estimate of annual foreign sales of MNCs which in its turn was calculated from an assumed ratio of foreign sales to the book value of international direct investment stock. In this particular report, that ratio was arbitrarily set at 2:1.[13] Let us compare this figure with the interwar situation.

Just before the outbreak of the Second World War, in 1938, total world exports came to $22.6 billion.[14] From John Dunning we learn that the gross value of long-term investments at that time had been in the region of $55 billion of which 25 per cent, or $13 billion, is reckoned to have been made up of *direct* investments.[15] Applying the 2:1 ratio to this figure gives us $26 billion as the value of international production, comfortably exceeding the value of international trade at the time.

I am presenting these figures for a purpose: demonstrating that which is *not* new enables us to see more clearly that which *is*. The use of global (in the sense of 'aggregate') trade and investment flows and expressing these as a percentage of 'global', again in the sense of 'aggregate', world product, creates an entirely false image of a 'global' economy that stretches from Anchorage to Cape Town, from Helsinki to Santiago de Chile. It does not; *not any more*! An ambitious net of capitalist catchment may have been thrown during the colonial era, but having caught the fish it has pulled back and settled comfortably on the shores of a relatively small part of the world. And it is in that part indeed that cross-national economic activity is being whipped up into a frenzy.

What is both a *new and consistent* feature of postwar foreign direct investment flows is the *geographic redirection* of such flows away from the periphery and into the core of the system. In the colonial period, right up until 1960, the Third World had received half of total direct investment flows; this percentage had declined to one-third in 1966, and to one-quarter in 1974. By 1988–9 it had dropped still further to 16.9 per cent.[16] But over half of this remaining trickle went to the regions of east, south and south-east Asia.[17]

In the data for south-east Asia, China dominates today as the single largest developing host country of inward investment. Because China has a very large population of 1.2 billion, this often distorts the picture on foreign direct investment (FDI) and growth in the developing world. But it is well-known that in China, both investments and growth are concentrated in the eight coastal provinces (mainly in the south) and in Beijing.

In their recent book *Globalization in Question*, Paul Hirst and Grahame Thompson have tried to discount this anomaly by including only the populations of the coastal provinces and Beijing in their summation of all populations in the ten most important developing countries in terms of inward investment. Together with the other nine most important developing countries hosting FDI, they constitute 758 820 million or 14 per cent of the world population; they receive 16.5 per cent of all global direct investment. Hirst and Thompson add to this the percentage of world population in the USA/Canada, EC and EFTA, and Japan who together receive 75 per cent of all direct investment flows, and they come to the staggering conclusion that only 28 per cent of the world's population receives 91.5 per cent of the FDI.[18] 'This means that nearly two-thirds of the world is virtually written off the map as far as any benefits from this form of investment are concerned.'[19]

World Capital Flows: Long-term Indirect Investments

Foreign direct investments are only one sub-part of all long-term international capital flows. The aggregate also includes so-called indirect flows: for example bank lending, bond issuance, export or commercial credits, official loans and grants, and today a plethora of financial instruments such as derivatives (options and swaps). When it comes to assess these wider international resource flows, it is almost impossible to compare the past with the present. This is not only because of the incompleteness of data and the unevenness of data collection in different historical periods, but more especially because of the interactive web of cross-penetration of such flows today as compared with the past. There was a time before the First World War when the world was sharply divided between creditor and debtor nations. A handful of countries in Europe were the creditor nations. Together they were responsible for 85 per cent of international lending, totalling by 1913 US$44 billion. Nearly 44 per cent of this went to the areas subsequently called the Third World, the bulk of the remainder going to the US, Canada and Russia.[20]

Today, however, creditor nations are also debtor nations. Cross-penetration of financial flows have cast such an immensely complex web of lending and borrowing that it has become almost meaningless to try to trace ownership of assets and liabilities to their respective national roots. National balance-of-payments statistics only give us figures for 'net' capital inflows and outflows. But these conceal a huge variety of international transactions, for example lending by American banks operating in Britain to Americans in American dollars, or to British residents in American dollars, or to American residents in Britain in sterling. Hence the difficulties in comparing the present with the past.

The figures on *gross* capital flows give us a picture of the cross-penetration of the world's financial markets and are therefore a more accurate pointer to today's integrated global financial system. As Clive Crook in his excellent survey of the world's financial markets has argued, during the 1980s the combined forces of innovation, technology and deregulation have brought about a real transformation in the world's financial markets.[21] The following figures on *gross* capital flows in the decade of the 1980s and those shown in Table 4.5 are mostly based on Crook's figures.

To begin with, national stock markets have all but disappeared. Between 1980 and 1990 the volume of cross-border transactions in equities alone grew at a compound rate of 28 per cent *per year*, from $120 billion to $1.4 trillion. The stock of international bank lending (that is foreign currency to home residents, domestic currency to foreign residents, foreign currency to foreign residents) rose from

Table 4.5 Gross capital flows, 1980–90 (US$billion)

Year	Stock of 'International' Bank Lending	Total of International Bonds	Global Stock of Principal Derivatives	Total Cross-Border Transactions in Equities	Global Stock of Foreign Direct Investment (FDI)	Combined GDP of the 24 OECD Countries
1980	324			120	551	7600
1982		259				
1986			1100			
1990				1400	1649	17100
1991	7500	1650	6900			
Growth Rate Multiple	23.15	6.37	6.27	11.67	2.99	2.24

Sources: FDI data: *World Investment Report* (UN, 1994). All other data: 'World Economy', *The Economist*, 19 September 1992.

$324 billion to $7.5 trillion over the same period. Add to this the growth of the international bond markets where companies issue 'I owe you's *offshore*, another increase of 537 per cent over the period from $259 billion to $1.6 trillion, plus the stock of principal derivatives (options, futures, swaps), and one begins just to glimpse the vastness of the transnational financial superbowl in which the national economies of the world are drowning. If we add up all these categories of international indebtedness (and include foreign *direct* investments), the total exceeds the total of the combined GDP of the OECD economies. And we are not even talking about the short-term transactions, such as in the foreign exchange markets where the *daily* value of such transactions already exceeds the monthly requirements of the total of world trade.[22]

It is widely held, not least by international organisations who try to keep track of these flows, that this 'cross-penetration' is testimony to a process of ever-deepening integration of the world's financial markets especially amongst the developed countries.[23] And it is further acknowledged that the integration of the world's financial markets has proceeded much more rapidly than that of the goods market.[24] Indeed, it is the integration of the global financial markets that is most often the reference point for the designation of the term 'globalisation' in the literature of international organisations.

Global Financial Deepening and the Structural Position of the Third World

In an extensive and critical review of the world's financial markets, the UNCTAD's *Trade and Development Report* of 1990 makes the interesting distinction between the '*internationalisation*' of finance, and '*global financial deepening*'. The latter occurs, it says, when – as now – the pace of growth of international financial transactions is very much more rapid than any of the underlying economic fundamentals, like trade, investment and output. For instance, between 1982 and 1988 the annual increment in the stock of world financial assets was, on average, about $3800 billion, whereas the annual average level of world fixed capital formation was around $2300 billion. The ratio of the size of the international banking market to total global fixed investment doubled in less than a decade.[25] Clairmont estimates that private, corporate and household debt

worldwide surpasses US$31 trillion, galloping, he says, at a com-
pound growth of over 9 per cent yearly, or three times faster than
world GDP and world trade.[26] Today more than at any time in
capitalism's history, the profits of finance capital are based on
fictitious capital formation, namely on debt and exponential debt
creation.

Surreptiously the phrases 'economic fundamentals' or 'the real
economy', as distinct from the weird world of high finance, have
crept into the vocabulary of politicians and journalists when having
to explain perplexing phenomena such as the rising value of a
currency during a recession, or a stock market crash during an
upswing in the economy. After the stock market crash of 1987,
which wiped more than 20 per cent of the value of all stocks and
shares, the then Secretary of State for the Treasury, Nigel Lawson,
hastened to reassure the British public that this would not affect the
'real' economy which was in good health and more or less independent from the goings on in the stock market. Indeed the financial
sector is now often dismissed as a casino society where speculators
play out their compulsive habits either without much effect on the
lives of any of us or with effects that can only be guessed at.[27]

On the other hand, there are many who fear that an overblown
financial sector sucks money away and out of productive investments and contributes to the 'short termism' that has come to
pervade the economy and the attitude of the business class. But
short-termism, and so-called paper entrepreneurialism,[28] are only
the more salient outcome of deregulation. Underneath there is
something more fundamental going on, *namely a change in the very
nature of money, and through it the relation between rich and poor,
advanced and less-developed sectors of the world economy.*

In abolishing the institutional barriers between the various functions of money, and in removing the restrictions regarding who can
deal in what kind of money, deregulation (pursued in nearly all
developed and underdeveloping countries with varying degrees of
robustness since 1980) has caused an enormous upheaval in the
structure of finance. On the one hand, banks were being cut out of
the profitable business of borrowing and lending, since companies
and all sorts of 'non-bank' banks or finance houses could issue
commercial paper direct. This is referred to as the process of
'disintermediation'. On the other hand, banks began to develop
new forms of business (so-called off-balance-sheet activities), creat-

ing a whole new breed of securities. Securitisation is often regarded as the single most important innovation following deregulation.

Simply put, securitisation means loan selling.[29] In the traditional, dictionary meaning of the word, a financial security is defined as 'something being given or pledged as guarantee especially for the payment of a debt'.[30] Note the tiny word 'for' in the expression 'for the payment of debt'. The quantum leap in financial innovation is that this word 'for' has now been dropped. The payment of debt itself became 'securitised' and offered as tradable paper; effectively, therefore, as money. For example, banks can pool together a variety of mortgages on houses, stores and office buildings, or even car and credit card loans, and next sell bonds backed by these 'receivables' in small chunks to individual investors who can either hang on to them and earn interest on their share, or in turn sell them in secondary markets.[31] Once that principle had been thoroughly understood and learnt there were no holds barred, and a weird and wonderful variety of novel financial instruments cropped up which would instantly convert any *expected future cash flow*, wherever and whenever it might occur, into instant spending power. As *The Economist* summed it up: 'The truth is that there is no longer any such thing as money. At least not in the sense required by monetarism and its siblings.'[32]

It is worth reflecting for a moment on the significance of the new form in which money appears, within the context of a globalised financial structure that has grown up in a world economy in which, nevertheless, the fundamentals of trade, investment, income and productive wealth remain highly unequally distributed across regions and nations. For the new financial instruments effectively delink borrowers from lenders and they do so on a cross-nation basis. The upshot is that people with relatively little money in one country can participate in the lending of funds to borrowers in another. Wealth, in short, has become highly mobile. The question is how the enhanced capacity of the global financial structure to switch money flows around the world economy interacts with the systemically uneven distribution of material activities of production and consumption.

On an optimistic reading one might agree with John Reed, the chairman of Citicorp, the biggest of American banks, that there is some good to be gained out of all this frenzied careening of monies around the world: 'you can translate the saving of that Japanese household into economic well-being for somebody in South Italy or Spain'.[33] But note that in this particular quote the banker was careful not to mention a Third World country. For, indeed, it is very unlikely that money will flow more easily from where it is concentrated and politically and strategically safe, to where it is scarce and subject to great political and strategic risks. And Reed himself is certainly aware of this when he recognises that the Third World today is 'unbankable':

There are five billion people living on earth. Probably 800 million of them live in societies that are bankable and probably 4.2 billion are living within societies that in some very fundamental way are not bankable. I think it's a great danger as we look out between now and the turn of the century that this distinction between bankable and the unbankable parts of the world could become more aggravated. We're forming this global economy which is very much a phenomenon of the northern hemisphere – Europe, North America, Japan – with some small additions. . . Many of the problems we have on the globe, be it the global environment or health, are problems of the 4.2 billion, not the 800 million.[34]

If we now look at the structural position of the Third World in the financial superbowl we encounter a curious paradox. On the one hand, and in line with the periphery's declining participation in the 'fundamentals' of the world economy surveyed above, its share of the total stock of international bank lending has declined to about 11 per cent.[35] Indeed, for most of the 1980s, new bank lending to the developing countries declined to the point of virtual extinction as the debt crisis took its toll and banks refused to lend anew to troubled sovereign debtors. Even the 11 per cent (or $512 billion) is an overestimate since it includes incremental values attributable to arrears; that is, it is not a summation of continuous fresh inflows. On the other hand, we also find an increased participation of Third World élites in the international financial markets. How is that?

Given that much of the Third World is unbankable in the traditional sense of the word, namely offering a safe return on investment, it is more likely that élites in the Third World will buy securities in the global markets rather than in their national markets. Studies by research staff of the International Monetary Fund on the scale of *capital flight* from the developing countries lend credence to this thesis. For example, between 1975 and 1985 an estimated \$165–200 billion were placed by individual investors from the Third World in the international financial markets.[36]

This is surely the critical difference between the earlier, expansive, phase of capitalism and today's 'imploding' phase. In the earlier prewar period, when nearly 44 per cent of all international long-term lending (including foreign direct investments) went to the regions of Africa, Asia and Latin America, it found its way into the development of railways, port installations, mines and factories. Capital accumulation and saving in the core of the world system through the financial intermediation of international portfolio lending, converted into fixed investments in the rest of the world laying the foundations for future wealth creation.

Today, however, the regime of privatisation and deregulation imposed by the World Bank and IMF structural adjustment programmes, have created a climate of what is euphemistically called 'financial openness' in which the Third World bourgeoisie are less restricted and more enabled than ever before to channel their nation's wealth to the financial markets and institutions of the core countries. In so doing, *they* can participate in the economies of the core of the world system, while their countries cannot. The intimate connection between the debt crisis, capital flight and the financial integration of the periphery into the world system will be discussed in Chapter 8.

Core–Periphery: From Structural Exploitation to Structural Irrelevance

I have tried in the foregoing analysis to substantiate my thesis of 'imploding' capitalism. By 'implosion' I understand an intensification of trade and capital linkages within the core of the capitalist system, and a relative, selective, withdrawal of such linkages from the periphery. Looking over the longer historical period, we have examined the relationship between the core and the periphery of the world system and found that the linkages between the two in terms of the volume of both trade and capital flows between them, which increased during earlier phases of the period, have since diminished. Moreover, even allowing for the shift in positions of some countries from the periphery to the core, it was also found that the proportionate share of populations in core and periphery has remained surprisingly constant from about 1880–1990.

Characterising the core and the periphery in the manner which we have done throughout this chapter, namely the core being western Europe, North America and Japan and the periphery covering the entire regions of Africa, Latin America and Asia, there is furthermore evidence that the gap between their respective shares of world income too has widened.

For example, in its 1992 *Human Development Report* the United Nations Development Programme (UNDP) calculated that in 1989 22.9 per cent of the world population estimated to be living in 'industrial' countries had 84.2 per cent of global GNP, compared with 77.1 per cent of the world population in the 'developing countries' who make do with just 15.8 per cent of global GNP. While the share of global GNP of each of these two groups has been practically constant over the period since 1960, their respective share of world populations, in this report, is said to have worsened with the 'industrial' group of countries comprising a declining share (from 31.5 per cent in 1960 to 22.9 per cent in 1989), while that of the developing countries has risen from 68.5 per cent in 1960 to 77.1 per cent in 1989.[37]

Going back over an even longer period, as in the previous section when we discussed economic exchanges between core and periphery, we come up against almost impossible limitations owing to the unavailability of comparable statistics. Economic historians have, however, attempted to *estimate* the GNP level of per capita incomes for 'developed' and 'underdeveloped' countries in earlier periods. One such estimate was made by Paul Bairoch in 1975, and goes back to 1900 using an implicit price deflator resulting from the calculations of the United States' gross product at constant prices. Bairoch notes a divergence between per capita income ratios between non-communist underdeveloped countries and the non-communist developed countries rising from 1:5 in 1860, 1:6 in 1900, 1:7 in 1929, 1:8.5 in 1953 to 1:13 in 1970.[38] This compares with the UNDP ratio of income for the same two groups of countries in 1989 of 1:18[39] (see Figure 4.1). Thus, the gap that almost a hundred years ago separated the rich world from the poor world has continuously widened, both during periods of capitalist expansion and during the more recent period of contraction.

Figure 4.1   Widening gaps in per capita income, 1860–1989 (weighted shares of world income of developed and underdeveloped groups of countries)

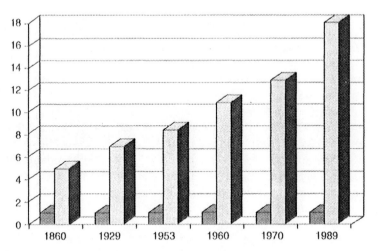

Key:

■■■ UDC – Underdeveloped Group of Countries.

☐ DC – Developed Group of Countries.

Source: 1860–1970 based on estimates in Paul Bairoch, *The Economic Development of the Third World* (London: Methuen, 1975), Table 53, p. 193. 1960–1989 based on UNDP *Human Development Report, 1992* (Oxford: Oxford University Press, 1992), Table 3.7, p. 37.

Three likely points of criticism to this very pessimistic assessment of the global economy need to be addressed. *First*, these are *relative* proportions. In absolute terms, for sure, the world capitalist system may well be seen to have delivered the goods for increasing numbers of human beings. The question which then must be put is: is this a victory for capitalism? Is this a triumph for the free market organisation of human and social life? In my view it is not. The moral justification in the liberal defence of the capitalist system is that it is welfare-maximising in the long run. But so far all that capitalism has been able to do is just about, or perhaps not even quite, to keep pace in the Malthusian race. Hardly a record to be proud of, in particular if one considers that to achieve this amazing 'triumph' the 'core' today uses 70 per cent of the world's energy, 75 per cent of its metals, 85 per cent of its wood and consumes 60 per cent of its food.[40] It is like trying and not even succeeding to win a race despite being given a very generous handicap!

The *second* point of likely controversy relates to the sudden emergence of China as the next giant. Nearly all the statistical data reviewed in this chapter is pre-1990. Since then, it is true, China has been 're'discovered in official international literature as a country with enviable growth rates, averaging 9 per cent per annum over the past decade. It is, more importantly, a country where since 1990 capital inflows (both international indirect lending and foreign direct investment) have been of an order of magnitude that dwarfs the share of all other regions of the developing world and that has done much to 'turn around', or so it would seem, the share of the Third World as a whole in global investment flows. Since 1990 the capital inflows into China have exceeded an estimated $54 billion. However, most of this has ended up in the three southern provinces of Guandong, Zhejang and Fujan, and from there has done a U-turn into the global financial markets of Hong Kong.[41] This is precisely what globalisation is all about.

A *third* point of criticism also relates to the 1990 end-date of the statistics surveyed in this chapter. It is confidently argued by some observers that the 1990s are witnessing a dramatic turnaround in the fortunes, not just of China, but of all the Third World. As an opening paragraph in *The Economist* in a 1994 upbeat assessment puts it:

A potentially dramatic new phase in the development of the global economy, in which growth is shifting towards poorer countries, is becoming ever more clearly detectable. It is being matched and stimulated by a massive strategic move by international investors into the so-called emerging markets. Suddenly the late 20th Century economy is beginning to look more like that of the late 19th Century.[42]

Even Africa, often regarded as beyond hope, is thought to be poised for growth and has caught the imagination of international fund managers.[43]

By all accounts, investment funds have recently been pouring large sums into the emerging stock markets of Latin America and

Africa as well as those of south east Asia, apparently completely reversing the declining trends of the 1970s and 1980s. But it is precisely at this point that we should beware of the chasm between the *fundamentals* of the world economy and the *global financial deepening* that I signalled before. For the 'strategic' shift that is occurring is nothing other than a shift in ownership of state property and resources, as the debt adjustment policies of the last decade work their way through to their logical conclusion.

The structural adjustment programmes of the World Bank and IMF have encouraged privatisation and liberalisation policies in the indebted countries. State-owned public utilities and national economic resources, such as mines, industrial companies and real estate, are being hived off to the private sector, and while national stock-markets are still small or in the process of being formed, liberalisation policies ensure that foreign investors get a large slice of the action. The inevitable under-capitalisations of these emerging stock markets prove an attractive hunting ground for the active money managers of core countries' investment funds and more speculative funds such as hedge funds. It is yet another example of frenzied international circulation of capital rather than a foretaste of real production and economic growth to come. The crash of the Mexican peso in 1995 following four years' frenetic 'paper' growth of the stock and estates markets is a case in point. Mexico is now back where it was ten years ago, facing a new cycle of debt and structural adjustment.

The question we must finally put is what are the chances of this circulating capital dropping down into expanded production and rising standards of living in the poorer countries? It seems to me that this question must be answered with reference to the new system of production that is at present coming about in the core of the world system. Variously referred to as a 'lean production system', flexible manufacturing, or post-Fordist system, these new production systems combine a transformation of the social organisation of industrial production with an infusion of information-driven technologies at every stage of the industrial process, from design to marketing. This new system of production has been called 'lean' because it uses less of everything compared with mass production: 'half the human effort in the factory, half the manufacturing space, half the investment in tools, and half the engineering hours to develop a new product in half the time'.[44]

In Chapter 5 we shall examine the various aspects of the new information-driven production systems. Here it suffices to point to their negative prospects for many, if not most, areas of the traditional Third World to be included in the expanded reproduction of capital. In a lucid article on the new international division of labour in the new informational economy, Manuel Castells has summed up the structural reasons for the marginalisation and exclusion of what he calls the 'Fourth World', that is those areas in the Third, Second *and* First World that are no longer relevant to the workings of the global informational economy:

> The more economic growth depends on high value added inputs and expansion in the core markets, then the less relevant become those economies which offer limited, difficult markets and primary commodities that are either being replaced by new materials or devalued with respect to their overall contribution to the production process. With the absolute costs of labor becoming less and less important as a competitive factor . . . many countries and regions face a process of rapid deterioration that could lead to destructive reactions. Within the framework of the new informational economy, a significant part of the world population is shifting from a structural position of exploitation to a structural position of irrelevance.[45]

5

From Fordist to Flexible Production

It has become a cliché to say that the world economy is in crisis, or, that it has been in crisis for over 20 years. Or that existing theories, whether of the neo-classical or Marxist variety, are no longer adequate to comprehend this crisis, and to predict how it is being resolved.

What we need is a sense of direction; a grasping of essentials, of emerging tendencies, of what Karl Mannheim, an eminent social philosopher writing during a previous period of crisis called *principia media*, those principal nascent features which will act as structural imperatives to other emerging features and which therefore may be expected to become the dominant features of the new epoch.[1] We need to know what these dominant features are; we want to know the contours of the new 'epoch'.

One thing the crisis has done thus far with illuminating clarity is to lay bare this need. Notwithstanding the contemporary postmodernist turn, there is a continuing intellectual current, to which I myself subscribe, that craves an understanding of order, of coherence, of comprehending how things hang together, for totalising stories, whether scientific theories or myths. We just have to know how everything fits. We seem unwilling to abandon the concept, or the experience, of society as a systemic unity of meaningfully related structures: technological, economic, political, cultural and ideological. But the experience of the crisis is that things do not fit any more. They are like shattered fragments of broken glass; beyond problem-solving, beyond being repaired with glue. The *angst* in the experience of crisis brings to mind Gramsci's dictum: that the old order is dead but the new order is unable to be born. And so the search is on for those *principia media*, those nascent features that will give us glimpses of a reconstituting new order. We want to know what the future holds.

The past 20 years have seen a good deal of 'epoch' sketching, a return even to grand social theorising: world system theory, regulation theory, postFordism, flexible specialisation theory, organised/disorganised capitalism; new times theory, third wave theory, even end-of-history theories. What this theorising has in common, is *first*, a preference for order over chaos; *next*, a belief in order as a condition for prosperity; *third*, the equation of order both with stability and with systemic wholeness; and *last but not least*, a definition of systemic wholeness in *its* turn as the product of compatibility of structures. Thus, there is a fascination with patterns of work organisation that match certain technological paradigms and that set the scene for wider industrial and political relations; or with the meaningful connection between economic production on the one hand and certain cultural forms and symbolic representations on the other; or with the link between intensified consumerism and multiple identities at the psychological level.

In this part of the book we engage with these debates and do some 'order' sketching ourselves. But we need to express a note of caution first:

1. To say something about a new order, one always finds oneself talking about the 'old order' from which the new one is said to be distinct. This means that the language of the old always informs the description of the new.

   The proliferation of labels, such as postmodernist, postmaterialist, postFordist or postindustrial, proves the point that we are leaving behind us a social order that was pretty much understood, and entering another the contours of which can be only dimly recognized.

2. Since, perforce, we have to try and understand the new in the language of the old, we impose an assumption of historical continuity that may not be justified. We always assume that we can read the future from our understanding of the past. Indeed it has been the hallmark of western philosophy to conceive of history as a 'story', with a beginning and an end, and thus a past that informs the future. But such an assumption precludes the

possibility that maybe this time around history is no guide to the future. Imagine this to be so with the very notion of 'social order'. What if the future is not like the past and what if it is marked by functioning anarchy instead?

Fordism

Henry Ford's celebrated invention, in 1908, of the car assembly line is credited with having ushered in the great era of mass production in manufacturing. But, actually, the assembly line was a mere enabling technical device. There was a real social innovation which preceded it, and that was Ford's concept of standardisation. Already in 1903, Ford had recognized that in the fabrication of complex products such as the motor vehicle the key to enhanced efficiency of production lay in the method of coordination of discrete sub-production processes and in the manner in which the various sub-parts were assembled into a whole. Ford reckoned that instead of making the parts first and then fitting them together to make the whole, as in craft production, to *make the parts fit prior to assembly* would make huge savings in the assembly stage. Thus he aimed for complete and consistent interchangeability of parts and for simplicity in attaching them to each other. To achieve this, he insisted that, for example, the same gauging system be used for every part all the way through the entire manufacturing process.[2]

The cost-savings of standardisation were subsequently further enhanced by minute division of labour, enabled by the time-and-motion studies of Frederick Charles Taylor which gave title to the production paradigm as 'Fordist–Taylorist'. Eventually, each worker carried out one simple manipulative task. This social innovation was completed with the technical innovation of the automated, moving assembly line which delivered the vehicles in various stages of assembly around the plant from task to task.

The results were awesome. In 1923, the peak year of his Model T production, Ford produced 2.1 million cars, compared with the one-car-a-day production of a craft producer like Aston Martin.[3]

Ford's invention was so crucial in shaping the postwar political economy that in much social science literature today this political economy is named after him. It was the period of 'Fordism'. But note that it took a good 30 years and the two biggest wars humankind has experienced before Ford's *techno-economic* paradigm was complemented by a whole ensemble of supporting macroeconomic institutions, social organisational forms, political settlements and even cultural values, which together and *only when they were in place*, permitted the economic benefits of that system to materialise to the full (see p. 46).

From Fordist to Flexible Production

It would seem that in the organisation of social life nothing ever fails like success. The social order of Fordism carried a number of internal contradictions which – as David Harvey comments – may be captured by one word: rigidity.[4]

The whole point about mass production as a profitable undertaking is that it achieves *economies of scale*. This means that the more that is produced of a standardised product, the more the unit cost of production comes down. More means cheaper. But the downside is, on the one hand, that there is a minimum scale required for economic operation, and, on the other, that the success of the operation depends crucially on *continuous* and uninterrupted expansion of market demand for that same product. The mass production system cannot cope flexibly with either cyclical recessions, or increased competition, or changing market tastes. The result is underutilisation of capacity, and overproduction, resulting in lay-offs, losses and ultimately closure.

By the late-1960s that distinctive period of mass production and Fordist accumulation had come to an end. The rigidities of the Fordist regime showed up with irrepressible frequency, culminating eventually in economic stagnation, contraction and continuing crises. There were many instances of rigidity at all levels,[5] but the most important was undoubtedly the deepening global inequalities discussed in the first part of this book. These put a limit on the further expansion of that particular system of mass production. There was a global demand crisis, and thus capitalism had to reconstitute itself on an entirely new basis. In a world economy where 20 per cent of the population has 150 times the spending capacity of the poorest 20 per cent, clearly a new production system was needed that could fully exploit consumer demand from the 'have-lots' in an ever fiercer climate of global competition.

During the crisis a series of novel social experiments and technical innovations (particularly the introduction of information-driven technologies) in the realms of industrial as well as in political and social life have begun to take shape. *The key concept that captures the nascent tendencies is flexibility*: flexible production, flexible work processes, flexible labour markets, flexible products, flexible education, flexible patterns of consumption, flexible savings and pension funds, and even flexible or multiple identities.

To understand the emerging contours of the new epoch we have to begin, as we did with Fordism, with the production process. Contemporary theories of social change, however hard they may try to escape from, or transcend, Marxism, cannot completely run away from the tentacles of technological and economic determinism. For it is key changes in the production process, namely certain technological innovations and the manner in which these become embedded in new forms of economic organisation, that form the point of entry of all contemporary analyses of social transformation, including that of the Regulation School, critical theory and institutional economics.

The reason that this should be so is because these new technologies and the associated new patterns of management, work and organisation in the workplace are at least visibly present, either already tangibly in existence in some places or visibly coming into being in others. And thus an impressive amount of literature from all sides of the political spectrum, right-wing and liberal, from the business community and the academic management world, as well as from the critical left, describes a cluster of properties of the new business, or enterprise, systems with a surprising degree of unanimity. It is therefore perfectly appropriate to speak, as many do, of a new technico-economic paradigm, or of a technological paradigm, or of a technological trajectory.[6]

According to institutional economists like Freeman and Perez:

a technico-economic paradigm is a cluster of interrelated technical, organisational and managerial innovations, whose advantages are to be found not only in a new range of products and systems, but most of all in the dynamics of the relative cost structure of all possible inputs to production. In each new paradigm, a particular input or set of inputs may be described as the 'key' factor in that paradigm characterised by falling costs and universal availability.[7]

I first want to describe the 'agreed' features of this technico-economic paradigm. I do this by summarising just one very influential text on the subject, namely Womack *et al.*, *The Machine that Changed the World*. Since it was published in 1990 it has sold several million copies world-wide, and it has become a standard text not just in academic management literature, but also in workshops, seminar groups, and other think tanks in the business community and in public policy-making circles.

Volume through Variety

Already in the 1950s, Toyota had invented a new organisation of the production process that combined the benefits of mass production with those of craft production. Because Japan in those days did not have a mass domestic market Toyota had to make the most of market segmentation, producing a wide variety of the same generic product (vehicles of all kinds) rather than, as Ford had done, use the same fixed capital investment for mass production of the same standard commodity. Toyota achieved this *not through making more of the same but by making a whole variety of products with the same general tool.*

For example, in Fordist automobile plants 'dedicated' machines were used to produce each one of the 300 sheet steel parts that go into a motor car. Mass producers used automated blanking presses and, next, stamping presses containing matched upper and lower dies. The same parts were stamped for months or even years without changing the dies. Toyota developed a simple technique for quickly changing dies so that a variety of parts could be stamped with the same machine without significant 'downtime'. Moreover, the changing of the dies could be done by the production workers themselves. This is the essence of what some have called 'Toyotaism'[8] and what Womack *et al.* refer to as 'lean' production, and this is why 'economies of scope' in contrast to 'economies of scale' is probably the most accurate descriptor of the new system's method of 'accumulation' or profit maximisation.

Customised Production

Once we understand the principle of volume through variety as the principle that combines the best of mass production with the best of craft production, we can anticipate the next step in the logic of lean production: namely customised production. Toyota gradually stopped building cars in advance for unknown buyers and converted to a build-to-order system in which the dealers became the first step in what came to be known as the *'kanban'* (or just-in-time) approach, sending orders for presold cars to the factory for delivery to specific customers in two to three weeks. Both dealers and customers became part of the 'extended family' of Toyota. Toyota has small or large equities in the dealer firms, while the dealers develop aggressive selling techniques which involve regular visits to customers, the building up of massive data banks on customer households, keeping track of the changes in these households and so on. Customers for their part have a real role in identifying weaknesses in the cars they buy, and in specifying the changes they want. Toyota goes directly to existing customers in planning new products. Brand loyalty becomes a salient feature of the lean production system. With his customary flamboyance in coining new terms, Alvin Toffler has identified the new consumer as a 'prosumer', that is a consumer who is indirectly, sometimes unwittingly, but for all that importantly involved in production and therefore partly contributes to his/her own exploitation.[9]

Just-in-time Supply Systems

The cost savings through the principle of volume – through variety rather than volume-through-bulk are enormous. It means less manufacturing space, and little or no inventory or 'work-in-progress'. These cost-savings are vastly increased when combined with the famous *just-in-time* (JIT) practice where components and parts are supplied literally only hours or days before they need to be assembled. This is a big change from mass production.

In mass production, the inflexibility of tools in supplier plants (analogous to the inflexibility of the stamping presses in the assembly plants) and the erratic nature of orders from assemblers responding to shifting market demand caused suppliers to build large volumes of one type of part before changing over machinery to the next, and to maintain large stocks of finished parts in a warehouse.

Toyota developed a new way to coordinate the flow of parts within the supply system on a day-to-day basis.

They simply converted a vast group of suppliers and parts plants into one large machine, like Henry Ford's Highland Park plant, by dictating that parts would only be produced at each previous step to supply the immediate demand of the next step. The mechanism was the containers carrying parts to the next step. As each container was used up, it was sent back to the previous step and this became the automatic signal to make more parts.[10]

This sounds nice and simple, but actually it masks real differences between Japanese and western conceptions and practices of capitalist enterprise and competition. For the relationship between Toyota, the assembler, and its suppliers of components is a classic example of Japanese 'group capitalism' (as in the *keiretsu*), and differs in important ways from either the centralised monopoly structure or the decentralised competitive structure of relationships that characterise large industry in the West. Both structure and strategy are very different.

In the West, typically, a large auto manufacturer will either obtain components and parts from in-house divisions or wholly-owned companies, or from independently-owned outside contractors, or indeed from a a mixture of both. In recent years the trend has been towards decentralisation. Neither works well because of the ingrained concept of competition in the bidding and the contracting, coupled with the mass-production practice of separating design (which is done by the assembler) from execution (by the suppliers, whether in-house or independent). The suppliers are simply given specific drawings of the parts they have to make and are then asked to bid in competitive tender. Cost comes first.

This derails the whole process right from the start: for the supplier will be so keen to win the contract that costs will be underestimated, setting the supplier on course for a development of a prototype that is bound to need adjustments both in price and in subsequent redrawings and new specifications, resulting in protracted renegotiations of contract and endless spiralling of costs. When volume production starts, the contract usually expresses a target for the supplier in terms of an 'acceptable percentage of bad parts'. It is not strictly the supplier's responsibility to improve on the design. The bad parts simply end up in the waste bin. Because of the essentially competitive nature of the relationship, including that between assembler and in-house suppliers (who are almost always separate 'profit' centres), information is not shared for fear that the assembler could use it to negotiate lower prices for follow-on contracts.

The Japanese model is quite different in conception. To begin with, the assembler and the suppliers are likely to have formed a 'group' of companies, on the model of the *keiretsu* in which the companies are partly related to one another through cross-equity structures. But these cross-equity structures are unlike our public equity structures. While shares may be traded on the stock market, the members of the group hold on to each other's shares because of the reciprocal obligations and rights that these equity holdings carry. Every *keiretsu* usually has a bank, an insurance company and a trading company. These make available cash resources to members of the group on a subsidised basis, for the whole purpose is to 'help' each other raise investment funds. This is very different from the Western practices of raising funds either through equity in stock markets or through interest bearing loans from banks, or bonds.

Members of the group, further, normally second senior personnel and re-assign managerial personnel to each other in times of need. There is, in other words, a sense of group commitment, and a preference for long-term stability in the relationships coupled with a sense of 'we all swim or drown together', that is completely different from the situation prevailing in the West.[11] And, what is more, seen in the context of lean production, it helps to explain the crucial aspect of collaboration between assembler and suppliers that is central to the success of the just-in-time system.

The Simultaneity Principle: Integrating Design, Manufacture and Component Supply

Toyota's lean production approach to components supply was to organise the suppliers into first, second and third-'tier' suppliers. These were functional suppliers and Toyota's assemblers dealt only directly with the first tier. In-house supplier operations were spun off into quasi-independent first-tier supplier companies in which Toyota retained a fraction of the equity and with whom it formed the same 'shared destiny' relationship as with the 'independents'. What is more, suppliers, instead of competing with each other, are joined in suppliers associations in which they share information and together try to improve on parts and component production. They work directly with the designers in product development, thus succeeding in bringing down the lead time between design, prototype and manufacture of the final product.

Instead of inviting the suppliers to cost–bid for contracts, the assembler establishes a target price for the car or truck and then, with the suppliers, works backwards, working out how the vehicle can be made for this price while allowing a reasonable profit for both the assembler and the suppliers. In other words, it is a 'market price minus system' rather than a 'supplier cost plus system'.[12]

Zero-defect and Total Quality Management

Apart from their invention of the just-in time-system, the Japanese lean production methods are probably best known for their quality control and total quality management (TQM). The latter is currently spurring frenzied imitation in the West, and a great deal of spurious management discourse has developed around it. For example, it is suggested that 'community spirit' in work teams and quality circles drives the Japanese workers to ferret out every defect in the production process because they feel responsible; they 'own' their product, and they are motivated by workplace democracy. Nostalgic dreams of the golden age of craftsmanship mesh with anti-socialist fervour in denying that anything like alienation or exploitation ever need exist in a capitalist society.[13] Indeed, it has become commonplace to use the word 'empowerment' to describe how the lean production system of quality circles, multi-skilling and team work affects the workers.[14] There are also dark stirrings of anxiety to the effect that behind the scenes lurk ancient cultural traditions of Japanese communitarianism and group life which explain and at the same time would sadly render indiffusable the practice of quality control to the mundane modern western man.

So what is the reality?

In mass production systems, because of the enormous investment in fixed plant and equipment, the prior concern is to keep the assembly line moving. If there is a defect, and there are plenty, it is – in an accounting sense – discounted for from the start, and physically dealt with at the end of the line where there are work stations to check and repair the mistakes.

This strategy of course has costly penalties attached to it. Some errors in one part may be recurring over quite an extended period or series, before being checked and stopped. They may have become embedded in a complex vehicle before being discovered, adding even greater costs of rectification. Also, in order to cope with the checking afterwards and the repair, the system of mass production relies on a whole army of so-called 'indirect' workers, that is workers who do not directly add value to the car on the line, but whose participation in the work process is simply intended to mop up the mistakes. In lean production, because of the small batches that are processed at any one time, there is none of that. Faults occurring in one batch are discovered instantly, and eliminated before the next order zooms along.

This waste-elimination is a consequence of the 'zero-defect' principle which constitutes a logical extension of the JIT principle. Flexible, just-in-time, production cannot work at all without perfect quality of materials and components since there is almost no stock to replace defective parts.

Within the Toyota company, and later on throughout lean or flexible production systems, the practice of checking for faults *during* the process of batch assembly instead of *afterwards* became ingeniously tied up with an entirely new concept of (self) management of workers. Critics have claimed that this signalled an intensification of labour exploitation. However, it seemed innocent enough to begin with: Toyota hit upon the idea to make the workers 'responsible' for the mistakes that were made, and it 'empowered' them to do what in mass production no shop-floor worker ever dared do: stop the production line. The workers were also grouped into teams not with a foreman but with a team leader/coordinator – all very democratic – and each team was given complete responsibility for their piece of the production line, including quality checking, tool repairs and 'house-keeping'. Each team was told that they 'owned' their product. The next logical step was to go beyond the zero-defect principle and give the teams responsibility for quality and workflow *improvements*. The periodic brainstorm to achieve such improvements within the team is referred to in industrial history by the name of 'quality circle'.

Quality circles and total quality management have been hailed as gigantic steps forward in the humanisation of the shop-floor. But they have also attracted some of the most damaging criticism, especially in recent years, as Japanese lean methods are being transplanted to western societies where labour emancipation and trade union consciousness as well as Marxist academic interest have a more robust tradition than in Japan.[15]

The Japanese Mode of Regulation

It is widely asserted in business and academic literature that the Japanese system of production organisation 'works' in Japan because it is embedded there in a complex of social institutional and cultural forms that are unique to the Japanese. In the parlance of the Regulation School which we discuss below, we might say that the Japanese system of production organisation is embedded in a societal mode of regulation. For example, work organisation on the shop-floor is woven into compatible production relations typified by what are often referred to as the three 'pillars' of Japanese employment institutions: lifetime employment, seniority-based wage systems and enterprise unions. These make for 'harmonious industrial relations' in which the workers throw in their lot with the company. The adversarial relationship between capital and labour is commuted into shared corporate interests in a competitive world.

The 'employment for life' institution and the hesitation employees have had in the past to sever their links with their employers has in turn been explained with reference to a strong attachment to the even deeper embedded socio-cultural institution of '*ie*'. *Ie* is the household economy which during the Meiji era was established as the basic unit of the Japanese economy. Paternal obligations towards the workers were foisted on the employers, while workers assumed filial piety and attachment to their employers. The '*ie*' thesis of Japanese corporate democracy thus presents an oriental form of social bonding as the determining factor explaining Japanese economic success.[16]

It is, however, not absolutely necessary to dig into the cultural recesses of Japanese life to explain its unique mode of regulation. Alternative explanations point to historical-structural conditions prevailing in the immediate postwar period, when the Japanese government, under American prompting, strengthened the rights of unions and imposed severe restrictions on the ability of company owners to fire workers. A historic class-compromise was reached in the late-1940s when workers negotiated lifetime employment, pay graded by seniority rather than by specific job function, and bonus payments linked to company profitability, in exchange for flexibility in work assignments and loyalty to the Company above all else.

Even so, the case for the culturist explanation of Japanese uniqueness remains strong. For example, it is difficult to understand the efficacy of 'implicit contracting' between large firms, and their extended network of 'independent' suppliers and distributors, without reference to the elaborate and deeply ingrained cultural system of '*giri*' (interpersonal obligations) pervasive in Japanese social life, or the 'situational ethics' which foster enduring forms of dependency and trust relations between people in work settings. The dominance of Japanese 'groupiness' as the social glue that explains collaboration in otherwise competitive situations is difficult to ignore.[17]

Internationalisation or Globalisation? The Japanese Model in the World Economy

Although the Japanese pioneered the development of flexible methods of organising production almost 40 years ago, it was not until the widespread industrial application of *information technology* since about the mid-1970s that flexible production spread to the West. Five key 'generic' technologies in particular have enabled firms to achieve the objective of flexible production. Computer-aided design (CAD) has become the principal automation technology for use in design activities, and computer numerical control (CNC) for control of machine tools. Industrial robots and automated transfer systems have almost completely replaced labour in fabrication and assembly, while process control systems have emerged as the replacement for supervisory staff offering instantaneous monitoring and control of production.[18]

The competitive success of Japanese manufacturing firms in global markets from the late-1970s forced companies in the West to follow suit and go 'lean'.[19] In the initial phase, they selectively adopted some of the best-known features of Japanese 'best practice' (such as customised production and JIT) together with the smart technologies described above. The UN Centre on Transnational Corporations, in its 1988 report, recognised flexible production together with the new information technology as one of 'the outstanding features of world development in the 1980s'.[20]

The outcome, however, was far from successful. In his book *Flexible Manufacturing Technologies and International Competitiveness*, Joseph Tidd describes the growing disenchantment with the new manufacturing systems among American and European manufacturers who had equipped their plants with ever more expensive, sophisticated technologies than the Japanese, but who nevertheless failed to match their Japanese competitors in terms of productivity or quality.[21] He argued that they failed to identify any dominant pattern of adaptation of international 'best practice',[22] and he concluded that the competitivenes of advanced manufacturing technology (AMT) will ultimately depend on *organisational* issues and market strategy, rather than smart technology [emphasis added].[23]

Nick Oliver and Barry Wilkinson, too, have observed how the enthusiastic application of Japanese lean production systems in British manufacturing during the 1980s failed to bring the great change that was hoped for. They write:

> It may be that the 'obstacles to Japanization' . . . are more deep-seated, perhaps more crucially embedded, than we originally believed. Nonetheless the imperative to change is still fixed in the minds of British managers and engineers, albeit often now along with the realization that the changes required are not so easy to implement as to conceptualise.[24]

The nub is that it is not enough to apply the new technology and to follow some new working methods. The lean production system was originally developed in Japan within a home-grown mode of regulation and its diffusion abroad requires a process of social adaptation, restructuring and reorganisation both at the firm-level and in the wider society.

In 1992, the Commission of the European Communities published a report entitled *What are Anthropocentric Production Systems?*[25] The report advocates the merits of the new production system and encourages its application through radical restructuring of industrial organisations. But the report invents a new term, *anthropocentric production system* (APS), although the key features of this production system are no different from lean production. So why then do they announce it as 'new' when they know that there had already been an all out drive for over a decade to introduce the new system?

What is new in this report is the recognition that lean production is not merely the application of new technology but a new *social* organisation of *production relations*, which adds up to a new way of thinking. The report argues that the 'comprehensiveness' of twenty-first century production methods, requires not just the acquisition of leading edge technology but also 'the integration of cultural, work and technological factors and their organisation'.[26] This recognition, it seems, has been brought about by the 'investment disasters' of the late-1980s.[27]

There are signs today that this lesson is now being learnt. At *firm-level*, the evidence by the mid-1990s points to either wholesale or selective adoption of the principal *organisational* features of lean production described above. Often these adoptions are couched in terms of local management discourse that disguise the degree of convergence of the process of industrial restructuring and work organisation now under way. For example, in the Anglo-Saxon world, human resource management (HRM) has been hailed as a 'new' management approach involving 'employee commitment, responsibility and customer satisfaction'. A recent survey by the British Labour Research Department found that no less than 87 per cent of workplaces used at least one or more of the following techniques: HRM, TQM and 'customer care'. Continuous improvement practices and multi-skilling are also spreading as are team-working and enterprise unions. These Japanese work organisations are diffusing both in industrial sectors and in service sectors, and they straddle the public/private sector divide.[28]

In the 1980s, when Japanese competitive success in export markets was followed by a steep rise in their direct investments in the advanced countries, the debates around Japanese 'best practice' culminated in debates about the full scale 'Japanisation' of the world. The presence of Japanese firms in global markets encouraged assertions, and raised questions, about the global diffusion of their national model through activities of transplants, emulators and competitors.

Broadly speaking, the debate divides into two polarised positions: culturists versus universalists. Culturists emphasise the national distinctiveness of the Japanese model, in particular the way it is embedded in culturally specific institutional complexes that cannot be diffused to, or learnt by, other societies. Universalists, on the other hand, point to the converging logic of global competition 'in which system standards and economic measures take precedence over nation state diversity'.[29]

Much of this 'global Japanisation' debate, however, is a red herring because it confuses firm-level adaptations and adoptions with wider, inter-firm, and macro-level modes of regulation. Here is where the research agenda of the Regulation School is pertinent.

The Regulation School

The Regulation School consists of a loosely networked group of intellectuals who study the present crisis and the emergence of a new social, economic and political order. Prominent amongst them are Michel Aglietta and Alain Lipietz of the so-called Parisian School. There is also a German School and an Amsterdam School.[30] Many stand firmly in the Marxist tradition, and acknowledge their Marxist roots. For example, Alain Lipietz, one of the pioneers of the group, describes his book *Mirage and Miracle* as a study about the current situation 'using Marxist analytical tools appropriately'. But in using the tools 'appropriately' they abandon the historical project for which Marx had designed the tools. There is no conception of social progress; no eschatological belief in the forward march of history; no political commitment to surrender the freedom of the intellect to a course that history has charted.

The Regulation School takes as its point of departure the concept of capitalism as a mode of production, but while the analytical concepts of Marx's historical and dialectical materialism are regarded as useful, they are nevertheless seen as having serious defects *because* they were coupled with the belief in progress. For the assumption of classical Marxism was that the contradiction of capitalism enhances the crisis which will lead to the end of capitalism and to a transformation of the capitalist mode of production to a new and 'better' mode called 'socialism'. But this belief has created difficulties, both in explaining the apparent success of capitalism in overcoming previous crises, and in addressing the nature of the crisis today from which Marx's historical hero, the victorious, revolutionary proletariat is lamentably absent.

A central task for the Regulation School, therefore, has been to ask how capitalism could survive even though the capital relation itself inevitably produced antagonism, contradiction and crises.

They accept here the Marxist dialectic, namely that the kernel social relation of capitalism carries within itself a contradiction which is worked out in two ways: the *political* conflict between capital and labour over discipline, domination, control, subjugation and the profit split (the capital relation problem), and the *economic* contradiction stemming from the operation of free, price-fixing markets (the capital logic problem).

But whereas classical Marxism views society as a structured totality driven to *certain* states of affairs by tendencies inherent within it, the Regulation School only admits to the notion of a structured totality driven by immanent contradictions and conflict, ultimately leading to crisis. The crisis itself is conceptualised as a *simultaneous* rupture and transformation of the system that may usher in a new mode of capitalist development in which, for a time, the contradictions are resolved and technological progress and economic growth is once more possible.

There are no *certain* outcomes predetermined by inherent tendencies. What the new mode looks like is entirely *contingent*, both historically and nationally. It depends upon the outcomes of specific, local, social and political struggles, strategies and compromises, and the pre-existing local institutional context. This emphasis on human agency and class struggle, and on local or national specificity, is the *voluntarist* aspect of the regulation approach with which it wants to transcend its structuralist bearings. Its research agenda is hence focused on precise, detailed and empirical analyses of the content and the actual contingent movement of capital, which is so diverse in its manifestations that it leaves considerable scope for historical and national variation.

The Regime of Accumulation and the Mode of Regulation

What is distinctive about the Regulation School, as the name suggests, is a concern with the *regulation* of the economy, the point being that (in their view) there is none (or at any rate no stable, growing economy) without it. Periods of growth and decline in the core of the capitalist system (the advanced countries) are understood through two key concepts: *a regime of accumulation* and *a mode of regulation*. A regime of accumulation is a relatively stable and reproducible relationship between production and consumption defined *at the level of the international economy as a whole*. Such was, for example, the case with the postwar regime of Fordism described above.

The merit of the Regulation School is that they have theorised this balancing of production and consumption (the regime of accumulation) as something that requires, simultaneously, a mode of regulation before it can actually materialise and its benefits be realized. According to Lipietz:

> *A regime of accumulation* describes the stabilization over a long period of the allocation of the net product between consumption and accumulation; it implies some correspondence between the transformation of both the conditions of production and the conditions of the reproduction of wage earners. It also implies some forms of linkage between capitalism and other modes of production. Mathematically, a regime of accumulation is describable by a schema of reproduction. A system of accumulation exists because its schema of reproduction is coherent: not all systems of accumulation are possible. At the same time, the mere *possibility* of a regime is inadequate to account for its existence since there is no necessity for the whole set of individual capitals and agents to behave according to its structure. There must exist a materialization of the regime of accumulation taking the form of norms, habits, laws, regulating networks and so on that ensure the unity of the process, that is the approximate consistency of individual behaviors with the schema of reproduction. This body of interiorized rules and social process is called the *mode of regulation*.[31]

From the perspective of the agenda of the Regulation School, the international diffusion of a certain techno-economic paradigm is only the entry point for a theory of social transformation. The structural properties of this new techno-economic paradigm are seen to define a set of micro- and macro-regulatory problems whose resolution is crucial to long-term success.[32]

Most of the empirical work undertaken by the Regulation School has been concerned with national variations in the modes of regulation and their adjustment to the specific international regime of accumulation that was dominant during the postwar period. This regime was the intensive regime of accumulation with mass consumption materialised by Fordist–Keynesian modes of regulation in

all advanced capitalist countries which guaranteed the stable relationship between mass consumption at the national level through
redistribution of income. Lipietz has repeatedly described the emergence of this mode of regulation as a 'historical contingent discovery'.

The welfare system was not intentionally established to serve the
steady development of mass production. Rather, what happened
was that during the period of crisis (which lasted from about 1913 to
1947) creeping welfare measures and state interventions in the
economy accidentally stabilised the regime of accumulation. Only
then did it become the fixed and dominant mode of regulation. But
this stabilisation crucially occurred under the *hegemony of the
United States*, which as sponsoring power provided the mode of
regulation for the international regime of accumulation. The international framework of global Fordism served as a stabilising configuration within which each national regime of accumulation could
develop, and to which it could connect.[33]

US hegemony first presented the Fordist model for development
to other countries and next financed them with Marshall Aid and
MacArthur plans for setting up new regimes of accumulation. It
institutionalised this international configuration by intertwining it
with US national, industrial and financial interests through the
medium of the Bretton Woods agreement and the establishment of
GATT, the IMF, the World Bank and the OECD. These contained
disturbances and maintained a set of rules which stabilised the
system through US overall hegemonic power (economic, ideological,
as well as political and military). The spread of the Fordist regime of
accumulation to other countries coincided with the strategic interests of the US financial and industrial community and thus global
Fordism formed an integral part of the US social transformation of
Fordism itself.[34]

Turning now to the *present* crisis, we can see that the adoption of
new flexible production systems and compatible firm-level organisational forms are indeed spreading internationally and are gradually
being accommodated within nationally-diverse social institutions
and practices in different countries.[35] But none of this adds up to
an international regime of accumulation, only to the *possibility* of
such a regime. Nor does the circumstance that Japan happened to be
the country of origin of the production model point to the emergence of a *Pax Nipponica*.

Japan is not a hegemonic power that can ensure a stable relationship between output and consumption at the level of the international economy as a whole, nor can it control the competition between different segments of international capital or coordinate the national state responses to recurring business cycles in the way that the US was able to do under the period of global Fordism. Furthermore, the application of information technologies to flexible production processes, and more especially the recent fusion of computer technology with telecommunications, has given the production model added structural characteristics that transcend and defy the socio-cultural embeddedness of the model in Japan itself.

Following the research agenda of the Regulation School we have to examine these structural properties of the now information-driven techno-economic paradigm to find the clues to the macro- and meso-level (inter-firm) regulatory problems which they pose.

The Regulation School generally reserves its position on the prediction of the future regime of accumulation by emphasising that when it emerges it will be the as yet unknown outcome of social and political struggles. Nevertheless, it is my view that when we examine these structural properties we shall discover that each and every one of them are global in scope and hence point towards the requirement of a mode of regulation that is global in origin. So long as this global mode of regulation is not yet in place, the regime of accumulation cannot be materialised. This implies that in the '*interregnum*'[36] the international spread of the techno-economic paradigm may be expected to lead to further crises and instability.

In the final sections of this chapter I run through these structural properties and identify their global character. This prepares the ground for the next two chapters in which the emerging features of a global mode of regulation are more fully traced.

Flexible Production and Global Markets

Because of all the emphasis in lean production systems on 'volume through variety', it is sometimes a little difficult to appreciate that, nevertheless, these production systems are *more* and not less dependent on maximum economies of scale such as can only be offered by the *combined* market size of the core regions in the world economy. First, the start-up costs of the generic technologies (automation technologies, CAD, CAM and CNC) are enormous, and in fact represent a shift from labour to capital intensity of awesome dimension. Second, these generic technologies are subject to very rapid technological obsolescence; this has led to very short product life-cycles placing an ever greater premium on access to financial resources, multiplant production and extensive marketing networks.

Thus, the size of the market remains all important. Kenichi Ohmae has coined the term 'Triad' countries to refer to the three core regions of the present world system: North America, the European Union, and the Pacific Asia Region. Ohmae argues that the global market of 'Triadian' consumers amounts to a total of some 600 million middle-class people 'whose academic backgrounds, income levels both discretionary and nondiscretionary, life-style, use of leisure time, and aspirations are quite similar'.[37] In these countries, moreover, the national infrastructure in terms of highways, telephone systems, sewage disposal, power transmission and governmental systems is also very similar. This permits corporations to treat the residents as 'belonging to virtually the same species'. They constitute the global market.

Flexible Production and Global Enterprise Organisation

Because of the sheer size of initial investments and the rate of technological obsolescence, today's new, high-tech, high value-added, products need to be brought out simultaneously in all three core markets of the world. This means that few companies are large enough to go it alone. In addition, there is a necessity to have a direct presence in each of the core regional markets because of other aspects of flexible production, such as the just-in-time supply and distribution networks, the simultaneous process of design and product development, and, more important still, there is in today's ever-threatening protectionist world a political necessity for multiple home bases. And therefore, according to the leading analysts, the key to competitive success in the future is for the truly global company to have top-to-bottom paper concept to finished-product manufacturing systems in each of the three great markets of the world. Womack *et al.*, for example, forecast a future dominated by multi-regional companies.[38]

For the moment there are signs that such multi-regional company development is evolving through strategic alliances between independent partners in each of the regions. A survey of 839 collaborative ventures identified between 1975–86 showed 31 per cent between EC partners, 26 per cent between EC/US, 10 per cent between EC/Japan and 8 per cent US/Japan. Most such agreements were carried out in high-tech industries: automobile, aerospace telecommunications, computer and other electrical industries. The vast majority of these ventures were formed between rivals.[39]

As we shall see in the next chapter, strategic alliances and other cooperative agreements between competing giants of industry, and between large corporations and complementary partners, such as cross-border, cross-regional and cross-industrial independent suppliers, are all indicative of the emergence of a new political economy of 'relationship enterprising' or 'economic networking'. Our traditional conceptual understanding of political economy and the dynamics between power and markets (see the introduction to Part I) has ill-equipped us to understand the precise nature of such networking. In the 'networked' or 'virtual' firm,[40] resources are allocated on the basis of a 'temporary' trust and commitment to collaboration that transcends our traditional understanding of resource allocation either through the competitive market mechanism or by administrative fiat arising from proprietary power. However temporary, such networked collaborative ventures between independent and/or competing corporations require a degree of trust and social commitment that cannot be backed up by national law (as in legal contracts). Nor can they depend on the exercise of power arising from proprietary claims as in wholly-owned subsidiaries of one corporation. As these cross-border alliances develop their own rules of engagement, so, step by step, a global governance structure, whether entirely voluntary or assisted by inter-nation government agreements may emerge.

Flexible Production and Global Capital–Labour Relations

The integration of design, production and management functions using the fusion of information technology with telecommunications importantly allows for a decentralisation in location and in ownership. There is no longer a need to co-locate engineering and design with manufacturing except in pilot production. The consequence of this is that at least in some industries *production capacity* itself is now sufficiently flexible to be viewed as a commodity. And, thus, large enterprises are presently evolving from firm organisation to a loosely confederated network structure in which many discrete fabrication activities and services are bought in the short-term relieving the buyer of the costs of accessing capacity by committing to its continued use.[41]

The decentralisation of operational activity fundamentally changes the capital–labour relation. Previously, under so-called 'Fordist' regimes of accumulation, capital hired labour power for the duration of the process of production itself. This meant that the wage had to cover the costs of reproducing labour ('necessary labour time' in Marx's terminology), while surplus value was extracted whenever the market value of the product exceeded the cost of the wage. Capital provided both working capital and investment capital. Working capital covered the costs of the wage. Labour was contracted and paid for a period of time rather than for its actual output.

Under conditions of flexible production two things happen: capital fragments into a thousand splinters of production capacity blurring the distinction between ownership of working capital and labour, and the output of labour is paid at the point of delivery.

The commodification of production capacity thus means that labour is exploited once more (as during previous epochs of craft production) through the mechanism of the market exchange, rather than during the process of production itself. But, as we shall see in the next chapter, the price for output is itself determined by global competition. While small companies bid for contracts, their labour works for free on the promise of pay once 'we have landed the contract'. If the contract bid fails, labour does not get paid, or is not paid its due overtime and so on. Thus *casualisation of labour*, through part-time employment, if-and-when contracts, and through self-employment and piecemeal work and so on, are all social changes that are being brought into place almost everywhere in the world.

It is immaterial for the conceptualisation of this ideal type whether one has in mind the casualisation of labour through part-time employment, or through if-and-when contracts, or whether one refers to the present expansion of the 'self-employed' small businesses sector, or the numerous forms of piecemeal work organised and distributed through 'affective' networks of communities based on kinship, ethnicity or religion as described by Piore and Sabel, for example.[42] Nor is it important that at the present time, as Hirst and Zeitlin[43] and others[44] have observed, 'hybrid' forms of production organisation straddling Fordist and flexible methods are the rule rather than the exception. The point is that there is an historical trend towards forms of production organisation in which *capital no longer needs to pay for the reproduction of labour power*. At the same time, participation in the global market means that the domestic market is no longer needed to serve the self-expansion of capital. Jobless growth is what the present phase of capitalism is all about. World-wide, the world's largest firms have shed over 400 000 workers every year over the past decade notwithstanding the upsurge of their combined revenues.[45]

It is this process of globalisation rather than any claimed imbalance in the national accounts between public and private sector growth (the fiscal deficit), nor any demographic imbalance (the greying population) that is the main reason for the perceived need to shed and restructure the welfare state which has become the dominant political project in all advanced countries since the 1980s.

At this point in our argument we need to consider the emergence of flexible accumulation in the light of another, seemingly independent, historical force, namely that of globalisation of finance and production organisation to which we turn in the next chapter.

6

Globalisation

'Globalisation' is a term that has been fashionable since about the mid-1980s, when it began to replace terms like 'internationalisation' and 'transnationalisation' as a more suitable concept for describing the ever-intensifying networks of cross-border human interaction. The concept covers a great variety of social, economic and political change, and it is therefore not surprising that different disciplines have assigned different meanings to it and that this has led to often spurious debates between them, particularly in respect of the question of whether globalisation is or is not happening.

Much of this rather spurious debate arises from a confusion of globalisation with its precursor movements, namely internationalisation (as in the increasing interwovenness of national economies through international trade) and transnationalisation (as in the increasing organisation of production on a cross-border basis by multinational organisations). Thus, for example, economic globalisation is often perceived as a process in which distinct national economies, and therefore domestic strategies of national economic management are increasingly irrelevant.

The world has internationalized in its basic dynamics, it is dominated by uncontrollable market forces, and it has as its principal economic actors and major agents of change truly transnational corporations that owe allegiance to no nation state and locate wherever in the globe market advantage lies.[1]

Such definitions are an open invitation to refutation. In their recent book, *Globalization in Question*, Paul Hirst and Grahame Thompson review the historical evidence of world trade and capital flows in relation to output, degrees of financial and monetary integration and the character of governance in the international economy. They come to the conclusion, much as we did in Chapter 4, that the level of integration, interdependence, and openness, of national economies in the present era is not unprecedented.

However, we must be careful not to confuse 'globalisation' with the integration of real territorial economies. As we saw in Chapter 4, the peak period of integration of real economies as measured, for example, by the amount of goods and services that cross frontiers as a percentage of all goods and services that are produced world-wide, was the year 1913 when that percentage (the export ratio of production) reached 33 per cent. Today it is about 31 per cent.[2]

As for the equation of globalisation with the growing dominance of transnational corporations in world production and trade, here too the overall picture that emerges is one of remarkable constancy, and not of dramatic change, in the long historical period. First in relation to total world output, the percentage share of world production subject to transnational corporate control has remained relatively stable[3] (see also Chapter 4); second, as Hirst and Thompson note, as far as the leading OECD economies are concerned international businesses are still largely confined to their home territory in terms of their overall business activity, that is in terms of location of sales, affiliates, declared profits, and research and finance.[4] Similar findings have been reported by others.[5]

Nor must we confuse globalisation with the integration of real territorial economies world-*wide*. While globalisation has proceeded in the last few decades, the geographical reach of world capitalism has actually receded. For example, if we take as an indicator of global reach the percentage share of all five continents in world trade, then we find that the percentage share of two continents, Latin America and Africa, in world trade has actually declined. Likewise the global reach of foreign capital flows (the percentage share of global foreign investments going to Africa and to Latin America) has declined by a wide margin since the colonial period.[6]

In fact, I have argued that the expansive phase of world capitalism is over. The expansive phase of capitalism was characterised by the *extension* of the fundamentals of economic activity, namely trade and productive investment, ever further into more and more areas of the globe; that phase has now been superseded by a phase of *deepening, but not widening capitalist integration*. I prefer to reserve the term 'globalisation' for that deepening phenomenon. To understand this 'deepening' phenomenon we have to start with the sociology of globalisation.

The Sociology of Globalisation

Even if today 'globe-babble' has penetrated the discourse of *all* social science disciplines, it is probably fair to say that sociologists have been at the forefront in efforts to give it a rigorous and consistent theoretical status.[7] In the work of prominent authors such as Roland Robertson, David Harvey and Anthony Giddens, we find distinctive formulations that may help us to overcome the limits of the globalisation discourse which has so vexed economists and international relations theorists. This is the aim of this chapter.

Roland Robertson: World Compression and Intensification of Global Consciousness

Robertson's writings are firmly welded to a conventional mainstream sociological theory of society as a social system. Social system theory is elaborated in Parsons'[8] well-known formulation in which any social system is thought to have four subsystems that are functionally related to serve the maintenance of the whole. These subsystems and their functions are:

1. The economic (adaptive function);
2. The political (mobilisation for collective purposes);
3. The social (integrative function); and
4. The cultural (providing the governing value system necessary for reproducing the system through time).

Robertson[9] argues that already for some time there has clearly been a process of social system building at the global level. In the economic sphere it predates even the rise of capitalism and the modern world because of the growing networks of international trade and production. It has also been actively fostered at the level of the political subsystem with the international cooperation between states and the emergence of international organisations. But as Malcolm Waters[10] notes in his succinct review of the evolution of

Robertson's theories, in his earlier work with Nettl, in 1968,[11] Robertson had argued that the process of globalisation was still being hindered by unresolved cleavages in the cultural arena which thus far had prevented full system development. There were three such cleavages: religious (between fundamental Islam and Christianity); legal-diplomatic between democracies and absolutist states (the West versus East divide); and industrial between cultures that emphasise norms consistent with industry (rationality, individualisation, impersonal authority) and those that do not (the North–South divide).

In more recent works, however, Robertson has come around to the view that the potential for a closing of these cleavages is today greatly enhanced. Globalisation at the cultural level has begun because of two things which he now introduces into his definition of globalisation: namely 'compression of the world' and 'global consciousness'. Compression of the world is the real experience of the way that interdependencies are being created in the economies of the world to such an extent that, today, the way we live our lives on this side of the globe has immediate consequences for people on the other side of the globe. Shifts in preferences of consumption in Europe and America, for example, deeply affect jobs in the Far East. Industrial processes of development and growth in one country can have environmental and ecological impacts in neighbouring countries. Big dam projects in India cause flooding in Bangladesh; an earthquake in Kobe, Japan, causes a fall in the dollar; and the forest burning practice of the Brazilian peasant colonists in the Amazon burns holes in 'our' ozone layer. This is what is meant by 'compression' of the world.

World compression is not a terribly new idea, what makes for its novelty in Robertson's work is that he argues that world compression intensifies 'global consciousness'. Global consciousness is manifested in the way we, peoples all over the world, in a discourse unified through mass communication, speak of military-political issues in terms of 'world order' or of economic issues as in 'international recession'. We speak of 'world peace' and 'human rights', while issues of pollution and purification are talked about in terms of 'saving the planet'. Thus, although in Robertson's view globalisation has been going on for a very long time, predating even the rise of capitalism and modernity, it has accelerated only in the last decade or so because it has moved to the level of consciousness.

David Harvey: Time/Space Compression

While for Robertson the point of departure of the analysis of globalisation is a well-worn conventional sociological theory, namely social system theory, there are others who have theorised it from a completely different angle, namely the concepts of space and time, and space/time compression.

Following the works of Pierre Bourdieu, a contemporary sociologist, David Harvey,[12] who is himself a social geographer, argues that symbolic orderings of space and time provide a framework for experience through which we learn who or what we are in society. Remember the commonsense notion that 'there is a time and a place for everything'. Certain behaviour that is encouraged in the classroom, for example, is not expected around the dinner table, and vice versa. In previous years, when we did not have so many students, academic tutors would sometimes try to create the informal atmosphere of home for their tutorials by inviting students to classes held in their homes, precisely to break the habit of 'habitus'. (Note that the Latin word 'habitus' means both location and habit.) Ordered space is a signpost for expected social practices, and serves as a reminder of these social practices. Let us think about this a bit more.

The organisation of space defines relationships, not only between activities, things and concepts, but by extension between people. The organisation of space defines social relations. Harvey argues that the development of cartography in the Renaissance permitted the objectification of space and the accurate measurements of land, thus supporting the emergence of private ownership in land and the precise definition of transferable property rights, thereby replacing the confused and conflicting feudal obligations that had preceded it. The organisation of space holds the key to power. Today, the freedom to move capital wherever it is needed world-wide gives the capital-owning international bourgeoisie a decisive advantage over the mass of workers who are restricted in their movements and migrations by the passports they carry.

Like space, time too represents a source of value and power. In capitalist enterprises the costs of production are calculated in terms of the time it takes to produce things, and labour is subjected to constant efforts by employers to reduce the time spent on a particular task. 'Economy of time', said Marx, 'to this all economy ultimately reduces itself.' The time-and-motion studies of Frederick

Taylor's scientific management gave Henry Ford a decisive advantage over his competitors, and eventually ushered in the world-wide system of production called Fordism. Bitter class struggles have been fought over the length of the working day. In the competitive battle today it is not even minutes but seconds that count. In a harrowing narrative of life on the shop-floor in a flexible production plant in the UK, Rick Delbridge *et al.* report how work intensification resulted in a saving of '0.85 seconds on standard time'![13]

Time, argues Harvey, also defines the value of money itself. In capitalist economies, accountants calculate interest rates as 'the time value of money'. The time of production together with the time of circulation of exchange are referred to as the *turnover time of capital*. The greater the speed with which the capital that is launched into circulation can be recuperated, the greater the profit will be. If an investment in this country gives me the value of my money back in five years, whereas in Singapore I can get it back in three years, then I am hardly likely to invest here, and I will prefer my money to go to Singapore.

Anthony Giddens: Time/Space Distantiation

However, the really important thing in all this discussion is the relationship between time and space. In capitalist economies, *space is expressed in time*. The distance needed to travel in order to do business or to transport commodities to their final destination, or to crosshaul intermediate products for fabrication, are all calculated in terms of the time it takes to cover the distance. Anthony Giddens, whose globalisation theory bears some resemblance to that of Harvey, calls this 'time/space distantiation', which is a measure of the degree to which the friction of space has been overcome to accommodate social interaction.

Technological progress has compressed the time–space equation enormously. Harvey has illuminated this equation in a graph that is described here. Between 1500–1840 the best average speed of horse-drawn coaches and sailing ships was 10 mph. Between 1850–1930 it was 65 mph for steam locomotives and 36 mph for steam ships. By the 1950s, propeller aircraft covered distances at 300–400 mph while today's jet passenger aircraft makes a cool 500–700 mph.[14]

All this refers to the transport and the covering of distances of material commodities and human bodies. But now think of the electronic age which we have just entered. Today's telecommunications using satellite TV and the linking of computers through cyberspace allow most 'disembodied' services, for example technological designs, managerial instructions and operational controls, as well as media images of wars and earthquakes and representations of consumer fashions, to enter the minds of people instantly anywhere in the global system. This shrinking of the world to a 'global village' amounts to a virtual *annihilation of space through time*. As Giddens sums it up:

> Globalisation can thus be defined as the intensification of world wide social relations which link distant localities in such a way that local happenings are shaped by events occurring many miles away and vice versa.[15]

Today people can have social relations and even organised community relations regardless of space; that is, regardless of the territory that they share. This has enormous consequences not only for the role of the nation-state as territorially bounded community, but also, as we shall see below, for the organisation of economic production on a cross-border basis. It permits the emergence of 'imagined' communities, cultures and even systems of authority and social control that cross borders. The other day I heard Mary Robinson, the President of the Republic of Ireland, say in a radio interview that Irishness exists not so much in blood and land but in shared culture and traditions. When the Ayatollahs in Iran decided to pronounce the Fatwa on Salman Rushdie it was not because they had stumbled across the book themselves, but because Muslims in Bradford had faxed them a copy of the offending pages. When the much maligned 'fat cats' of recently privatised British utilities are villified for their perks and pay they can still sleep at night without undue embarrassment or shame because their peer group, their own social reference group, is a community of utility chiefs and other boardroom fat cats across the Atlantic with whom they are probably more immediately and continuously in touch through e-mail, telephone, fax and video-conferencing than the people in the street where they live.

What these examples show is that while we still have local lives as physical persons, we also now experience phenomenal worlds that are truly global. It is this globalisation as shared phenomenal worlds which today drives the processes of economic globalisation.

Such privileging of the sociological aspect of globalisation is not to deny the importance of other factors, more especially the dynamics of historical capitalism which – as Wallerstein and many others in the Marxist tradition have argued – always had a 'globalising' imperative from the beginning. The development of transnational corporations and the growth of international finance in particular, testify to a complex multi-causal logic of globalisation. Rather, what is being argued here is that, owing to the present reconstitution of the world into a single *social* space, that self-same historical process has now lifted off and moved into a new ballpark. If, previously, global integration in the sense of a growing unification and interpenetration of the human condition was driven by the economic logic of capital accumulation, today it is the unification of the human condition that drives the logic of further capital accumulation. In the next section, I shall clarify this theoretical position.

The Economics of Globalisation

I suggest that time/space compression drives the economics of globalisation in three principal ways. *First*, the 'shared phenomenal world' supports the emergence of a global market *discipline* as contrasted with the existence of a mere global market-*place*. *Second*, the annihilation of space through time compression re-orders the way economic activities are being conceptualised and, as a consequence, organised. Whereas, before, it was common to classify economic activities *either* into three categories: primary, secondary and tertiary (agriculture, industry and services), *or* – as in more recent works on international economics – into a chain of high value-added and low value-added activities, today it makes more sense to re-order economic activities into two: 'real-time' activities where distance and location are no longer relevant as a determinant of economic operations, and 'material' activities where there is still some 'friction of space' that limits choice of location. As we shall see below this twofold conceptualisation is beginning to inform the organisation of transnational business today, and, as a result, the global organisation of work. *Third*, money itself has become a 'real time' resource permitting a degree of international mobility that is qualitatively different from anything witnessed in previous eras. In summary, I suggest that economic globalisation has three key features:

1. A global market discipline;
2. Flexible accumulation through global webs; and
3. Financial deepening.

A Global Market Discipline

To begin with, it is important that one makes the distinction between a global market-*place* and a global market *principle*. A global market-place exists when there is an international division of labour and, consequently, an international market exchange between different goods and services that are produced in different nations. Such international trade dominated the prewar and immediate postwar period. It was essentially *complementary*; that is, countries that specialised in the export of one type of product would exchange that product for other types that they did not produce themselves.

As a result of the growth and organisational evolution of multinational companies, this pattern of *inter-product trade* gradually has given way to *intra-product trade*. There is no longer a neat division of labour between countries. There is now export competition between producers in different countries in the same product lines. Countries that are high volume exporters of cars are also high volume importers of cars. How did this situation come about?

Liberalisation and technological progress have steadily altered the way in which international production is being undertaken. At first, multinational companies adopted *simple* integration strategies where they set up foreign affiliates producing, typically with technology obtained from the parent company, the same standardised commodities that previously had been subject to cross-border trade. Second, parent companies would set up foreign affiliates engaging in a limited range of activities in order to supply their parent firms with specific inputs that they were in a more competitive position to produce.

Next, multinational companies began to adopt *complex* integration strategies where they turned their geographically dispersed affiliates and fragmented production systems into regionally or even globally integrated production and distribution networks. Thus, multinational companies (by this time, that is the 1970s, often referred to as 'transnational' companies or even 'global' companies) farmed out different parts of the production process to different affiliates in different national locations. Each subsidiary took part in the production process, but not one single affiliate produced the whole product from beginning to end. The hallmark of this global fragmentation and organic integration of the production process was an enormous increase in international trade in components and semi-processed manufactures. This began in the 1960s and soon overtook the growth in world trade itself.[16] Telling evidence of this global integration at the level of production is found in data on intra-firm trade. Whereas in the early 1970s intra-firm trade was estimated to account for around 20 per cent of world trade, by the early 1990s that share was around one-third, excluding intra-TNC transactions in services.[17]

For many observers and analysts of the world economy, this development of an integrated international production system is sufficient evidence of the emergence of a truly 'global economy'. And in some ways it is. That is to say it prepares the *structural* conditions for the emergence of a global economy. For it means that a global market *principle* (a dominant standard of price, quality and efficiency) begins to impose itself on the *domestic* supply of consumer goods, intermediate and half-processed goods, technology, and indeed the factors of production, capital, labour and raw materials. As a consequence of the shift from inter-product trade to intra-product trade, global competition has intensified. Instead of being complementary, international trade has become *predatory* or 'adversarial', as Peter Drucker puts it.[18]

The corollary of global competition is that even goods and services that are produced and exchanged *within* the national domestic sphere have to meet standards of quality and costs of production that are set globally. A good example is the United States, the country with the largest domestic market. As Stephen Cohen reminds us in a revealing statistic: whereas in the early 1960s only 4 per cent of US domestic production was subject to international competition, today over 70 per cent is.[19] The contrast between the global market-*place* and the global market *principle* can not be put more sharply, for in the 1960s the US-dominated international manufacturing trade contributing 25 per cent of all international trade flows, whereas in the 1990s its share of world manufacturing trade has dropped to just 12 per cent.[20]

However, of still greater significance is the manner in which such structural integration is becoming *internalised* in the behaviour of economic agents, be they entrepreneurs or workers, consumers or producers. If the expression 'market principle' refers to a structural constraint, I use the expression 'market discipline' to address the internalisation of this structural constraint by individual agents in their own conduct. Writers of the Regulation School which we discussed in Chapter 5 have tried to stretch their concept of 'mode of regulation' to include the internalisation of relevant social values and norms. For example, Aglietta[21] speaks of the 'socialisation of the mode of life', Boccara refers to 'anthroponomic factors',[22] while Alain Lipietz uses the term 'habitus' borrowed from Bourdieu to indicate that values and norms that might sustain a mode of regulation are internalised in individual conducts.[23] Yet, as Bob Jessop has pointed out, none of these writers have managed to pinpoint the precise process of transformation because they have failed to theorise how modes of regulation *actually become* internalised in individal conducts.[24]

Our discussion of time/space compression and the 'shared phenomenal world' clarifies this internalisation process. For, it is the *awareness* of global competition which constrains individuals and groups, and even national governments, to conform to international standards of price and quality. We are constantly reminded, in the experience of others' own daily lives, but even more so in the way that this experience is reinforced by media coverage of events occurring elsewhere, that unless we conform to these standards we will lose the competition, lose our own jobs. Workers come to accept that it is 'proper' that jobs should be lost because their company 'has to' move elsewhere where wages and social conditions are less demanding.

In 1992, the American Hoover company was faced with pressures for higher wages from its Dijon workforce and it decided to move the plant to Glasgow. The point about the 'discipline' of the global market is that such companies do not actually have to move. It is sufficient for them to 'threaten' to move. Time/space compression has permitted us all to share in the phenomenal world of the Dijon workers (and in that of numerous other victims of company relocations elsewhere), and this has created a social discipline on workers all over Europe, indeed all over the world, that unless they toe the line, companies can move plant abroad. Because of the existence of a global market discipline, it is sufficient for a company to merely *threaten* to set up a plant abroad, for it to successfully drive down the wages to the globally competitive level. Charles Sabel reports on German plants where charts of defect rates for particular processes are displayed on videoscreens next to equivalent data for their Brazilian subsidiaries.[25]

Thus, while global competition has created the structural conditions for the emergence of a global market discipline, it is time/space compression that creates the shared phenomenal world that supports and reproduces this discipline on a daily basis. And not just on workers. Companies, too, know they to have to adopt the best quality and the most efficient costs, and engage in constant innovation, because they know that otherwise they will lose their markets and someone else will move in. The same holds true at the consumer end of the organisation of economic life. Consumers in China can see on their satellite TV screens western lifestyle products which they will want, regardless of their government's desire to limit foreign imports and give a boost to local producers. The Chinese government even tried to ban satellite television for that reason, but to no avail.

To give another example: when traders in the London or Tokyo stock market see on their screens the price of dollar interest rates move up by just one notch, they will immediately want to move out of yens and pounds and buy US dollar-denominated bonds, thus putting pressure on other governments to follow suit soon and raise interest rates too.

Flexible Accumulation Through Global Webs

As the costs of transporting standard products and of communicating information about them continue to drop (another example of time/space compression), modern factories and state-of-the-art machinery can be installed almost anywhere in the globe. Routine producers in the UK and the US therefore are in direct competition with millions of producers in other nations. In his book, *The Work of Nations*, Robert Reich, the influential Secretary of State for Labor in Clinton's administration, gives spectacular examples of the speed with which factories and productive capital investments have become footloose. For instance, until the late-1970s, the American telephone and telecommunications company AT&T had depended on routine producers in Louisiana to assemble standard telephones. It then discovered that producers in Singapore would perform the same tasks at a far lower cost. Faced with intense global competition they then had to switch to cheaper routine producers in Singapore. But already by the late 1980s they switched production again, this time to Thailand.

Routine production is no longer the preserve of deskilled jobs in industrial plants. The fusion of computer technology with telecommunications makes it possible for firms to relocate an ever-widening range of operations and functions to wherever cost-competitive labour, assets and infrastructure are available. The new technologies make it feasible to standardise, routinise and coordinate activities which previously were subject to the friction of space and therefore regarded as non-tradable. They enable such activities to be turned into 'real-time' activities. Take, for example, data-processing services of all kinds. Airlines employ data processors from Barbados to Bombay to punch in names and flight numbers into giant computer banks located in Dallas or London. Book and magazine publishers use routine operators around the world to convert manuscripts into computer readable form and send them back to the parent firm at the speed of electonic impulses. The New York Life Insurance Company was dispatching insurance claims to Castleisland, Ireland, where routine producers, guided by simple directions, entered the claims and determined the amounts due, then instantly transmitted the computations back to the United States.[26] British Telecom has all its software computer programming done by programming specialists in India.

The next evolutionary step in this process of global integration of production comes when the global market principle becomes imposed upon *production capacity* itself. In some industries production capacity is now sufficiently flexible to be viewed as a commodity, something that can be instantly bought and sold on the market. Harvard Business School researchers, Ramchandran Jaikumar and David Upton studied a number of manufacturing industries and came to the conclusion that in some cases world-wide manufacturing capacity can be allocated by competitive market forces through the use of information technology linked with cell-based manufacturing technologies.[27] They argue that in many industries, the application of CAD and CNC means that manufacturing concerns can establish small, independent cells that operate effectively and economically with only a modest capital investment. These production units can be organisationally and physically separated from design, marketing and engineering. Such independent providers of flexible capacity are next networked to the company in a kind of internal electronic market. This is now referred to as the IntraNet, as distinct from the InterNet. They compete with each other for subcontracting orders.[28]

This is what is meant here by flexible accumulation through global webs. The United Nations *World Investment Report, 1994* provides several examples of it. The NIKE footwear company with annual sales of nearly $4 billion subcontracts 100 per cent of its goods production. NIKE itself currently employs only about 9000 people, while nearly 75 000 people are employed by its independent subcontractors located in different countries mostly in the Third World. NIKE has a performance-oriented inventory control system on its computer network and it gets orders from retailers in advance in return for guaranteed delivery times and discounts, making it possible for it to organise timely production (through its computer network) from its different producers located abroad. The subcontractors are all networked to the parent company. The parent company is really no more than a marketing and research and design company. Benneton and IKEA too rely on their computer networks to receive and place orders and monitor sales.[29]

Thus, transnational enterprise is evolving from company organisation to a loosely confederated network structure (global web) in which many discrete fabrication activities and services are bought in for the short term. This relieves the buyer of the costs of accessing capacity by committing to its continued use. By organising their suppliers not as wholly-owned subsidiaries but as independent agents, the contemporary transnational is in a position to combine the advantages of market competition with all the advantages that used to be associated with 'administrative fiat'; that is, company control over productive operations by wholly-owned subsidiaries.

Economic networking has been made possible by the fusion of telecommunications with computer technology (time/space compression). But there are also important social and institutional requisites that need to be brought into place to ensure its success.

Much of the work of the Regulation School and the new 'institutional economics' addresses these social and institutional requisites (see Chapter 5). What is argued here is that these *requisites* must be regarded simultaneously as structural *consequences* of the converging logic of global competition in which system standards and economic measures take precedence over nation-state diversity. We shall return to this in Chapter 7 where we consider the consequences of globalisation.

Global Financial 'Deepening'

We have referred before to the phenomenon of 'financial deepening' which occurs when the growth of financial transactions far exceeds the growth of the underlying economic fundamentals of production and trade.

In the 1980s the growth of the financial or 'symbol' or 'balloon' economy outpaced the growth of the fundamentals of trade and investment in the OECD countries seven times, and at a conservative estimate the total annual value of transactions in the world's financial markets is now twice the total value of world production.[30] Peter Drucker, the doyen of the management community, claims that '90 percent or more of the transnational economy's financial transactions do not serve what economists would consider an economic function'.[31] As Frederic Clairmont writes in his usual, colourful language:

> Today, more than at any time in capitalism's history, the profits of finance capital are based on debt and exponential debt creation. Private, corporate, and househeld debt worldwide surpasses US$31trillion, galloping at a compound rate of over 9 per cent yearly, or three times faster than that of world GDP and world trade. It is clear for whom the bells are tolling. The tocsin is heard.[32]

What this means is that, evidently, money is increasingly being made out of the circulation of money, regardless of traditional restrictions of space and time as when money transforms into bricks and mortar. The financial revolution since the 1980s has been characterised by a potent fusion of financial deregulation on the one hand with powerful advances in telecommunications and information technology on the other. The upshot of this has been a tremendous increase in the international mobility of capital. This mobility refers not only to the speed and freedom with which money can now move across frontiers at the press of a computer button, it also, more significantly, refers to the way it is being disconnected from social relationships in which money and wealth were previously embedded. It is because of this 'disembedding' that globalisation entails a process of intensification of linkages within the core of the global system, while its counterpart 'peripheralisaton' becomes a process of marginalisation and expulsion that cuts across territories and national boundaries, rendering areas within the traditional core subject to the same processes of expulsion as large swathes of territories in Africa, Latin America and Asia. Hence the structure of core–periphery becomes a social division, rather than a geographic one.

Let us explore the meaning of this heightened international mobility of capital a bit further. In particular let us examine why this should represent a form of *imploding* capitalism rather than a further expansion of world capitalism.

When our pension funds invest in, say, the Hong Kong stock exchange, which has seen a rise of 300 per cent in 1993 alone, they can then benefit from the rising values of the stock and, if they are clever fund managers (which we certainly hope they are), switch out of that stock exchange when it goes down and invest in another rising one somewhere else. There is no need for them or us to wait and see what happens to the companies that build skyscrapers in Hong Kong or sell textiles back to Europe. But of course the connections between the world of high finance and the economic fundamentals of world trade and production are not completely severed. There is still no such thing as a free lunch. What has happened, rather, is that the integration of the world's financial markets and the development of a whole range of novel financial instruments, permitted since the deregulation of these markets, have made it possible to connect up the arteries of real production and trade, and thus squeeze the last drop of surplus out of workers and peasants all over the world, in a manner that makes these innumerable threads that lead to our pension fund invisible and therefore unchallengeable.

To stick to the same example: the rise and rise of the Hong Kong stock market owed in large measure to Chinese provincial authorities investing borrowed money in Hong Kong's stock market and real estate, with dire consequences for the Beijing government's ability to hold the value of its currency and pay the peasants in northern China for its grain procurements. The world is now like this: if our pension fund works well for us, the peasants in northern China will just have to go a bit more hungry. If we, as we did during the consumer boom of the 1980s, push up interest rates through our incautious use of credit cards, it has knock-on effects for the interest rates that Brazil pays on its loans, and this in turn prejudices the livelihood of peasants in Brazil.

The speed with which money can move across borders removes the need to anchor it firmly in (national) social relationships. Globalisation makes national social solidarity (as expressed in transfer payments to the old, the sick, the unemployed and the lower income groups) *dysfunctional* from the point of view of the rational economic interests of those who participate in the global economy. This process is being sharpened by recent deregulation in the core countries which encourages the globalisation of small private investors and undercuts the last remaining vestiges of national social solidarity. The privatisation, for example, in the area of pension schemes (a transition from 'defined benefit' or occupational and state pension schemes, to 'defined contribution' schemes or 'personal' pension schemes) is a case in point.

Thus today, in the advanced countries, the pressures for globalisation (maintaining liberal and deregulated markets for finance and trade, and resistance to policies of protection for national territorial economic activities) come not just from a tiny group of international capitalists, that is from those dominant fractions of corporate capital that have global interests, but also from a broadly-based stratum of society, the 13 per cent of senior citizens and those with an eye to their pensionable future, whose continued survival, to put it bluntly, is better secured in the rising economies of the Far East than by reproduction of the labour power (and pension premiums paid) by the shrinking younger generation that steps into their shoes. As *The Economist* has put it:

Ageing populations in rich countries and freer flowing capital the world over are changing the way people save and invest. American and British institutional money is flooding foreign markets.[33]

This de-territorialisation of economic rationality as it affects not just organised capital but the mass of middle-class individuals in bourgeois societies is a key consequence of globalisation.

In this chapter we have argued that globalisation today is essentially a *social* phenomenon that drives cross-border economic integration to new levels of intensity. In our discussion we have already touched on some of the consequences of this process and we shall examine these consequences more fully in the next chapter. It is worth noting two points in conclusion. One is that globalisation is a *process*, not an end-state of affairs. There is no such thing as a global economy or a global society yet! Whether the process of globalisation continues along the pathways which I have identified depends largely on whether and how national governments resist the process or go along with it. This, in turn, depends largely on a correct identification of, and policy response to, the key elements of globalisation. The sceptics in the globalisation debate make rather much of the continuing, indeed in some cases apparently enhanced, exercise of sovereignty and regulation by national governments. And yet, as we shall see in the next chapter, much of this regulation amounts in effect to no more than a regulation *for* globalisation.

7

Global Regulation

Let us retrace our steps thus far in this part of the book. In Chapter 5 we began our story of the present crisis and transformation process by describing the principal features of a new techno-economic paradigm of industrial production, called flexible production.

We next looked at the Regulation School's attempt to theorise the process of social transformation. We recall that the School's central tenets are that capitalism, instead of destroying itself in consequence of the internal contradictions which are its inherent and systemic properties, time and again proves able to overcome the self-inflicted crises by complete transformation. Total renewal is what makes possible the reproduction of capitalism, involving not only production technology and the organisation of economic life but also the complex of institutions and norms which ensure that individual agents and social groups behave according to the overarching principles of economic life. In the language of the Regulation School such overarching principles constitute the regime of accumulation. But this regime of accumulation in turn is materialised through an appropriate mode of regulation, in the shape of relevant norms, habits, laws and governing insitutions.

The methodological problem with the Regulation School's approach is that it is doomed to have merit only in hindsight, as an explanatory theory after the fact. It cannot predict outcomes. This is so because during the period of crisis and transformation itself (as now), when a new regime of accumulation is *in statu nascendi*, the corresponding mode of regulation is not yet in place. Thus we cannot say with any degree of certainty or precision what the key features of the new mode of regulation are, and as long as we are unable to describe these features the regime of accumulation itself is not fully there to be described either. To usher in a period of stable economic growth, that is to be fully established or materialised, a regime of accumulation has to match production and demand at the level of the international economy as a whole. We are not there yet. All we have to go by are certain directional tendencies – these we identified in Chapter 6. They are: the emergence of a global market discipline, flexible accumulation through global webs, and financial deepening. But, note that these directional tendencies so far are all on the production side. An appropriate mode of regulation would have to provide not just the institutional mechanisms, coordinating complexes and norms and values that regulate the supply side in the global economy, but also those that govern the demand side. The recognition of this problem has led some writers to advocate an international version of the Keynesian order that governed the economies of the industrial countries earlier in the postwar period.[1]

More complicating still is the circumstance that the Regulation School rejects a mechanistic and deterministic form of theorising, where, for example, one would deduce (and thus predict) the emerging contours of a mode of regulation from an understanding of the 'logic' of the techno-economic paradigm and the way this drives the process of accumulation. But instead, the Regulation School reserves its opinion about the future shape of things to come by stressing the voluntaristic genesis of any mode of regulation as the outcome of locally and historically-specific struggles.

For the Regulation School, the international diffusion of a particular techno-economic paradigm is only the entry point of a theory of social transformation. The structural properties of this paradigm are thought merely to define a set of micro- and macro-regulatory *problems* whose resolution, while crucial to long-term success, is nevertheless the contingent outcome of locally and historically-specific struggles.

Finally, we have also noted that in the case of the two previous capitalist transformations (for example imperialism and Fordism) the Regulation School had observed that the hegemony of a dominant state in international relations (for example Britain or the US) had ensured that *its* mode of regulation became the model of development of other national modes of regulation, while its hegemonic position provided the sponsoring power to ensure stability for the international regime of accumulation within which each national regime of accumulation could develop and to which it could connect.

But where does that leave us today? We have seen that the present crisis and transformation process crucially evolves within a context of a hegemonic vacuum in international relations, and further that the structural properties of the techno-economic paradigm are global in scope. Following on from this, we saw in Chapter 6 that the structural properties, or at any rate the directional tendencies of the emerging regime of accumulation, are also global in impact. Hence my designation 'globalisation' for that emerging regime of accumulation.

Our task in this chapter is therefore to examine the contours of a corresponding mode of regulation. We need to home in on the governance structures and institutional complexes that are growing up as resolutions to the micro- and macro-regulatory problems posed by the emergent global regime of accumulation.

In the following section I identify three key domains in which we may already discover the emergent forms of a global mode of regulation. These domains are: (1) capital–state relations; (2) capital–labour relations, and (3) core–periphery relations.

Capital–State Relations: Global Governance and the Internationalisation of the State

Globalisation restructures the relations between state and capital. It has led to what Robert Cox refers to as the *internationalisation of the state* in which the state becomes a vehicle for transmitting the global market discipline to the domestic economy.[2] Cox argues that the globalisation of the world economy gives rise to a global class and social structure that deeply affects the forms of state. Elsewhere he suggests that globalisation is led by a transnational managerial class[3] that consists of distinct fractions but which together constitute what Susan Strange has called the international 'business civilization'.[4]

The term 'business civilization', however, has a positive ethical connotation that is arguably not warranted. It is perhaps better to refer to a transnational business 'culture' of shared norms and values that underpin and interweave with the structural power of transnational capital. Together these are gradually becoming institutionalised in a plethora of organisational forms and institutional practices: within international organisations such as the World Bank and the IMF; in interstate summit agendas and agreements (for example GATT) and other forms of cooperation between nations; within emerging institutional forms of 'élite interaction' between members of the international business class, state bureaucrats and members of international organisations;[5] and within the administrative bureaucracy of national governments.

As Stephen Gill and David Law[6] note, there are elements of a common perspective, or a hegemonic ideology, emerging on the role of international business and private enterprise which cuts across and unites all of these institutional forums. At the heart of this 'neoliberal' ideology is the idea that private property and accumulation are sacrosanct and that the prime responsibility of governments is to ensure 'sound finance': they must 'fight inflation' and maintain an attractive 'business climate' in which, amongst other things, the power of unions is circumscribed. These ideas both underpin, and are the result of, the 'structural power' of capital that is so internationally mobile that the investment climate of each country is continually judged by business with reference to the climate which prevails elsewhere.

Under the previous epoch of world order, under *Pax Americana*, there was also a world economy and internationalisation of production, but the role of the state was still largely autonomous. States had the *recognised* responsibility for *domestic* economic progress and capital accumulation, employment and welfare, under the *aegis* of the hegemonic structure of the American-led Bretton Woods-managed world economy, which laid down the rules of interstate competition and coordination. All states, advanced and underdeveloped alike, had a recognised 'developmental' role. Although the prevailing ideology was supportive of free markets and of the internationalisation of capital, it was nevertheless, as John Ruggie has argued, a period of 'embedded' liberalism,[7] that is to say liberalism 'embedded' in the nation-state. This contrasts with today's globalisation which we might describe as a period of 'unembedded' liberalism.

A good example of the institutionalisation of 'unembedded' liberalism may be gleaned from the recently concluded Uruguay GATT agreements, in particular the protocols relating to so-called 'trade related investment measures' (TRIMS) and 'trade related intellectual property rights' (TRIPS). These severely circumscribe the sovereign rights of all states (including those of the developing

countries) to regulate foreign investment and external trade in order
to foster perceived developmental needs.[8] For example, under the
TRIMS protocol a number of domestic measures which used to be
'normal' and 'accepted' elements in any development strategy must
be phased out, for example local content requirements, domestic
sales requirements, trade balancing requirements, remittance and
exchange restrictions.[9]

Equally corrosive of independent developmental state action is
the agreement on TRIPS. This agreement strengthens international
property rights of foreign investment and it extends international
patent protection to a whole gamut of products and processes
previously not subject to patent. Take, for example, genetic material
collected by agribusinesses or pharmaceutical companies, which are
harnessed to fabricate a particular industrial process or product.
These products and processes may now be patented by the corporations and sold back to the country in which the genetic material
originated, under international property rights protection. Under
GATT provisions the recipient country has to allow free competitive
entry for such products and processes, and, furthermore, it must
prohibit the development and use by local companies of 'identical'
products and processes. As Kevin Watkins has argued, this provision amounts to an act of unbridled piracy by transnational capital:

> . . . the main beneficiaries will be the core group of less than a
> dozen seeds and pharmaceutical companies which control over 70
> per cent of the world's seeds trade . . . this attempt to incorporate
> into the GATT a biotechnology patenting code dictated by
> corporate interest appears an act of unbridled piracy. The over-
> whelming bulk of genetic materials used in the laboratories of
> western companies are derived from Third World crops and wild
> plants. . . Once incorporated into a patentable invention, they can
> become the property of the company which can claim royalty
> payments and restrict access to them, even claiming royalties
> when they are imported into the country of origin.[10]

Although developing countries, spearheaded by India, fought
hard during successive phases of the Uruguay round against both
TRIMS and TRIPS, they eventually bowed to the hegemony of the
neo-liberal trade agenda. Nothing illustrates this better than the
agreed statement of the United Nations Conference on Trade and
Development in February 1992:

The Conference recognizes that the establishment and implementation of internationally agreed standards of protection for intellectual property rights . . . should facilitate international flows of technology and technology cooperation amongst all partipating nations, particularly to developing countries on terms and conditions agreed to by the parties concerned, and notes the important role of the World Intellectual Property Organization and the important efforts in the ongoing GATT Uruguay Round negotiations in this regard. The Conference further recognizes that a national regime for the adequate and effective protection of intellectual property rights is important because it can create market incentives for indigenous innovation and the transfer, adaptation and diffusion of technologies.[11]

Whereas up until that time UNCTAD had been the platform where developing countries demanded adjustment of the international patent system to their development needs, it now expressed the belief that adoption of adequate and effective IPP laws and related efforts in WIPO and GATT would facilitate technology transfers to developing countries.[12]

The structural power of transnational capital has not just informed the policy agenda of *deregulation*, it is also responsible for the drive to *privatisation* of the state sector in all countries of the world.

Throughout the 1980s, the advanced countries witnessed a vigorous policy of privatisation of the public sector involving first public utilities and next welfare services. In Britain, for example, in the 1980s a total of £60 billion of state assets was sold at knock-down prices to the private sector.[13] In addition, Britain has pioneered 'Government by Contract', or 'arm's length' government which involves the government in contracting out to the private sector everything from the issuing of passports to the prison services, setting up quasi-independent agencies (Quangos), unaccountable and undemocratic, for the purpose. When the Tory government first took office in 1979, there were about 770 000 public and civil servants in government service; by 1995 there were reckoned to be only some 50 000.[14]

Privatisation is often presented as a policy response by governments to the fiscal deficit arising from welfare burdens of their ageing populations and from the rise in unemployment resulting from recurring recessions. However, this only partially explains it. For privatisation has involved huge transfers of monies from the public sector to the private sector in the form of subsidies and tax cuts and, most importantly, it has created an infrastructure for the private sector to trade with, and carry out services for, the public sector which continue to be paid for by the state through various forms of out-contracting.[15]

In indebted Third World countries, privatisation has been imposed by multilateral agencies within policy frameworks provided by 'structural adjustment programmes' (see Chapter 8). The World Bank and the IMF, who have a firm lever over the economies of many indebted countries in the Third World, use the arguments of neo-liberalism to impose privatisation. By 1992 more than 80 countries around the world had privatised some 6800 previously state-owned enterprises, mostly monopoly suppliers of essential public services like water, electricity or telephones.[16] Because of the fragility of domestic stock markets in these countries, the shares for these utilities were bought up by international financial conglomerates. The same processes of global governance, of course, are visible in the ex-centrally planned economies of eastern Europe.

Thus, with the globalisation (as opposed to mere internationalisation) of the world economy, there is a tendency for states to become instruments for adjusting their economies to the pressures of the world market. Adjustment to global competitiveness is the new categorical imperative.

From a point of view of theory we need to conceptualise the emerging governance by the global capitalist class as a complex process that institutionalises structural power through the widespread adoption of cultural values and legitimating ideology. But this legitimating ideology, while parading under the banner of 'deregulation' and 'privatisation', yet draws in governments in an ever-widening circumference of 'regulation' in the form of policy initiatives and legislation. These include monetary and fiscal policies, industrial legislation, social policies, the restructuring of the welfare state, and even the reconstitution of social obligations; for example, an ideological attack on alternative lifestyles, and prioritisation of traditional family values through social policy initiatives.[17] As we have argued elsewhere, this list also includes the transformation of 'higher education' from a critical activity to short-term training for the labour market and research 'relevant' to industry.[18]

The difficulty for any theorist of regulation is that the forms of regulation of the new epoch are – compared with the past – quintessentially a form of *de*regulation. That is the paradox. Deregulation in one sense implies a dismantling of state-sponsored forms of regulation of the market, a shrinking of the public sector, indeed even a diminution of the public domain. Yet as we have seen, national governments adjust their economies to globalisation by regulating *for* deregulation. It is this confusion over regulation and deregulation that explains why there is so much controversy within international relations theory and international political economy literature between those who hold so called 'declinist' views of the nation-state, and those who claim to observe a strengthening of national authority.

Capital–Labour Relations: The New Global World of Work

At the beginning of 1994 there were at least 120 million people registered unemployed world-wide. To this figure must be added an estimated 700 million workers who were *under*employed, that is engaged in an economic activity that does not permit them to reach a minimum standard of living.[19] What is new about these statistics is that they include some 35 million people who are registered unemployed in the advanced countries.[20] Furthermore, any recent declines in unemployment levels in the latter are almost wholly attributable to growth in part-time and self-employment.[21]

Debates about global employment patterns are dominated by two agendas: on the one hand there is the 'relocation' debate which focuses on the extent to which jobs in industry in the core regions of the world economy are being relocated to the periphery. On the other hand there are debates around the restructuring of the labour market in the core countries, where core activities in manufacturing are increasingly either shed or 'externalised' into producer 'service' activities.

The 1970s, and still more so the 1980s, witnessed the global restructuring of industry and a redistribution of jobs through integrated international production enabled by the new technologies. The haemorrhaging of jobs in the core countries benefited the periphery, particularly Pacific Asia. A French government report in 1993 estimated that in the last 20 years no less than 6.6 million jobs left the EC and the US for the Far East.[22] US manufacturing employment in the developing countries as a whole grew almost five times the rate of such employment in the developed econo- mies.[23] Today the developing world as a whole contributes 19 per cent of manufacturing exports as against only 7 per cent 20 years ago. Two-thirds of this comes from just one region in Pacific Asia, namely South Korea, Taiwan, Singapore, Hong Kong and the regions in mainland China near Hong Kong.[24]

Optimists argue that the loss of jobs in manufacturing activities in the core economies will be compensated for by a growth of service industries, including services related to manufacturing itself. 'New U.S. Factory Jobs aren't in the Factory' ran a headline in *Business Week*, in 1994, arguing that support industries with their high component of knowledge skills constitute a second tier of manu- facturing industries. While a smaller percentage of the US workforce will be in production, a much larger percentage will be supporting this production in computer software, robot making, and countless services that will add jobs to supply the 'leaner' manufacturers.[25]

Robert Reich, in his bestselling book *The Work of Nations* comes up with supporting statistics. Between 1975 and 1990 America's 500 largest industrial corporations failed to create a single net new job, and their share of the civilian labour force fell from 17 per cent to under 10 per cent. At the same time the number of people describing themselves as 'self-employed' began to rise, and by the late-1980s America was adding about 1.3 million new enterpises to the economy each year (compared with a mere 93 000 in the 1950s), most of them small businesses.[26] The same transformation is in evidence in other advanced countries.[27]

Attempts to theorise the contemporary transformation in global capital–labour relations are made especially difficult by the fact that today's advanced information-driven production systems have ren- dered the conventional conceptual distinction between capital and labour crude to the point of uselessness.

Information society theorists typically argue that, today, knowl- edge and information are replacing capital and labour as the source of value.[28] While this is a contentious issue which many who stand in the Marxist tradition may not accept (including many adherents of the Regulation School), at a minimum we have to recognise that knowledge and information have become a key, independent, source of added value, a fourth factor of production alongside the conventional trio of capital, labour and land (raw materials). The reason why knowledge is a key source of added value has to do with its extreme 'fungibility': when applied to the other factors of production it releases them for other use. Computer-programmed laser cutting in the garment industry enables the reduction of waste, and thus the saving of cloth, that no amount of skill of the human hand could ever hope to achieve. Robots release labour for other activities. Computer-driven technologies reduce the capital costs associated with fixed plant and equipment, and warehouse space for inventory and stock. And unlike the other factors of production, knowledge and information do not diminish with use. Rather the opposite; the more knowledge is being used and shared the greater the likelihood that new knowledge, and new added value, will be created.

But who has this knowledge? Is it capital, is it labour, both or neither? This depends on whether we are talking about 'embodied' or 'disembodied' knowledge. To the extent that knowledge is embodied in tangible products and processes, to that extent it is clearly able to be owned by capital; indeed it is a part of capital. For example, with the advent of micro-electronic-driven numerical systems, it has become possible to incorporate the knowledge and experience of the skilled operator into a controlling programme held on a paper tape. Somebody 'owns' this paper tape. Likewise, computer-operated management information systems that control and automate materials/logistics flows (so-called MRP systems) as well as other operational and oganisational informations systems (CAD/CAM and cellular manufacturing systems) are knowledge systems that are embodied in 'hardware', that is physical, tangible assets. But the distinction becomes blurred with expert systems embodied in software (over which claims to ownership are notoriously difficult to establish and enforce) and it disappears altogether with the expertise lodged in the brains of those who invent the software.

The distinction between embodied and disembodied knowledge to some degree, of course, also applied in a previous era. Scientists in company research laboratories, design engineers, managers at all levels, clerks and other administrative 'white collar' workers, lawyers and accountants, advertising and marketing staff, all these were 'knowledge' workers whose expertise was not actually encapsulated in tangible physical assets. Nevertheless, excepting a relatively small proportion of independent and self-employed professionals, they were not normally able to turn this knowledge to economic advantage without their expertise being incorporated within the organisational boundaries of a corporate firm. Knowledge was 'organisationally' embedded. This gave the legal owners of the firm, that is the owners of 'capital' in Marxist terminology, the opportunity to 'appropriate' knowledge or mental labour in the same way as they appropriated physical, unskilled labour, hiring the exercise of mental abilities for a specified period of time, most often on an exclusionary basis. For a while, despite all the evident complexities that this entailed, it was thus possible for Marxist theoretical analyses to conceptualise such white-collar staff as 'similar' to blue-collar staff, that is as labour whose surplus value was being extracted by 'capital' in the course of production.

What is new today is the advent of desk computers and the fusion of computers and telecommunications. These technological advances, notably electronic data transmission and video conferencing which facilitate 'teleworking', have enabled 'knowledge' workers to be involved in, and contribute to, the business of a firm without being employed by it. Conversely, it has made it possible for firms to 'externalise employment'. The result has been a fundamental transformation of corporate organisation, away from bureaucratic centralisation, all-embracing size and the associated hierarchical command structure, and towards loosely networked structures of 'adhocracy'.[29] In the 'post-entrepreneurial' firm, as the influential American business analyst, Rosabeth Moss Kanter terms it,[30] both routine activities of general overhead and administrative services, and special project activities are 'externalised'. Many employees are either being replaced with outside contractors, or becoming contractors themselves, or staff departments are being spun-off as independent contractors and consultancies. As firm managers and professional staff are disappearing, so bureaucratic career ladders are crumbling; full-time employment is giving way to 'contingent' employment, including part-time, just-in-time, contract work and temporary employment. In the US, in the 1980s, more than half the new jobs created have gone to contingent workers.[31]

New forms of regulation are emerging to deal with the new situation of externalised employment. These new forms of regulation are best summed up as institutional practices around 'connectivity'. They involve an exhaustive bureaucratisation of quality assurance and advance process certification methods permitting final product assembler companies to identify 'best' suppliers and trace liability in the event of defects.

For example, lead or assembler companies need to assure themselves of the quality of the intermediate product or service prior to its use. Flexible, just-in-time production does not allow for quality assessment of goods and services at the point and time of delivery. Instead what is required in the global market is quality assurance through advance process certification. The global networked firm or global web thus organises, as it were, an internal market of 'best suppliers' (suppliers who have achieved the company's approval rating and who work to company specification). National governments eager to ensure that their domestic firms can compete within these global webs, and who may be called upon in cases of liability disputes, are drawn in as a regulating force. For instance, the British government has institutionalised quality certification through the introduction of British Standard 5750 (BS5750) which has subsequently been harmonised with the International Standard ISO 9000. This standard certification applies equally to businesses in the private sector and the public sector.[32]

Thus, once again, we see that there are indeed new forms of regulation emerging which coordinate human activities in the new circumstances created by the global process of accumulation. In an exciting new theory of connectivity, Charles Sabel suggests that the practice of coordination develops its own discipline of collaboration through 'learning-by-monitoring'. Third party registrars such as the ISO 9000 series of standards permit the evolution of a *lingua franca* of discussion of projects among independent advanced firms and their suppliers, without them having to rely on either proprietary systems of fiat, or some mysterious cultural glue that has often been used to explain Japanese collaborative arrangements between independent units.

> By linking learning to monitoring the new institutions (for example ISO 9000) allow initially wary partners to begin cooperating in ways which may eventually so align their understanding of the world and so their mutual interests that they come to trust each other in ways not contemplated at the start.[33]

Core–Periphery Relations

The complex integration strategies of international production together with the new forms of coordination which are enabled by the new technologies, coupled with the operation of the global market principle, are together altering the landscape of the global division of labour. It is no longer one that strictly follows economic geography.

There was a time when the geography of the global division of labour ran parallel with the sequential transformation of goods-in-production from low value-added activities to high value-added activities. To explain this we need to first say a bit about the concept of value-added.

'Value-added' is the market value of a firm's output minus the market value of the inputs it purchases from other firms. Essentially, therefore, it is the sum of the factor incomes, the wages and profits of the firm. The concept of a value-added *chain* arises because in the transformation of a raw material, say, cotton, to an end consumer product, a garment in a shop window, there is a *sequence* of intermediate stages of fabrication and processing: spinning, running, dyeing, weaving, cutting, designing, sewing, wholesaling, advertising, marketing and retailing. At each stage, the labour involved adds value to the process of transformation, making the product progressively more expensive to the final consumer. Moreover, at each stage, capitalist entrepreneurs intervene to organise the discrete activity in the chain, each in turn adding a mark-up to make some profits for themselves. This implies that the market price for the final product incorporates all the wages and mark-ups of all the previous stages. The history of multinational enterprise may be summed up by saying that it has moved from trying to internalise all these stage-like transactions within its own organisational embrace, to once more, as under global networking, externalising all or many of these stages and transactions.

It may thus be seen that the concept of a value-added chain expresses a sequential progression from 'lower value added to higher value-added' activities. But there is more to the hierarchical progression than mere sequencing of transformation. The historical development of capitalism on a world scale, for all the reasons which we have spelt out in the first part of this book, also, and additionally, concentrated 'higher value activities' at the final, consumer, end of the chain (the consumer markets in the rich countries), while largely (though not exclusively) leaving low value activities in underdeveloped lands. There was a double effect, therefore, in so far as the wages of labour at higher stages of the transformation process are likely to be higher, and therefore the pass-on prices, than at the lower end of the production chain. Furthermore, the more specialised the final product, again more typically at the rich consumer end of the chain, the higher the profit mark-up for such products due to the effect of limited demand. For all these reasons, bulk or volume production which is concentrated at the lower end of the chain yields lower value-added than specialised, high-tech products which are concentrated at the higher end of the value chain.

Today something curious is happening. As Paul Krugman has put it, it is now possible to 'slice up' the value chain in a different way, and locate the labour intensive slices in the production of those goods traditionally viewed as skill, capital or technology-intensive, in low-wage locations. A classic example is the notebook computer. It looks like a high technology product, but while the American microprocessor and the Japanese flat-panel display are indeed high-tech, the plastic shell that surrounds them and the wiring that connects them are not, so the assembly of notebook computers becomes an industry of the 'newly industrializing economies'.[34] Also, as we have seen in the previous chapter, many information-intensive activities previously classed as 'high value-added' activities are today 'real-time' activities that may be carried out anywhere in the global system.

Thus, the global division of labour is rendering a core–periphery relationship that cuts across national and geographic boundaries, bringing on board within the core, segments of the Third World, and relegating segments and groups in both the traditional core of the system and in the Third World to peripheral status. Core–periphery is becoming a social relationship, and no longer a geographic one.

This new social core–periphery hierarchy threatens to become still more uneven than was previously the case. Many high value-added activities that are contributed by 'disembodied knowledge workers', are not only 'externalised', they are also extremely *mobile*. Marketing experts, computer consultants, legal affairs specialists, financial accountants and top managers can go to wherever they can obtain the highest price for their services. Conversely, because of the operation of the global market principle, payments for their services are being equalised across national boundaries, increasingly therefore at the highest price. In the recent row in the UK over the payments and perks for top managers in the utilities sector, these emoluments were defended with reference to figures such managers might earn in other countries. But at the lower end of the value chain exactly the opposite is happening. Low value-added activities are still typically tied to tools and equipment, that is to knowledge embodied in capital, and/or to the location where raw materials are extracted. At this end of the international production chain it is capital and not labour that is mobile, a situation that is perpetuated by political intervention designed to stem the free migration of labour. The mobility of capital here implies that wage rates equalise at the lowest possible denominator, and this includes wage rates for such activities in the advanced countries.

How is the social core–periphery relationship managed and regulated? In a previous era, world system writers used to point to the regulatory function of the 'semi-periphery'. Both Wallerstein and Galtung, for example, dwelt on the emergence of semi-peripheral nations as 'go-between' nations. They argued that a core–periphery system based on unequal rewards must constantly worry about rebellion. To avert this, 'middle-sectors' are created which tend to think of themselves primarily as better-off than the lower sector, rather than worse-off than the upper sector. Standing in-between the exploiters and the exploited, such middle-sector nations (for example Brazil, Mexico and the newly industrialising countries of south east Asia) were themselves both exploiting and exploited. They sought trade with both core and periphery, exchanging different kinds of products with each and achieving intermediate wage levels and profit margins. Their political role, too, was one of mediation between First and Third World.[35] This existence of a middle layer in the hierarchy of nations gave the world system a dynamic quality which allowed for the upward and downward mobility of nations and thus permitted the reproduction of the overall core–periphery hierarchy over time.

How does this work in the present global system where the core–periphery hierarchy is no longer a geographic division between nations, but a social one that cuts across nations? Today it is quite common in postindustrial society literature to talk of the emergence of 'two-third societies' in the advanced countries, where one-third of the electorate is marginalised by long-term unemployment. But this is a rather crude picture that omits reference to what is in fact an emerging middle layer of semi-periphery, again one which cuts across nations but which, however, does not perform the same function of mediation as its predecessor. Indeed the political function of stabilisation of the global system rests today on the *politics of exclusion* of those disadvantaged groups and segments in all societies that can no longer perform a useful function as either producers or consumers within the global market.

In his book, *The State We're In*,[36] Will Hutton outlines an emerging 30/30/40 society in Britain. He argues that developments in the labour market have led to a new categorisation of British society. There is a bottom 30 per cent of unemployed and economically inactive who are a marginalised disadvantaged group (in my view, a better term for this social segment is 'excluded'). Another 30 per cent is constituted by those who, while in work, are in forms of employment that are structurally insecure. Finally there are only 40 per cent who can count themselves as holding tenured jobs which allow them to regard their income prospects with any certainty. I suggest one might include in this category those with secure future incomes from capital investments.

Hutton's key concern is with the middle layer. They are the very people whom we have identified before as the growing army of part-time, casualised contract workers, workers sacked and then rehired as self-employed, temporary, part-time, self-employed and agency workers. Not only are they insecure in their present job prospects, they also have to meet the exigencies of an uncertain future, with pension and health provisions and other forms of collective insurance against risk previously secured by the welfare state, diminished or being phased out.

While Hutton rails against this new three-tier society as inefficient from a national economy point of view, as indeed it is, I want to draw attention here to its functioning from the point of view of globalisation. For there are similar three-tier structures growing up in other nations, developed and underdeveloped alike. The difference between underdeveloped and developed countries is solely in the size of the various segments, with the excluded sector in the Third World often approaching 50 per cent, with the middle group a narrow band of between 20 and 30 per cent.

Global competition pits the members of the middle sector against each other both within and between nations. Thanks to pro-flexibility[37] and anti-union legislation, pursued with varying degrees of resolve in different countries, they are also fragmented and deprived of the organisational instruments of collective organisation and action which were the hallmark of the social-democratic settlement in national economies of the advanced countries in the postwar era. Permanent high levels of structural unemployment, the visible presence of disadvantaged groups (the third sector) in their midsts, and what Hutton aptly calls 'fear of the future', keeps this stratum in check. For its part, the free mobility of capital coupled with the existence of a global market and global labour pools, removes the need for capital to worry about the reproduction of labour power or domestic markets.[38]

The Politics of Exclusion

The key to preservation of this new emerging order is therefore, for the present, not an economic problem but a law and order problem. It is a problem of how to deal with the excluded segments of society. The politics of exclusion takes many forms. We can see examples in the shooting of street children in Brazil and Columbia, and in the anti-immigration laws and the policing of the Mediterranean waters around 'fortress Europe'. We witness it in the policy of 'mass incarceration' in the US where over two million people (disproportionately black, young and unemployed) languish in jail at any one time. We see it happen in the politics of Aids research where 90 per cent of research and investment is spent on the development of drugs for the treatment of the 8 per cent of people who have Aids in the developed countries, while snuffing out the funds and the research agendas for cheap vaccines to prevent the further spread of Aids in the Third World. After all, as one World Bank official observed: 'if Aids falls disproportionately on the poor in these countries then the fact that they will die of it will have a positive impact on the economic growth of these nations'.[39]

At the other end of the spectrum we also observe the politics of exclusion in more subtle, less immediately visible forms. Take for example the privatisation of mass public space and the gradual replacement of public by private forms of security and surveillance.

In Britain today more private security guards patrol private shopping centres, recreational parks and offices than there are policemen on the beat. Such privatisation of mass public space entails a diminution of citizens' rights. Unlike the rights constitutionally secured to citizens for free access to the 'Queen's highway', today sections of the 'unwanted' public may be kept out on private orders.

Finally, in still more subtle ways, we detect the politics of exclusion in the discourse of local community politics that is informing the agenda of inner city regeneration programmes in Britain and elsewhere in the advanced countries. These programmes ingeniously appropriate the language of community politics, traditionally the preserve of the Left, to contain territorially and ideologically the disadvantaged groups of the population.

Already in the 1980s we have seen a timid embrace on the part of the deregulating and privatising governments of advanced countries of the concepts and practices of community development, community management, community capacity building, community enterprise, community development corporations and even community credit unions.[40] These diverse forms of generously-funded community-oriented programmes combine an expressed denial of the growth of personal wealth (otherwise the 'normal' practice in the global system) with a specifically local focus and reliance on community participation. They are in tune with the neo-liberal governments' calls for greater self-help, active citizenship and a reduced dependency on the state. They have rightly been condemned for calling upon people with the fewest resources to help those most in need.[41] They have also, thus far, failed to make a dent in the spiral of job losses caused by globalisation, and their contribution in economic terms is extremely marginal.[42] But they have one great merit, namely of organising the poor and the marginalised to care for and contain and control themselves.

PART III
THE POSTCOLONIAL WORLD

Introduction

In Part II we described the transformative directions of the world capitalist system. While it is over-ambitious to pin one label on the totality of all the complex, interactive changes, some writers nevertheless suggest that these changes add up to a transformation of capitalism from its modern stage to a postmodern stage.[1] This stage is characterised by new flexible systems of production, a predominance of high-tech industries, economic enterprise orientation towards niche markets and consumerism, globalisation of markets and of forms of regulation, fictitious capital formation, and the ascendancy of a hegemonic neo-liberal ideology.

Crucially, as Frederic Jameson has argued, this transformation does not permit developing countries to complete the project of modernity. For international capital, moving rapidly from one low-wage situation to the next, only cybernetic technology and postmodern investment opportunities are ultimately attractive. Yet, in the new international system few countries can seal themselves off in order to modernise at their own time and pace. Thus, the disappearance of the 'Third World' is a constitutional feature of postmodern or, what I prefer to call, globalised capitalism.

Acknowledging that the Third World is no longer a unitary category nor has a homogeneous identity, the aim in this part of the book is to capture the differential impact on, and responses to, globalisation in those regions of the world that used to be gathered under the label 'Third World'. Nevertheless, in describing those regions and those responses as 'postcolonial' I borrow a theoretical concept for which I first must give some justification and offer clarification. For what indeed is the point of erasing one unitary label only to scribble in another?

Part of the answer, pragmatically, lies in the popularity that the concept enjoys today. And since a central purpose of this book is to introduce key contemporary trends and issues, I cannot ignore the rising tide, even institutional endorsement,[2] of postcolonial studies

153

which claims as its special provenance the field that used to go by the name of Third World studies or development studies.

But over and above this, I do believe that the concept has heuristic value because of its timeliness: it has entered the lexicon of development studies simultaneously as the product of, engagement with, *and* as contestation of globalisation. In the reshuffled order of the global economy, where First Worlds have appeared in the Third World, and Third Worlds in the First World, postcolonial studies opens up three windows, or angles of vision. *First*, such studies dispute that one can infer 'identity' by looking at material relations alone. The politics of cultural identity and recognition have become as important as the politics of redistribution; and, as Nancy Fraser argues, they can support the politics of redistribution.[3] *Second*, postcolonial studies puts a referent emphasis on the cultural *complexity* of identity formation. Today, cross-border migrations have resulted in fragmentation and heterogenous mixes of belonging and loyalties and political allegiances in which class and nation have become 'decentred' as a source of identity. *Third*, postcolonialism is suggestive and reflexive of a world no longer structured along binary axes, be they First World/Third World; north/south, east/west or socialist/capitalist.

The concept is, however, far from being unproblematic. While it seems to be succeeding in 'destabilising' the development debate, it has also been accused of intellectual escapism and critical paralysis.[4] Let us first examine the concept and these debates more fully before deciding on how we can best make use of it in organising the chapters in this part of the book.

The Postcolonial: Condition and Discourse

The term 'postcolonial' is a member of a family of 'post' literatures of which 'postmodernism' is the all-embracing, generic term. And, as is the case with all this 'post' literature, the word 'post' pulls us into a semantic trap. For it expresses an epistemological break with the all-encompassing totality of western thought and scientific tradition, while also signalling an epochal sequentiality. The problem, however, is that those who make the epistemological break reject the 'foundationalism' and the 'essentialism' that underpins the historical analysis by which the epochal succession is diagnosed. Needless to say, this has led to largely fruitless debates between the two camps.

In her critique of postmodernism, Ellen Meiksins Wood reminds us of how the sociologist C. Wright Mills had formulated this intellectual conundrum: the crisis of reason and freedom which marked the onset of the postmodern age, he said, presented:

> structural problems, and to state them requires that we work in the classic terms of human biography and epochal history. Only in such terms can the connections of structures and milieux that affect these values today be traced and causal analyses be conducted.[5]

But, comments Meiksins Wood:

> this statement is in nearly every particular anti-thetical to the current theories of postmodernity which effectively deny the very existence of structure and structural connections and the very possiblity of 'causal analysis'.[6]

Exactly so, and thus it is with postcolonial theory! In fact, much of the debate surrounding the use of the term 'postcolonial' repeats *mutatis mutandis* the debates around the term 'postmodern'.

In regard to postmodernism, those writers who have engaged with it from a historical structural, or Marxist, perspective, for example David Harvey and Frederic Jameson, have done so by resorting to the only theoretical option available under the circumstances, namely to distinguish between postmodernism as 'condition' and postmodernism as 'critique'. And, again, so it is with the concept 'postcolonial'. Following Arif Dirlik who has thus tried to bring the postcolonial discourse into the arena of global political economy,[7] I intend to treat postcolonial discourse as a 'cultural condition' or 'logic' that corresponds to the specific geopolitical and economic configuration of what we have earlier referred to as postmodern or globalised capitalism. In short, we shall understand what 'postcolonial' *is* from an understanding of *how* and *why* it all began.

On a strict semantic interpretation one would think that the word 'postcolonial' refers to the period after independence, that is after formal colonialism ended. Yet this is *not* what the term is intended to mean today. Ella Shohat in her crisp interrogation of the concept describes it as:

a designation for critical discourses which thematize issues emerging from colonial relations and their aftermath, covering a long historical span (including the present).[8]

This also covers, pointedly, the postindependence, neo-colonial, period which was stabilised under the American-led Bretton Woods postwar order. Thus, 'postcolonial' implies a movement going beyond anti-colonial nationalist theory as well as a movement beyond a specific point in history, that of colonialism *and* Third World nationalist struggles.

Noting how historical specificity collapses under chronological diversity, Shohat asks, somewhat impatiently: 'When, exactly, then, does the "post-colonial" begin?'[9] To which Arif Dirlik quips the reply: 'When Third World intellectuals have arrived in First World academe'.[10] The term originated, in the mid-1980s, among Third World scholars in First World universities, who were caught up in diasporic circumstances owing to the crisis of the Third World and the failure of the developmental and democratic project in many Third World countries. Whether forced into exile, or as voluntary émigrés, they have regrouped around a discourse of identity that owes less to geographic location and national origin than to *subject position*. This confluence of historical and biographical details can explain much of the epistemology and the substantive theory that was to emerge.

As Arif Dirlik notes, the release of postcoloniality from the fixity of Third World location, means that the identity of the postcolonial is no longer structural but *discursive*. That is to say, it is the participation in the discourse that defines the postcolonial. The postcolonial discourse or critique:

resonates with concerns and orientations that have their origins in a new world situation created by transformations within the capitalist world economy, by the emergence of what has been variously described as 'global capitalism', 'flexible production', 'late capitalism' and so on, terms that have disorganized earlier conceptualizations of global relations, especially relations comprehended earlier by such binaries as colonized/colonizer, First

World/Third World, and 'the West and the Rest', in all of which the nation state was taken for granted as the global unit of political organization.

But here comes the epistemological twist: even as postcolonial discourse thus engages with global times, postcolonial critics, with few exceptions, do not interrogate that relationship because they repudiate a foundational role to capitalism in history.[11] By ignoring the political economy approach they have invited criticisms of being apolitical and ahistorical and even complicitous in the 'consecration of hegemony'.[12]

So much for the 'condition' of postcoloniality. Let us now turn to postcolonial discourse, or postcolonial critique, itself.

In First World academe, Third World scholars found a welcome home and symbiotic environment in the burgeoning discipline, and polemics, of 'cultural studies'. Cultural studies began as literature critique in English literature and linguistics departments, and likewise did postcolonial studies. The central terrain and mode of questioning in studies such as *The Empire Writes Back*,[13] *Colonial Discourse and Postcolonial Theory*[14] and *Decolonising the Mind*[15] are literature and literature criticism. This, too, matches the careers of Third World intelligentsia, many of whom first found a voice through literary writing.[16]

Cultural studies, in Raymond Williams' classic definition, investigates the creation of meaning in, and as a formative part of, a whole way of life, the whole world of sense-making (descriptions, explanations, interpretations, valuations of all kinds) in societies understood as historical material organizations.[17] Its terrain of inquiry is 'mass' or 'popular' culture in all its manifestations: language, film, magazines, TV soaps, shopping, advertising and so on. It is political and polemical (and massively irritating to structural Marxists) in so far as it argues that the masses are not mere passive recipients of a culture wickedly designed by capitalists to suck them into consumerism, exploitation, and subjugation, but instead are actively participating and contributing. Their participation can be deliberate, creative, selective and even subversive.

Culture is also the vehicle or medium whereby the relationship between groups is transacted. The emancipatory promise and purpose of cultural studies is to discover resistance and subversive creativity in the cultural relation between dominant and subordinated groups, and helping to reverse it, as when Frantz Fanon once argued that 'Europe is literally the creation of the Third World'. Cultural studies does this *first* by deconstructing the texts, words, names, labels, definitions of the situation that have been authored by the dominant groups, and *next* by giving people of all subordinated groups – blacks, gays, women, peasants and indigenous peoples – their voices back through a 'new historicism', or through a new style of anthropology as in ethnographic accounts of local cultural practices of resistance and protest. *Third*, Cultural studies is emancipatory in so far as it links, through its interventions, the experience of these diverse social groups, and potentially brokers new political alliances between them.

Within this broad field and style of enquiry, postcolonial discourse nestled organically to engage in a radical re-think and re-formulation of forms of knowledge and social identities authored and authorised by colonialism and western domination. For example, it critiques both the idea and the practice of 'development' as well as the concept of the Third World as part of a Eurocentric discourse of control and subordination. Much of this literature re-writes and 'counter appropriates' the history of the 'subalterns' (the subordinated 'others') making their voices of resistance heard (past and present), reversing orientalist thought, and decolonising the mind. The goal is to undo all partitioning strategies between centre and periphery as well as all other 'binarisms' that are the legacy of colonial ways of thinking, and to reveal societies globally in their complex heterogeneity and contingency. In this way postcolonial discourse aims to reconstruct the identities of subordinated peoples, give them back their pride of place in history and with it the confidence to build on the record of their own 'hybrid position of practice and negotiation'.[18]

The concept of 'hybridity' occupies a central place in postcolonial discourse and it is a good example of the 'reverse value-coding' that Gyan Prakash speaks of as one of the strategies of the discourse.[19] In colonial days 'hybridity' was a term of abuse, signifying the lowest possible form of human life: mixed breeds who were 'white but not quite'.[20] In postcolonial discourse, by contrast, hybridity is celebrated and privileged as a kind of superior cultural intelligence owing to the advantage of 'in-betweenness', the straddling of two cultures and the consequent ability to 'negotiate the difference'. Re-interpeting Fanon, for example, Homi Bhabha argues that the liberatory 'people' who initiate the productive instability of revolutionary cultural change, are themselves the bearers of hybrid identity.[21] In Development Studies, an analysis in terms of hybrid cultures leads to a reconceptualisation of established views. Namely, that rather than being eliminated by modernity, many 'traditional cultures' survive through their transformative engagement of modernity.[22] In the ensuing chapters we shall encounter illustrations of this 'hybridisation' in each of the 'zones' of development that we shall be discussing, whether it be the Confucianisation of modernity as in East Asia, or the postdevelopment trajectories of Latin American peasant communities and slum dwellers.

Postcolonial Formations

One does not have to buy into the whole of the postcolonial discourse to appreciate that the concept has merits in helping us get a handle on the diversity of development and underdevelopment trajectories in these global times. For it is the colonial and neo-colonial experience and the manner in which the aftermath interacts with globalisation that illuminates the different outcomes, namely a different postcolonial formation in various parts of the world system at the present time. As the titles of these chapters suggest, we shall study these various forms of the postcolonial condition in four major zones of the world. While the word 'zone' still carries with it a notion of area-specific location, there is nevertheless a certain fluidity and ambiguity between the area-referential emphasis and the subject-positional one.

Thus, in Chapter 8, we look at the peripheralising consequences of globalisation prevalent in many parts of the Third World, but we focus on how these have become exemplified and, in a manner of speaking, have gone furthest in subSaharan Africa. Debt, and deregulation following punitive structural adjustment programmes, have more tightly integrated the wealth of many Third World élites in the global economy, while politically emasculating the states in these regions and thus undermining their capacity to relaunch any national territorial developmental project. Moreover, the imposition of the neo-liberal orthodoxy, coupled with the insistence on electoral reform and democracy, has not only undermined the state but contributed directly to the descent into anarchy and civil war in many countries in Africa. The ensuing political emergencies have drawn in the international donor community in a form of containment activity that may be summed up as the *management of exclusion* rather than a programme of development and incorporation. It is a management of exclusion that is becoming characteristic of the manner in which other areas at the edge of the global system are being treated too.

In Chapter 9 we examine the postcolonial condition of militant Islam. We argue that the failure of the neo-colonial, developmentalist period has interacted with the historical cultural tradition of Islamic spiritual renewal and its subjection to cultural imperialism, feeding a process of cultural denial of globalisation and modernity. While we shall not develop the theme of its resonance in other parts of the world, including the diasporic Muslim communities of the West, it is clear that this anti-developmental postcolonial position, again, is one in which the area referent and subject position become fused. The *anti-developmentalism* of militant Islam is different in its origins and expression from both the *management of exclusion* in subSaharan Africa and the *postdevelopment* response in Latin America.

The global process of transformation is neither even nor unopposed. In Chapter 10 we look at the experience of the 'developmental' states in East Asia which testify to the possibilities of national territorial accumulation and defensive regional alliances. It is an experience that owes as much to the end of the cold war and *Pax Americana*, as it does to the very same historical process of capitalist expansion and integration which peripheralised and marginalised other areas and communities in the world system. Here too, there are lessons to be learnt from the locally-specific contestation of this postcolonial condition that may hold out the promise of successful replication in other areas of the periphery of the global system too.

Chapter 11 looks at Latin America, where the postmodern turn in Development Studies has gone furthest in promoting a postdevelopmentalist philosophy of liberation. Postdevelopment theory and practice is different from antidevelopment sentiments in so far as it does not deny globalisation or modernity but wants to find some ways of living with it and imaginatively transcend it. Much of the creative thinking about the new social movements and the development of civil society originates on this continent. Yet, as before, the hybrid forms of struggle and local experimentations with alternative social and economic organisation are not exclusive to Latin America but are also found elsewhere, including the heartland of the traditonal core of the capitalist system. Thus, these 'postdevelopments', too, reflect conditions, and inspire responses that may be of relevance to other social groups and localities within the global system.

8

Africa: Exclusion and the Containment of Anarchy

We have argued that with globalisation the world capitalist system has reached a new and higher level of integration. It has, in the words of Peter Drucker, become a 'transnational economy, one that is shaped and driven, not by production and trade, but by money flows'. These money flows he calls 'the symbol economy'.[1] The symbol economy has its own dynamics and is not determined by the real economy. However, as mentioned before, the connections between the world of high finance and the fundamentals of world trade and production are not completely severed (see p. 129). The electronic integration of the world's financial markets and the development of a whole range of novel financial instruments, permitted since the deregulation of these markets, have made it possible to connect up the arteries of real production and trade, and thus squeeze workers and peasants all over the world for their last drop of surplus in a manner that makes invisible, and therefore unchallengeable, the innumerable threads that lead to the pension funds, the share prices and the bank accounts in the core of the world system.

We have also argued, with Manuel Castells (see p. 89), that the present transformation of the global economy reduces many parts of the Third World to a position of 'structural irrelevance'. But this is not to say that in the period of transformation itself those parts of the Third World do not have a function: between 1982 and 1990, creditor nations received $1345 billion in debt service, most of it coming from the heavily indebted nations of Africa and Latin America.[2] Structural irrelevance is the *outcome* of this process of accelerated pillage under debt-peonage.

In this chapter we will first examine in a general way how the debt crisis of the 1980s has had a dual function:

1. To enable the periphery of the world capitalist system to be managed in the interest of the core countries; and
2. To more effectively extract an economic surplus from it.

These more general sections permit us to refer back to them when we discuss similar issues and problems in the chapters on Latin America and the Middle East. Next we shall look at the structural consequences of the neo-liberal stranglehold in Africa where it has reduced or eliminated the integrity of what were fragile nation-states and pushed them into anarchy and civil wars.

Debt and the Internationalisation of Capital[3]

In the 1970s, the massive expansion of Third World debt began at the precise moment when Third World economic nationalism reached its peak and, it seemed, its near actualisation in OPEC generated petrodollar recycling. In 1974 the General Assembly of the United Nations adopted the (now defunct) *Declaration on the Establishment of a New International Economic Order*, followed in 1976 by the (now equally defunct) *Charter of Economic Rights and Duties of States*. This charter for the first time enshrined the right of nationalisation and the right to regulate the compensation for these nationalisations as a principle of international law. Petrodollars helped fund state nationalisations of foreign-owned enterprises and ambitious development programmes.

Paradoxically, the easy access to Arab petrodollars, which were all too eagerly recycled by international banks who were caught in a monetarist freeze in their core country markets, also encouraged the *privatisation* of Third World debt. By the end of the 1970s commercial lending and public lending had reversed their traditional post-war positions, with commercial lending to the Third World now outstripping public lending by a ratio of 3 to 1.[4]

As Naylor[5] has shown, against the backdrop of ambitious development programmes, the privatisation of Third World debt in its turn created the very conditions for the massive diversion of foreign borrowing by private individuals to personal deposits in foreign banks. The strategies deployed encompassed every trick of deception: from stolen airline tickets to phoney invoicing, overvaluing the costs of imports and under-reporting the receipts from exports with the differences stashed abroad, smuggling drugs and commodities, currencies and precious metals, and last but not least, commissions and kickbacks price-tagged to officially-recorded borrowing but banked in safe havens abroad.

Already in the early-1980s when the debt crisis broke, official estimates put the figure of capital fleeing Third World countries at between $80–100 billion, or about 25 per cent of Third World outstanding debt. But, interestingly, it was not until the very end of the debt decade that the international banking community openly pointed the accusing finger at flight capital. For example, according to figures estimated by the Bank for International Settlements, by 1989 the amount of assets held abroad by Latin American residents *exceeded* their countries' outstanding debt to commercial banks.[6] Flight capital had become recognised as an essential cause as well as consequence of the debt crisis.

Financial Integration and Deregulation

After Gorbachev and *glasnost*, the globalisation and deregulation of the world's financial markets is probably the most significant historic event of the 1980s. It is a subject which we have already discussed in the context of more general forces towards globalisation in Chapters 4 and 6. There are, however, two principal aspects of financial globalisation that are directly relevant to the debt crisis, and which are therefore worth repeating here. The *integration* of the global financial markets means that money can now be raised, borrowed, lent, lent on, invested and transferred around the globe at the press of a computer button. *Deregulation* implies that the institutional separations between different functions of money, and by corollary between different ways in which money can be used as a source of making more money, are disappearing. This combined process of financial integration and deregulation has facilitated the merging of two streams of capital flow: private capital fleeing the Third World (some of it quite illegal from the national treasurer's point of view – in fact, diverted booty), and mainstream corporate and institutional funds that are raised on the money markets. As Naylor has put it:

Recycling had taken a bizarre new twist. An ever growing number of off-shore banking centres and tax havens competed for the increasingly large supply of hot and footloose money fleeing the developing countries. The hot money was then lent through the eurobanking system funding loans to developing countries in need of hard currency to bolster their foreign exchange positions drained by capital flight.[7]

Money laundering has become easy. It is much more difficult now for public or national regulatory bodies to track down illegal funds; indeed with deregulation the concept of illegality has been whittled down to its minimum moral denominator, namely to include only those monies which are clearly derived from drug smuggling. After all, the present world-wide ideological regime of monetarism dictates that money *must* be free to flow across frontiers. The point is that since the core of the capitalist world system has now moved to this higher level of financial integration, its institutions do not recognise or respect the right of national governments in the periphery to control their currency areas.

Debt Crisis and Solutions: the 1980s

If the 1970s marked the massive expansion of Third World debt, the 1980s became the decade when the chickens came home to roost. Why was this so?

The core creditor countries, amongst which the USA is today still dominant,[8] issue and control the value of the currencies in which most debts are denominated. In a world economy dominated by global financial markets, by money careening around the globe at a frenetic pace, the principal national economic objective of the core countries has to be, and indeed has become, one of maintaining the competitive strength of their currency *vis-à-vis* each other, fighting domestic inflation that threatens this competitive strength, and trying to catch as much as possible of the careening capital flows into the net of their domestic currency areas. The trade wars of yesterday have been replaced by investment wars. However, the prevailing monetarist ideology with its emphasis on deregulation and privatisation, and on reduction of the size and influence of the public sector, permits only one instrument to achieve this objective: manipulation of interest rates.

It is therefore no coincidence that the 1980s, at least until the Louvre Accord in 1986, stands out as a period of historically unprecedented high and rising interest rates of the core currencies. Most of the outstanding stock of Third World debt was originally contracted at low and fixed interest rates in the mid-1970s. They were, however, rescheduled in the early-1980s when floating (and rising) interest rates prevailed. The sharply increased commercial world market interest rates of that period (of between 13 and 16 per cent) coupled with the resulting improvement in the value of the core denomination currency (the US dollar) have throughout the 1980s *added* to the debt service burden of the Third World.

The upshot has been that since 1983, and for the very first time in the postwar period, *officially recorded* capital outflows from the Third World to the core countries have annually exceeded the monies flowing to it.[9] Clairmonte and Cavanagh,[10] in an article published in 1987 and covering the period 1981–6, have added to these figures an estimate of flight capital and profit remittances. Together these have lifted the total net financial transfers over the period 1981–6 to a figure well over $250 billion, representing the total financial contribution of the Third World to the advanced, core countries over that period. This figure in today's prices, the authors point out, is four times that of the $13 billion in Marshall Aid with which the United States financed the postwar recovery of Europe.

The Role of the IMF and the World Bank

Since the debt crisis broke in 1982, when Mexico first declared a moratorium on its international debt payments, the IMF and World Bank have been commissioned and dispatched to the frontiers of the global economy to exact payments from and supervise the credits to the Third World. In this capacity they have been able to profoundly affect the organisation of production and trade in the periphery to the benefit of the core of the world capitalist system.

To be fair, these international institutions were catapulted into the role of debt collector by force of historical circumstance rather than design. The privatisation of the world's financial markets which began in the 1970s, and the concommitant rise of private lending to the Third World in that period, ruled out direct government intervention on the part of the leading industrial nations. Karl Otto Pohl, IMF Governor for the Federal Republic of Germany in 1982, summed up the bankers' position during a visit to Buenos Aires:

> The IMF is our only hope. It is the only institution that can lend money and impose conditions for doing so. No government can do this, nor any bank.[11]

In all debt rescheduling exercises in the 1980s it has been the seal of approval of IMF/World Bank as expressed in official memoranda of agreements and letters of intent exchanged between them and the debtor countries which has released, in complex and interactive packages, official and commercial credit flows.[12]

There were basically two groups of seriously indebted countries. On the one hand, there were the 15 so-called 'Baker' countries. These were the middle-income countries, mostly in Latin America, plus Nigeria, the Philippines, and former Yugoslavia. On the other hand, there was a group of some 20 least-developed countries, mostly in subSaharan Africa. The difference between the two groups, apart from the size of the debt and level of economic development, lay in the composition of their debt. The former group incurred their debt mostly through private lending, the latter mostly through 'official' credits. Yet, the terms and conditions of the rescheduling packages have been remarkably similar, whether introduced under IMF stabilisation agreements (as in the case of the former) or under IMF/World Bank structural adjustment facilities (as in the case of the latter). In both cases the scope and detail of the combined IMF conditionality rules and the World Bank's structural adjustment contracts have amounted to a degree of economic intervention in the debtor countries which matched, perhaps even exceeded, the direct administration of bygone colonial governments. Inside the ruled countries the IMF came to be known as the 'International Ministry of Finance'.

Structural adjustment is the generic term used to describe a package of measures which the IMF, the World Bank and individual western aid donors have persuaded many developing countries to adopt during the 1980s, in return for a new wave of loans. As Adrian Leftwich writes, the aim of adjustment was to shatter the dominant postwar, state-led development paradigm and overcome the problems of developmental stagnation by promoting open and free competitive market economies, supervised by minimal states.[13] Between 1980 and 1990, World Bank structural adjustment loans increased from 7 to 187 in 60 countries.[14]

The inventory of IMF/WB prescriptions is by now well-known. It includes currency devaluation, deregulation of prices and wages, reduction of public spending on social programmes and state bureaucracies, removal of food and other subsidies on basic necessities, trade liberalisation, privatisation of parastatal enterprises, and the expansion of the export sector; the latter – in the case of agriculture – often at the expense of food production. The officially-stated aims of these policies was to stabilise domestic economies, to stimulate economic growth and to ensure the country's ability to earn the foreign exchange needed to service its foreign debts.

Dismantling the Developmental State

The privatisation of debt in the 1970s would have been bad enough had it been consistently applied, but in their intervention in the debt crisis in the 1980s the World Bank and the IMF exacerbated the problem for Third World countries by operating a wickedly double standard: in order to secure debt servicing on the part of the peripheral countries, they had to ensure the legitimation and the acceptance of *public* responsibility for the debt, however privately incurred or fraudulently diverted: *the debts had to be nationalised.* This was done technically by inserting cross-default clauses in rescheduling packages, and it was done ideologically and institutionally by propping up concepts of national sovereignty and the legitimacy of individual rulers, many of them spectacular thieves, as well as by recreating the fiction of local currencies though on this occasion merely as a method (through imposed devaluations) for mobilising the surplus created by a plurality of unrelated individuals and economic activities, and press-ganging all of it into one vehicle which would transport the combined wealth out of the country and into the core of the world system.

At the same time that they did this, however, they sought to *denationalise the economies* themselves by imposing various forms of deregulation, liberalisation and privatisation, indeed the dismantling of the public sector.

Combining these two contradictory strategies was not, it has to be recognised, an easy task. At the ideological level it made the bailiffs walk a tightrope between, on the one hand re-affirming the notions of national sovereignty and national economy, while at the same time, and on the other hand, confining development economics and any hint of Keynesian notions of national economic management to the dustbins of history. They had to uphold the state and destroy it at one and the same time!

The bailiffs have squared this circle by differentiating between the political/juridical state and the bureaucratic state. While the one was upheld – including the position of fraudulent leaders – the other was torn asunder. The IMF did not instruct such leaders to bring their stolen loot back into the country but rather to sack thousands of public employees. The developmental, bureaucratic state was in all literature including much left-wing literature criticised as the real cause of Third World poverty and underdevelopment. This was the message of the 'counter-revolutionaries' in development theory and of many who claimed to be standing in the Marxist tradition as well.[15]

The public sector and particularly state-owned enterprises were condemned for being managerially inefficient, corrupt, and creating market distortions and depleting national budgets. In an ingenious turning of the screw, state-owned enterprises were sold off in 'debt-for-equity' swaps. International corporations were persuaded to buy up Third World debt that was being traded in secondary markets at considerable discounts and then convert these debtor-country IOUs into local currency equivalents pegged to sell-offs of designated public assets.

By the end of the decade this twin-track policy had come full circle in the debt-for-equity swaps and other market-based debt reductions: in the privatisation of public assets, governments of debt-ridden countries sell off the state companies to pay down the debt they have legitimated. And when debt conversions, finally, came to be seen as one means of bringing flight capital back, the magic circle was complete: *roundtripping* as it is called in financial circles, not only affords Third World capital-exporting élites some form of amnesty, it is also extremely profitable to them. Having at one time transferred the nation's capital out of the country at overvalued exchange rates to bask in the sun of tax and safe havens abroad, they now come back to buy up the remainder of the nation's wealth at knock-down prices.[16]

Structural Adjustment in Africa: The Social and Economic Record

The 1980s saw 29 subSaharan African countries accept the IMF/WB medicine. Even in the stated objectives of the multilateral agencies themselves, the results have been very disappointing. In fact so disappointing that a World Bank-sponsored report in 1992, given the frank title 'Why Structural Adjustment has not Succeeded in subSaharan Africa', was retrieved from the publishers, re-issued with a less controversial title and embellished with an introduction which pointed out that the analysis was anyway flawed because it failed to distinguish countries that merely signed up to a reform programme from those that carried it out.[17] Since then the World Bank has issued a more upbeat report on the lessons of structural adjustment in subSaharan Africa.[18] Unsubtly shifting the blame for failure on to the governments of the countries themselves (for not having implemented the World Bank/IMF adjustment policies properly), it argues that only six countries got their macro-economic fundamentals 'about' right (Ghana, Tanzania, Gambia, Burkina Faso, Nigeria and Zimbabwe). This, the report claimed, has resulted in restored export competitiveness with low inflation and improved fiscal balance. But even these star performers, although eventually returning to positive GDP per capita growth rates, had deteriorating rates of investment. The other countries which implemented the policies only partially or not at all, or which backslided, have paid the price with negligible or deteriorating growth.

Taking the subSaharan region as a whole, per capita incomes declined by 30 per cent over the period 1980–8,[19] and while it is true that political crises and civil wars in many countries have contributed to this staggering loss of income, the adverse international economic environment (as partly mediated through structural adjustment and debt management policies) can be held responsible for most of it. Cynthia Hewitt de Alcantara and Dharam Ghai argue that this is so, first, because of the *simultaneous* deterioration in nearly all of the countries of the region incuding those relatively free from internal turmoil, and second because of the *magnitude* of the deteriorating external financial position of subSaharan Africa over the period. Based on UN figures, they note an annual loss of $6.5 billion over the period, even without taking account of capital flight. This total amounted to roughly one-third of total annual imports, 45 per cent of export earnings, 10–11 per cent of the region's combined GDP and 60 per cent of gross capital formation.[20]

Outside of IMF/WB circles, few observers have a positive word to say about structural adjustment. Non-government organisations (NGOs) working in the field in Africa are particularly scathing in their critique,[21] none more so than Kevin Watkins of British Oxfam. He sums up his devastating critique as follows:

> . . . the application of stringent monetary policies, designed to reduce inflation through high interest rates, has undermined investment and employment. At the same time, poorly planned trade-liberalisation measures have exposed local industries to extreme competition. Contrary to World Bank and IMF claims, the position of the poor and most vulnerable sections of society have all too often been undermined by the deregulation of labour markets and erosion of social welfare provisions, and by declining expenditures on health and education. Women have suffered in extreme form. The erosion of health expenditure has increased the burdens they carry as carers, while falling real wages and rising unemployment have forced women into multiple low-wage employment in the informal sector.[22]

Structural Adjustment: Intensifying Global Relations

Even if the structural adjustment programmes have achieved little or nothing from the point of view of national territorial development and the improvement of standards of living of the masses in African countries, the programmes have been a resounding success when measured in terms of the acceleration of the process of globalisation. Structural adjustment has helped to tie the physical economic resources of the African region more tightly into servicing the global system, while at the same time oiling the financial machinery by which wealth can be transported out of Africa and into the global system.

Commodity specialisation and debt go hand in hand. Both the World Bank and the IMF have used their leverage on indebtedness to require that production be concentrated on commodity exports. The consequence of this has been a flooding of the commodity markets which forced prices downwards. During the 1980s, the terms of trade for subSaharan African commodities fell more rapidly than for any other region of the globe.[23] Moreover, the forced pace of export specialisation reversed the share of gross domestic product between industry and agriculture from 32 and 28 per cent to 26 and 31 per cent respectively in 1980 and 1987.[24]

Secondly, forced privatisation was a standard feature of all structural adjustment programmes. In the words of one senior World Bank manager who resigned after 12 years service:

> Everything we did from 1983 onwards was based on our new sense of mission to have the south 'privatised' or die; towards this end we ignominiously created economic bedlam in Latin America and Africa.[25]

According to the World Bank 400 industries were privatised in Africa in the 1980s. These included public utilities such as telecommunications, electricity companies, railways, and credit organisations.[26] Inevitably, while national stock markets are still small and in the process of being formed, these privatisation policies ensured that foreign investors got a large slice of the action. The under-capitalisation of the emerging stock markets proved an attractive hunting ground for the active money managers of core countries' investment funds and more speculative instruments such as hedge funds.[27]

Democracy and Economic Reform

As the debt decade wore on, the *political* nature of the structural adjustment programmes, and of bilateral and other multilateral (for example EU) programmes, became ever more strident and outspoken. Previously, western governments and multilateral agencies, while professing a genuine interest in liberal democracy and human rights, had nevertheless been quite happy to openly sponsor repressive authoritarian regimes for the sake of a stable political climate.

The World Bank, forbidden by its own articles of agreement to use overtly 'political' criteria, was likewise apparently disinterested in the nature of regimes.

However, in the drive for structural adjustment, western governments during the 1980s became more and more outspoken in their preference for electoral, multiparty democracy as a precondition of further loans and grants. The World Bank, whilst still unable to insist on 'political' adjustment, began to favour a none too subtle form of 'good governance' which it defined as including the following features: an efficient public service; an independent judicial system and legal framework to enforce contracts; the accountable administration of public funds; an independent public auditor, responsible to a representative legislature; respect for the law and human rights at all levels of government; a pluralistic institutional structure; and a free press. All this adds up, as Adrian Leftwich writes:

> to a comprehensive statement of the minimum institutional, legal and political conditions of liberal democracy, though the Bank never stated this explicitly.[28]

For its part, the European Union formally adopted political conditionality as an 'aid regime principle' in 1989, while the United States added a 'democracy initiative' under the auspices of USAID in 1991.[29] Today, almost without exception, African states have moved in the direction of competitive multiparty systems with contested elections either having been held or to be held shortly. Between 1988 and 1993, the United Nations has monitored ballot-box elections in some 30 subSaharan countries.

What explains this curious change of heart? Adrian Leftwich identifies four main influences: the experience of structural adjustment lending; the resurgence of neo-liberalism in the West; the collapse of official communist regimes; and the rise of pro-democracy movements in the developing world and elsewhere. In short, we might say: the new world order.[30]

How does this 'democracy is good, state is bad' agenda assist economic reform? The link between democracy and debt restructuring in the case of Africa is the more puzzling since it assumes a positive correlation between democracy and economic development. But such assertions are *not* made by the leading international organisations when commenting on and 'explaining' the success of economic development in the newly-industrialising countries of East Asia. As we shall see in the chapter on East Asia, in relation to that part of the world the new orthodoxy singles out the virtues of strong, authoritarian and dirigiste states as the most important factor contributing to the development of the region.

Many analysts have zeroed in on this apparent contradiction, arguing that while prescriptions of a minimal liberal state treat the state as a pariah, economic reforms nevertheless depend on a pro-active interventionist government. Reform cannot be delivered without local capable hands bolstered by an efficient bureaucracy.[31]

For such authors the suspicion then arises that there is a hidden purpose behind the ostensive ignoring of this obvious contradiction. Falling back on classical structuralist explanations, some have explained away the contradiction in terms of concepts like 'low intensity democracy', arguing that electoral reforms merely permit changes acceptable to international capitalism to be put in place with greater ease and less resistance than in more overtly author-itarian regimes.[32] They have also pointed out that economic reform policies benefit certain factions of African élites with close links to international capital.[33] Others have argued that the emphasis on quality of governance merely serves 'as an efficient means of focusing responsibility on governments of developing countries, both for past ills *and* for implementation of reform packages.[34]

While, thus, one view in the academic literature regards the new political conditionalities in the manner of serving up old wines in new bottles, that is as new ways of serving the interests of international capital, there is also a new turn in the analytic literature on Africa which explores the 'new donor agenda' more widely and rather differently, namely as reflective of a generalised re-consideration and re-formulation of bilateral and multilateral relations with Africa and, indeed, with other marginalised, politically unstable, areas of the global economy. As we shall see further below, there is a new kind of postmodernist type of analysis which examines the political conditionality of the economic reform agenda as a discourse which, whether intended or not, both creates and manages a new relation-ship between the 'new world order' and Africa. This is a relationship of *exclusion*, rather than of continuing incorporation. But before we turn to this literature, we examine how far economic reform itself has contributed to fragmentation and political instability.

Economic Reform and Anarchy

In many African countries, the imposition of the neo-liberal ortho-doxy, including privatisation of the public sector, the emasculation of the state apparatus and the insistence on electoral reform, has directly contributed to the descent into anarchy and civil wars. Recent wars have scarred Angola, Sudan, Sierra Leone, Liberia, Somalia and Rwanda. Banditry, warlordism, and low-intensity conflict have come to prevail in some other parts of the continent too.

What is the link between neo-liberal reform and the descent into chaos? Surprisingly, today, there is relatively little theoretical litera-ture that addresses this question. Although there are studies which report on the empirical connection beween structural adjustment and food riots,[35] there are few attempts to theorise the link between reforms, weakened state apparatuses and disintegrating state–civil relations. One plausible explanation, however, is offered by William Reno.[36]

In a compelling study of the reform process in Sierra Leone, Reno argues that neo-liberal reforms dissolve the 'patrimonial' state form that emerged after de-colonisation and encourage disaffected élites to strike out on their own. After independence, the newly-indepen-dent states in Africa were typically weak, they lacked legitimacy and were confronted by formidable coalitions of rent-seeking strongmen using alternative, often tribal, power bases. The patrimonial state form emerged naturally to deal with this situation. In the patrimo-nial form, rulers use the state's resources available to them to buy off the opposition. The larger the state sector, the greater the amount of monies and lucrative positions of privilege which are in the gift of the rulers. Undoubtedly this state form created unwieldy, inefficient and corrupt administrations, and led to economic decline and debt. But what is often overlooked is that it *also* kept the peace.

Imposed neo-liberal reform, by contrast, attacks the patrimonial state, cleanses out the corrupt bureaucracy and yanks state officials out of the framework of patron–client politics. In its efforts to get the state budget under control, the IMF has even negotiated with governments to subcontract tax collection to foreign firms. But this manner of reining in the rent-seeking state and its officials dissolves the patrimonial glue that holds the society together. It brings about fragmentation as erstwhile clients are now forced to seek their own benefits independent from the central authority. This hastens the collapse into 'warlordism'. As Reno sums up the situation for Sierra Leone:

> . . . much recent fighting, especially its territorial spread, is directly related to the elimination of opportunities for powerful strongmen under "reform" and the efforts of these strongmen to strike out on their own for personal gain. Meanwhile, ordinary citizens conclude that Freetown has less and less to offer in the way of services or protection from predations of wayward élites. The reformist state is attacked from two sides – from below, by those who believe it will have little to offer them, and from above, by clients who make irresistible claims on reform policies.[37]

World Bank and IMF officials protest their innocence as country after country tumbles into civil strife and despair. After all, all *they* had wanted to do was to 'free' poor peasants from corrupt state marketing boards, and liberate urban enterprise from the punitive shackles of bureaucratic licences and petty government regulations. Their grand design was to use the economic discipline of global markets to promote social restructuring. But this strategy backfired because Africa is simply too far behind to make a living in the global market. Because of its structural irrelevance to the global economy, any enforced return to global markets as agent of economic discipline can therefore not even be excused on grounds that the adverse effects of adjustment will be 'temporary'.

Nor, it seems to me, can the officialdom of the international institutions be excused on grounds that they could not have foreseen the political consequences of their neo-liberal programmes. Theories of the patrimonial state and the positive function of corruption in it had been part of mainstream political development literature in the 1960s and 1970s. Political scientists like Samuel Huntington had commonly viewed political corruption as the only means of integrating marginal groups into a disjointed social system.[38] Some were objective enough to recognise that the growth of corruption, for example in England in the seventeenth and eighteenth centuries, was a necessary alternative to violence, a historically inevitable step in the long haul towards the institutionalisation of a political structure and administration relatively independent from the competing demands of economic agents.[39] It is the tragedy of Africa that history has not given it time to catch up.

The Reverse Agenda of Aid and Global Management

As I intimated earlier, some of the analytic literature on Africa today explores the political conditionality of the 'new donor agenda' more widely as articulating a generalised re-consideration and re-formulation of bilateral and multilateral relations with Africa and, indeed, with other marginalised areas of the global economy. Pathbreaking theoretical work by Mark Duffield, for example, theorises that the new aid agenda reverses earlier developmentalist goals of 'incorporation' of peripheral areas into the world system, and instead now serves as a policy of management and containment of politically insecure territories on the edge of the global economy.[40]

What is particularly striking about some of this literature is its epistemological orientation which is reminiscent of, though not openly indebted to, postmodern 'discourse' critique. That is to say there is a preoccupation with *when* and *why* particular statements, like 'pluralist democracy', or 'institutional capacity', 'strengthening civil society', and 'human rights' came about, how these statements have merged into a consensus agenda mediated through collective structures of consultation and coordination between previously disparate donor countries, and – last but not least – how these statements translate into practices of policy which, using Michel Foucault's phrase, 'systematically form the objects of which they speak'.[41] For this is the epistemological difference between the modern (Marxist) and postmodern critiques of knowledge, namely that where the former merely expose the use of theories, policy statements or doctrinal assertions as ideologies that legitimate anterior, existing social practices, the latter study such statements as constituting the very conditions of their historical appearance. And thus, some analytic studies of the New Aid Agenda now seem to appreciate that social relations within African countries and between Africa and the global economy, are being shaped through the discourse of the New Aid Agenda itself.[42]

Political conditionality is the deliberate use of 'aid' to improve 'governance'. We have already discussed the definition of 'governance' in World Bank-speak. Ostensibly it is aimed at creating an enabling environment for economic reforms. Leverage through 'aid' may be achieved through threats of withdrawal of promised monies in the event that certain conditions of project or programme-implementation are not met. Some people may be quick to retort that in this sense aid was always politically conditional. This is true, but the difference is that in the past the recipients of aid were mostly national governments or programmes designated with their approval, and this offered the donors the excuse to say that aid was 'non-political', that is not interfering in the internal affairs of state.

However, what characterises the new political conditionality today, is that *per force* of its own conceptualisation of good governance and an enabling environment, it wilfully and openly *does* meddle in the internal affairs of state, targetting a plurality of actors, be they non-governmental organisations, micro-businesses, local communities and grassroots organisations. Also they pay for programmes and projects that stimulate and strengthen pluralist local structures. This re-direction of 'aid' away from national governments and towards civil society has become known as the 'reverse agenda'. As the British Overseas Development Institute (ODI) put it in 1995:

> One manifestation of a growing common ground has been the way that most donors have broadened their aid objectives . . . [they] now view action to enhance human rights and democratic processes as a constituent part of their development agenda. Additionally, many donors have taken up 'strengthening civil society' as a specific aid objective.[43]

NGOs and the Politics of Exclusion

In the *Symphony of the Damned*, Mark Duffield[44] uses discourse analysis to deconstruct the new or reverse aid agenda. He argues that with economic globalisation has come a new discourse of development. Previously development was theorised as a process of societal convergence between hierarchically conceptualised state-societies (rich–poor; developed–underdeveloped). In this theorisation the state was seen as the accepted engine of growth. The failure of modernisation in many parts of the Third World, however, brought the critique of 'top-down' approaches, the disparagement of big government and the state, and thus made way for 'bottom-up' interventions that are concerned with the vulnerability of the poor and that aim to strengthen local structures and empower local communities.

Duffield next contextualises these donor adaptations within a wider reshaped world view in which cultural pluralism has replaced universalist preoccupations and goals. In the West, cultural pluralism, or multiculturalism, has been the liberal establishment's answer to racism. That is to say, it has replaced biologically-derived notions of racial superiority with an appreciation of cultural difference. On the positive side, the discourse of multiculturalism aims to promote societal harmony and integration by encouraging mutual respect and recognition. The idea that violence can be avoided fosters the organisational adaptations among international aid agencies and donor governments towards civil society and democratisation in the periphery, in the same way as it supplies the motivation and operational logic for multicultural activities at home.

Unfortunately, the fundamental premise of multiculturalism has *also* bred a darker, oppositional structure of beliefs which has been labelled 'the new racism'.[45] The basic, generic assumption, namely, that cultural difference is both natural and unavoidable has *also* fed into notions that these differences are immutable and that they have an innate and nonrational quality which 'inevitably' leads to inter-ethnic conflict. Today this new racism has come to underpin popular explanations for the growing political instability and inter-communal conflicts in the marginal areas of the global economy. A special variant of the new racism as applied to contemporary Africa has come to be known by the label 'the new barbarism'.

One influential version of this theory appears in the work of Robert Kaplan,[46] who interprets the collapse into anarchy as an unfocused and instinctive response, rooted in nature, to mounting pressures resulting from environmental and economic collapse. Contrarily, other writers give the 'new barbarism' a positive connotation. Richards, who is credited with having coined the term in 1995,[47] actually welcomes the new barbarism as a form of liberation. He describes the often grotesque acts of warlord violence and terror as rational reponses to the failure of modernity, and as potentially exhibiting new and innovative ways of knowing and interacting with the environment. Thus, argues Duffield, both assertive cultural pluralism *and* the new racism are mirror images of a common structure of beliefs. They share a common glass of cultural pluralism, yet each foretells a different future.

Humanitarian Relief and Complex Political Emergencies

Drawing conclusions from the previous two sections we may argue
that both the economic reforms imposed under structural adjustment and the new or reverse agenda of aid have, at minimum, put an
extra spin on the centrifugal forces already present in weak, underdeveloped states of Africa. The advent of humanitarian relief to
cope with the ensuing political emergencies has, furthermore, the
effect of protracting such crises by making them more 'complex'.
According to Duffield, the possibility that humanitarian intervention encourages fragmentation is a factor that makes a political
emergency 'complex'.[48]

Since the mid-1980s, as several countries in Africa have fallen into
chaos and political conflict, humanitarian relief operations have
increased six-fold. As emergency food and medical aid has been
rushed in to support war victims, the legal mandates of relief
agencies (UN connected *and* independent NGOs) have been re-
framed: whereas previously it was nearly impossible to operate in
non-government controlled areas, today the organisational options
have been widened to effectively include all situations of contested
governance. This further undermines the responsibilities previously
held by governments.

The agenda of cultural pluralism, again, informs the nature and
direction of relief operations. That is to say, it is stubbornly
apolitical – less concerned with power and power relations, or with
rights and wrongs, or with human rights abuses, than with managing and containing the situation. Relief agencies intervene in the
hope that by feeding the victims they will somehow free up the
warring parties and allow them to eventually resolve the conflict. In
this way cultural pluralism translates into cultural functionalism: the
idea that natural order and stability will resume in due course.

However, because of their robustly apolitical stance they are
unaware that their humanitarian aid is gradually being incorporated
into the socio-political fabric of the internal conflict. For cultural
functionalism prescribes a stance of balance and even-handedness
which legitimises both or all of the warring factions. Such legitimation operates not only at the ideological level but also materially.
For example, humanitarian relief agencies negotiate access for
emergency deliveries of food and medicine equally with all warring
parties, routinely having to offer a proportion of the aid to warlords.

Such aid is diverted immediately and commutes into a fresh supply of arms. A further step in this process of 'incorporation' occurs when warring parties use the promise of relief aid as a means to mobilise local populations for practical and political purposes. Duffield illuminates this process in his description of how bush air-strips have been cleared for relief operations in the southern Sudan.

Thus, with Duffield, we conclude from this sorry tale of the West's present relations with Africa that there is an emerging system of global governance with methods and instruments geared to containing and managing symptoms rather than removing causes.[49] The lack of political will to remove such causes attests to a process of disengagement from the periphery of the world economy.

9

Islamic Revolt

Today there are 28 countries in the world, with a total population of 836 million, in which Muslims have an overall majority. Many more countries have sizeable Muslim minorities. The total world Muslim population is around 1.2 billion, or one-quarter of the total world population. And even in Europe, heartland of Christianity, Muslim immigration and conversion has led to Islam being the second largest religion.

In the past 20 years or so a number of apparently related political and social events all over the world have led western commentators to speak of a militant Islamic revival. The defining moment no doubt was the overthrow, in 1979, of the Shah's pro-western monarchy in Iran, and the establishment there of the modern world's first theocratic Islamic Republic. In Lebanon, the Hamas movement sponsored by the Muslim Brotherhood has since forced an increasingly bitter split within the Palestinian struggle against Israel. In Sudan, Islamists are preventing the military junta from making concessions to the non-Muslims of the south, thus dragging out the civil war there. In Algiers, the fundamentalist party, the FIS, won the elections in 1990 only to find its victory at the ballot box snatched from it by the imposition of martial law (backed by western governments), resulting in near civil war. In Egypt, the tourist industry has been badly affected by attacks from fundamentalists, and the Mubarak regime only holds on to power by a massive, and precarious, security clampdown involving the imprisonment, without trial, of thousands of fundamentalist Muslims. In India, tensions between Muslims and Hindus, always simmering just below the surface, have been threatening to boil over since the Muslim revolt in Kashmir, and the destruction by Hindus of the mosque in Ayodhya. In Afghanistan there is an ongoing civil war between rival Islamic groups, while in Turkey recent elections have yielded a clear victory for Islamist parties. The disintegration of the Soviet empire has created new Muslim states searching for identity in Islam. Terrorist attacks in the West, alleged or real, have raised the spectre of the *jihad*, or holy war, being fought out abroad as well as at home. As *The Economist*, in 1995, summed it up in colourful language 'Islam at its most ferocious is cutting a bloodstained path to the front of the world's attention'.[1]

In a provocative article in *Foreign Affairs*, in 1993, Samuel Huntington predicted a new clash of civilisations.[2] The nation-state, he said, is disappearing as the primary unit of international relations and, therefore, conflict and competition between the world's peoples will in future be worked out at another level, chiefly among the larger units known as cultures or civilisations. He identified as the most important amongst a total of eight, three such civilisations: the West (the Euro-American culture), the East (the Confucian culture) and Islam. His article is well worth reading, particularly as a counter argument to the facile statements of the 'end of ideology' or 'end of history' theologians (for example Fukuyama[3]). The latter are based on an economic/technological deterministic interpretation of an inevitable course of human evolution. Huntington, on the other hand, says: 'The great divisions among humankind and the dominating source of conflict will be cultural'.[4]

Huntington argues that precisely because of economic modernisation and social change throughout the world, people are being separated from long-standing local identities while at the same time the nation-state is weakened as a source of identity. Religions move in to fill the gap left by the nation as a source of identity. A complementary factor which he theorises relates to what Giddens, Harvey and other writers on globalisation have variously referred to as the 'time/space compression' or distantiation phenomenon.[5] The increased cross-border social interaction of people around the world has the paradoxical effect of signifying the larger social or cultural or ethnic group people belong to as a source of identification for 'the other'. By way of example, Huntington quotes Donald Horowitz:

an Ibo may be . . . an Owerri Ibo or an Onitsha Ibo in what was
the Eastern region of Nigeria. In Lagos he is simply an Ibo. In
London he is a Nigerian. In New York, he is an African.

Civilisation according to Huntington is the 'highest' cultural
grouping of people, and the broadest level of cultural identity people
have short of that which distinguishes humans from other species. It
is defined both by common objective elements, such as language,
history, religion, customs, institutions, and by the subjective self-
identification of people.[6]

As far as the immediate future is concerned, Huntington expects
the clash between civilisations to rage between the West and Islam.
However, it is a mistake to argue, as he does, that this is so because
of the potent contradiction between oil and poverty. For, excepting
the combined population of 10 million who live in six very rich Gulf
States, the vast majority of Muslims live in countries with minimal
or no oil resources. These countries belong to the world's poorest
and middle-income groups.

More decisive for a correct analysis of the roots of the contemporary Islamic revolt, in my view, is the circumstance that the
Islamic world contains within it millions upon millions who do
not have any prospect of being incorporated into the new global
system while – likewise – Muslim minorities in the advanced
countries often find themselves excluded from the global system as
well. The analysis presented in this chapter is that, rather than the
West's domination of oil, it is the failure of the national developmental strategies in the neo-colonial period, coupled with the
present episode of globalisation, that drives the contemporary
Islamic crescent. Islamic resurgence is best understood as a politics
of identity in reponse to exclusion, rather than (as was the case
during the heyday of Arab nationalism) as a response to subordinated incorporation. But this politics of identity has neither brought
a new model of society, nor has the organisational programmatic
unity to become a geostrategic factor.

In developing this analysis I put forward two themes that appear
to prevail in much of today's discourse about the Islamic revolt:

1. The continuity of spiritual renewal throughout Islam's history;
    and
2. The cultural impact of the West's historical confrontation with
    Islam.

Spiritual Renewal

Islam is more than a religion; it is a complete way of life. It concerns not only God's relationship with His people, but it also orders social relations amongst people including legal, contractual institutions, social and political institutions, and issues of economic propriety and practice. G. H. Jansen, in his book *Militant Islam*, quotes two fundamentalist Islamic scholars as saying that:

> Islam provides guidance for all walks of life, individual and social, material and moral, economic and political, legal and cultural, national and international.[7]

Islam is particularly detailed about matters relating to family, marriage, divorce and inheritance; it also addresses questions of dress and etiquette, food and personal hygiene, in short the obvious and public signifiers of identity and belonging, potentially therefore the insignia of lifestyle politics.

The two principal sources for Islam are:

1. The *Qu'ran*, the book of direct revelations by God to the Prophet Muhammed through the archangel Gabriel; and
2. The *Sunna*, literally, the 'trodden path', which is a compilation and codification of the sayings of the prophet plus the official biography of the prophet's life, this including all the things He *did* as well as said.

After the prophet's death in 632 BC (AH 10) naturally it took a while to compile and codify the entire body of holy scriptures. There was confusion, interpretation and counter-interpetation, by competing schools of law, until sometime around AD 900 consensus amongst the scholars triumphed. From that moment 'the Gates of the *ijtihad* were closed (*ijtihad* meaning independent judgement). This implied that from then on no further augmentation to the scriptural body could be countenanced, and that henceforth only past precedent counted.

As an aside we should note at this point that while the above description of religious authority holds for the vast majority of Muslims, who are called Sunni, there is a sizeable minority, called Shi'ites, for whom, by contrast, religious authority centres on an inspired person, the Imam. Shi'ites have constituted themselves as a separate sect since the early days of Islam, and at first traced the authority of religious inspiration through a direct line of succession from Ali, cousin and son-in-law of the Prophet Muhammad. The fact that the twelfth and last Imam, Muhammad al-Mahdi, disappeared in AD 878, did not become an effective bar to this divine basis of authority. On the contrary, He became the 'Hidden One', still in this world and in contact with his chosen agents who have the right to pronounce *ex cathedra* an opinion on any matter affecting the *Sharia*, or canon law. In Persia at an early date the Shi'ites lent themselves to the nationalist movement, which in time displaced the Arab domination by purely Persian rule. In this way Shi'ism ultimately became the national religion of Persia, later Iran.[8] The Ayatollah Khomeini successfully led the revolution that overthrew the Shah, and claimed to be the incarnation of the twelfth Imam.

Although the system of authority thus differed between Sunni's and Shi'ites, and led to mutual enmity between them, both systems have features which make for powerful religious revivals. In the case of the Shi'ite religion the withdrawal of the Imam and his continued existence as the 'Hidden One' periodically would fire up hopes of messianic return and salvation that enabled strong personal leaders to emerge as new Imams leading social revolt agaist the orthodox establishment. In the case of the Sunni religion, as we see below, it was the doctrine of the *ijhitad* that allowed social protest to be battled out at the level of theological disputes and in this way challenge existing powers.

According to Ernest Gellner,[9] the sociological significance of the *ijtihad* was twofold, and it implanted a deep dialectic into the very heart of Islam: on the one hand it provided a power-base for the scholar/jurists, the learned men, *ulema*, who could pontificate on the basis of analogous reasoning, and declare any conduct or event in changed historical circumstances to be or not to be in accordance with Islamic law. This gave them a power-base independent of temporal authorities, and therefore there was always an institutional separation between political and religious authority. On the other hand, the subordination of the former to the latter meant that in principle, as Gellner has put it,

> a socially and politically transcendent standard of rectitude was ever accessible, beyond the reach of manipulation by political authority, and available for condemning the *de facto* authority if sinned against it.[10]

Thus, despite the *institutional* separation between politics and religion, there was never a *cultural* separation between the two. In this sense Islam was not a secular civilisation. Where Christ had accepted the separation between God and Caesar and had advised to 'render unto Caesar the things that are Caesar's', Muhammed and Islam never recognized such separation in their universe of discourse and belief.[11] Further, the non-manipulability of divine law proved time and again a source of legitimacy for acts of self-correction, as when the disgruntled, oppressed masses could translate their grievances into the discourse of theological disputation, challenging political authority on those grounds. As we shall see below, much of the present Islamic revolt may be interpreted in precisely those terms.

Thus, the spirit of renewal has been immanent in Islam as a cultural belief system. But it was also sourced by the peculiar material circumstances and social relations of production of the historical environment in which it developed and consolidated. As Simon Bromley writes, in the course of its history Islamic civilisation came to straddle two social formations, each grounded in a different ecology and economy. On the one hand, there was the urban society of the Sultanates (consolidated during a period of five century rule in the Ottoman Empire). It was a society of state officials, military personnel and Islamic scholars (*ulema*). Together, these, in tacit cooperation with the merchants, maintained order and networks of trade and finance and exacted tribute from the surrounding peasantry. On the other, beyond the compass of the urban social formation lay the tribal forces that remained outside central control. In these regions,

> the tributary state was unable to control the rural areas, essentially because of the greater weight of pastoral nomadism with its mobile means of production, armed populations and absence of urban growth.[12]

These two different social formations, Gellner states with absolute confidence, gave rise to,

> the really central, and perhaps most important feature of Islam namely that it was internally divided into a High Islam of the scholars and the Low Islam of the people.[13]

While high Islam was puritanical, scripturalistic and mindful of the prohibition of claims to mediation between God and man, low Islam or folk Islam was simple, adaptive and flexible, inspired by saintlike mystic heroes (*sufis*) and centred on grassroot *tarikas* (Muslim brotherhoods). Periodically the two religious styles would clash as when the scholars of high Islam would launch 'a kind of internal purification movement' in an attempt to re-impose itself on the whole of society.[14]

The West Confronts Islam

Compared with all other areas of the world, the world of Islam has had the unique if dubious distinction of having always been regarded by the West as a *cultural* adversary – a cultural 'other'. No doubt rivalry over exclusive claims to a one and indivisible transcendent God had a lot to do with this, as had the shared location of their respective Holy Land, and their geographic proximity. And no doubt the original contest of wills on the battlefield during the crusades helped strike enduring terror in the hearts and minds of Europeans and Muslims alike.

But of greater significance probably is the fact that in confronting Islam, from the time of the Crusades and in distinct episodes since, the West came to define itself. The need to know the enemy became an inspiration for self-identification as well. While, thus, as in Edward Said's celebrated account,[15] 'orientalism' was a product of western culture, equally it may be said that the West's concept of its own culture and society derived from the same discourse. It is this dependency engendered through binomial opposition, in different phases of their intertwining histories, that explains the West's special fear of Islam and Islam's enduring search for self-identity.

In his overview of the history of the West's image of Islam, Maxine Rodinson opines that:

> The image of Islam arose, not so much as some have said from the Crusades, as from the slowly welded ideological unity of the late Christian world which led both to a clear view of the enemy's features and also to a channeling of effort towards the Crusades.[16]

The fight having become more concentrated and better focused, the enemy must of necessity be given sharper, more specific features and thus his image must be simplified and stereotyped. In these stereotypes Islam was given a systemic civilisational unity that it did not possess.

Later, in the medieval period, when Latin Europe was beset by internal factions and struggles, the ideological conflict with Islam lost its pre-eminence. But in Europe, internal ideological strife also sowed the seeds of a relativity of belief which in fact opened up a certain ideological space for Christian scholars to pursue the study of Islam with some 'objectivity'. From there, Islam graduated to become a subject of curiosity and exoticism, as witnessed in the flourishing of Arabia scholarship notably in the fields of philology, arts and religion. With the birth of the sciences, followed by the Age of Reason, Islam even became an unwitting partner in the project of Enlightenment.

> People could now view the religious faith which competed with Christianity in an impartial light and even with some sympathy, unconsciously seeking (and obviously finding) in it the very values of the now rationalised trend of thought that was opposed to Christianity.[17]

However, in the nineteenth century, specialist knowledge about Arabia and Islam turned into 'orientalism', a special discipline devoted to the study of the East. But it was a special discipline which henceforth would serve European imperialist conquest. While buttressing the confidence of Europe in its own cultural superiority, it cast the Muslim in the role of contemptible victim, in need of correction. This was so because the specialist knowledge of Arab language, customs, religion and art, transmitted itself to other fields of scientific equiry (notably social philosphy, later sociology and economics) in its most vulgarised, mechanistic form, driven as it was by the general ideas of the time which attributed a boundless influence to religion, language and race as explanatory factors in the diverse trajectories of human social evolution.[18]

This particular form of social theorising climaxed in Max Weber's enduringly authoritative typification of West and East, whereby the oriental became no more than a mirror image of the occidental. As Edward Said writes:

Weber's studies . . . threw him into the very territory originally charted and claimed by Orientalists. There he found encouragement amongst all those nineteenth century thinkers who believed that there was a sort of ontological difference between Eastern and Western economic (as well as religious) 'mentalities'.[19]

This ontological difference became theorised in a self-serving contrast of identity and progress: while the West was economically dynamic *because* it was universal, rational, pluralist and secular, the Orient was economically stagnant *because* it was particularistic, traditional, despotic, wallowing in religious obscurantism, and therefore stagnant.

As Rodinson writes:

In the Middle Ages, the Oriental had been regarded as a fierce enemy, but nevertheless on the same level as Western man; in the eighteenth century enlightenment and the resulting ideology of the French Revolution the Oriental was, underneath his disguise, essentially a human being; but in the 19th century he became a creature apart, imprisoned in his specificity, an object of condescending praise. Thus the concept of *homo islamicus* was born, and is still far from being overthrown.[20]

The end of the First World War resulted in the demise of the Ottoman Empire. Against the backdrop of fierce competition between European nations, the scramble for the Middle East and its vast oil resources began. Everywhere the Europeans established two new principles: the freezing of boundaries and the freezing of dynasties. Arbitrarily drawing lines in the sand, they made permanent territorial boundaries which had either been non-existent or constantly shifting.[21] In a cynical move that would pre-empt any future pan-Arabism or pan-Islamism, the colonial powers drew the circumference of states in such a manner as to ensure that there were oil-rich territorial states with small populations and oil-scarce states with large populations.

This new age of imperialism again changed the cultural and political relationship between the West and Islam. This time it was marked by an 'active tide of imposing responsibility on the local peoples', turning the unchanging oriental passivity into militant modern life.[22] In the creation of Arab protectorates, mandates, and outright colonial territories there began the process of imposed political state-formation, which dialectically grew into independence movements,[23] and it was sealed by constitutional sovereignty granted at various moments in the interwar and postwar epoch.

We return to the refractory effect of the imposition of artifical nation-states in a moment. First a word about how the impact of the West was received and resisted in the Islamic world. Jansen reminds us that since 1500 scarcely a decade or even half a decade has passed without some Muslim area somewhere fighting against the encroachment by some western power.[24] Rioting and internal armed uprisings were endemic, especially after the First World War. For the Muslims these were all wars both in defence of Islam and in defence of hearth and home. Mostly they took place at the local level, at the grassroots of popular 'low Islam', rather than at the level of the urban scholars of 'high Islam'. This was hardly surprising since the European conquests were frequently accompanied by a vigorous policy of support for the Christian missionary effort. Many a time this forced the Muslim brotherhoods to go underground, and to become 'secret' societies. The creation, through conversion, of Christian communities, deliberately fostered and favoured by the colonial powers and living as separate enclaves amidst the mass of Muslims, had the paradoxical effect of keeping Islam militant.[25]

Education and Orientalisation

It is probably a function of the rising pre-eminence of cultural studies in the Humanities today, that recent literature on the Arab world singles out European education and European cultural domination generally as the most important, lasting and damaging legacy of the colonial period. In the introduction to this part of the book we have referred to cultural studies and its connection with postcolonial studies, so we shall not dwell on it here. Edward Said in his path-breaking book *Orientalism*, and again in its sequel *Culture and Imperialism*,[26] has probably done more than anyone to redefine imperialism in terms of cultural power. Taking as his frame of reference Michel Foucault's notion of 'discourse', he has examined orientalism as a discourse in which power and knowledge are dialectically linked. European imperialist power in the nineteenth and twentieth centuries drew on knowledge of the Orient to rule and

manage, and in so doing *produced* the Orient: politically, socio-
logically, militarily, ideologically, scientifically and imaginatively.
While European culture gained in strength and identity by setting
itself off against the Orient as a sort of surrogate and even underground self, the Orient itself became 'orientalised'.[27]

The most tangible concretisation of this orientalisation was
effected through colonial educational policies. Jansen writes:

> foreign rulers with rare unanimity and unusual purposefulness
> and pertinacity, sought to give as little education as possible, the
> wrong sort of education when it had to be given, and also to bring
> about a schism in the soul of the Muslim community.[28]

The local education system was either destroyed or allowed to
collapse through benign neglect, while new schools using European
languages and curricula were introduced. A new breed of intellectual
élites was selected and nurtured and sent abroad for higher education, including, perversely, the study of subjects like 'Islamic' and
'oriental' studies. There they learnt to see the Orient through
occidental eyes. Jansen turns up the arresting statistic that until
1955, 95 per cent of all books written about Islam were written by
western scholars.[29]

The colonially imposed yet arbitrary process of state-formation
combined with this conscious policy of educating native élites who
would see their own world through European eyes; it succeeded in
forging a deep rift between modernisers and reformers on the one
hand and traditionalists and neofundamentalists on the other.
Nevertheless, all these movements also had a common origin.
Indeed, in one sense all these groups may be classed as 'Islamists',
or representative of 'political Islam'. As Oliver Roy points out, from
a sociological and intellectual point of view they were products of
the modern world, and more particularly of their subordinated
position in the West's dominated world system. Thus, in this sense,
the Islamist movement was and still is a Third Worldist movement.
It conceives of itself explicitly as a sociopolitical project, founded on
an Islam defined as much in terms of political ideology as in terms of
religion.[30]

But where the modernisers (in different ways and with different
emphases on secularisation) sought to reform or rationalise Islamic
thought and institutions in order to bring them into line with the

new order introduced by the Europeans (particularly the 'order' of the interstate system and of developmentalism), and the reformers sought to Islamise the western model, attempting to create a synthesis between modernity and Islam, the neofundamentalists and traditionalists are obsessed with the corrupting influence of western culture. They reject the western model and eschew any compromise with it. Instead, they seek a return to the scriptures and a lifestyle signifying, in dress, in body language, in social practices of conviviality and prayer, and most prominently in respect of the status of women, the exclusivity of the true believer as a member of a select and holy community. As Roy says, 'Neofundamentalism entails a shrinking of the public space to the family and the mosque.'[31]

After independence, in the neo-colonial period, the modernisers were in the ascendancy, but in more recent times radical reformers and neofundamentalists have begun to hold sway. The reasons for this are both external and internal: the dependent development project of the modernisers was corrupted by continuing and divisive interventions of the West in the pursuit of its strategic interests in oil, and 'legitimated' with reference to the cold war. For its part, the political establishment failed to deliver material benefits or a coherent system of meanings.

The Failure of Dependent Development

The defeat in the Yom Kippur war and the economic crisis that followed put paid to fragile attempts at pan-Arab unity which had been the hallmark of the radical reformers in the immediate post-independence era. It meant that everywhere Arab nationalism had to give way to ever more 'pragmatic' and corrupted leaderships dancing to the tune of the US and IMF/World Bank donors and aid givers. As their hold over their populations weakened, they became still more dependent on military and other handouts from their western masters.

Meanwhile, the conservative regimes of the oil-rich Gulf states became increasingly implicated in the geo-strategic interests of the US and the West. The Shi'ite Islamic revolution in Iran was followed by a cynically-exploited divide-and-rule backed war with Iraq which did much to identify the Iranian revolution with Shi'ism and Iranian nationalism. Conservative Arab states financed a Sunni fundamentalist pole of attraction outside their own borders in order to break the momentum of the Islamic revolution. The second Gulf War spread even more confusion in the Arab world by organising a conservative Arab and western coalition against Iraq.

A structuralist understanding of the geo-political dynamics that led to the Gulf war of 1991 may help us understand the forces that give rise to the present neo-fundamentalist crescent as well. In the structuralist perspective which we have adopted in much of this book, the advanced capitalist countries, with the US at the head, form the core of the system, the rest is either semi-periphery or periphery. But we have also seen that the capitalist world system is continually developing towards higher, more complex forms of integration. Periodically this forces a reshuffling of the relations between the parts, and a destruction and reconstruction of the formal political organisation of these relationships.

Following the Second World War, and within the context of the emerging bipolar world order, the process of decolonisation and the creation of a multitude of sovereign states within the periphery of the capitalist system was an appropriate reconstruction of formal political relations which served to maintain the interests of the core within the periphery. But it also, inevitably, did open up opportunities for national development and liberation for those peripheral states which played the sovereignty card to the full, and which knew how to play off the superpowers to their nation's advantage. There is no doubt that Saddam Hussain and his Ba'athist Party had succeeded in doing just that. We may not like the way he had set about this task, and morally condemn the fascist brutality which accompanied the building of a militarily-powerful, industrially-advancing and even socially-commendable welfare state, but we cannot deny that national economic and social progress had been made.

The pertinent historical as opposed to moral question one should ask is: what was it that blocked internal advance towards progressive democratisation and instead propelled this brutal leadership into external aggression? It is here that a structuralist analysis, without condemning or condoning, directs attention to the entire web of core–peripheral and semi-peripheral relations in the region which had reached a crisis point due to the combined effect of global capitalist integration and the collapse of the bipolar world order.

What was the structure of these relations and why was it in crisis? The core has, of course, economic interests in the oil of the Middle East. But this is only a starting point. In order to access the oil, in the past it was in the interest of the oil companies backed by the political power of the imperialist core countries to make deals with local feudal rulers, kinglets, or sheiks in exchange for concessions for exploration and so on. Now, when one is only interested in a raw material like oil, and not in labour or consumer markets, one's profit strategy at that stage dictates a preference for dictatorships rather than democratic regimes. A sovereign ruler is all that is wanted. *Oil and dictatorship go together.*

The same reasons prompt a divide-and-rule strategy, that is an uneven distribution of populations over the oil-rich regions. Small countries with lots of oil and small populations are less demanding than large ones. After the demise of the Ottoman Empire at the conclusion of the First World War, such deliberately uneven divisions of states were drawn up under British and French colonial rule. There are six very rich Gulf states (joined together in the Gulf Cooperation Council) with a combined population of ten million, and six very populous states outside with a combined population of about 200 million. It is these latter states that particularly have to cope with the displaced and restless Palestinians within their borders who lost their land to the Israelis.

When, however, oil prices did eventually increase as a result of organised cartel-type rebellion in the oil producing countries (1973), the links between the peripheral and semi-peripheral states in the region and between them and the core became more complex. Arms trade and financial links, *in addition to* oil now formed a triangle of interests, consolidating the interests of the rulers of the small states with the core. This is the significance of the developing integration of the world capitalist system.

For every 100 dollars the West spends on oil in the Middle East, $40 comes back in arms-trade and roughly another $40 comes back into our banks underpinning the financial system in the core nations. Noam Chomsky nicely illustrates this point with a joke going around on Wall Street at the time of the second Gulf War:

Why do the United States and Kuwait need each other? Answer: Kuwait is a banking system without a country and the United States is a country without a banking system.[32]

While a blanket of secrecy is wrapped around the exact amount of oil dollars invested in the West, the highest estimate of Gulf countries' investments in the USA alone amounts to $1 trillion. In 1989 Kuwait earned more income from its vast overseas investments located in the capitalist metropoles than from its domestic oil production ($8.8 billion as compared with $7.7 billion).[33]

The interwovenness of the 'reformist', 'modernising' Muslim élites in the Third World with the core of the western capitalist system, increasingly widened the gap between them and the masses of the populations whom they rule and who are dispossessed. Much of the rise of neofundamentalist Islam can be understood as a popular and anti-imperialist protest movement. But two features which are unique to the Islamic tradition give it its vitality: the tradition of spiritual renewal and the concept of '*umma*' (the community of the faithful). While the former permits, at least in principle if not in practice as we shall see below, the conversion and re-absorption of governmental élites and 'exploiters' in the revivalist movement, the latter gives priority to the world-wide community of Islam and denies its nationalist or even supra-nationalist (as in pan-Arabic) pretensions. This, I believe, makes a historical fit with the de-nationalising forces of globalisation.

What has been worrying the West since the late 1980s is that increasingly within Sunni territory a fundamentalist interpetation of Islam as a potent popular, anti-western force is rising. For the real strength of neofundamental Islamists lies in their peaceful, community-based activities. The Muslim Brotherhoods, so-called, offer welfare, health care and educational services to thousands of people neglected by the secular state.

The Rise of Islamist New Intellectuals and the Politics of Anti-developmentalism

After independence, having been given the mantle of sovereignty, the modernising, westernised élites set about the task of social and economic development. As Bromley has noted, whether they adopted a capitalist model or a socialist model, the outcomes in terms of social structure were not all that different. *First* of all, everywhere the state became the main site of surplus appropriation. This was so regardless of whether the source of revenue was oil exported under the aegis of international oil cartels, and the state thus became a 'rentier-state', or whether in the absence of oil, nationalist élites – as in Egypt, Iraq and Sudan – occupied the state centre to secure more or less complete control over internal resource mobilisation, if not state control over all property. The point is that in both cases what was lacking was a degree of separation between the institutions of rule and surplus appropriation. This, as Bromley points out, led everywhere to an absence of the conditions for democratic participation, and ushered in the politics of clientelism.[34]

Second, in the oil-poor, populous countries, strategies of import-substitutive industrialisation became stranded on the same rocks of deepened foreign indebtedness as they had in Latin America. By contrast, the oil-rich countries with small populations had income far in excess of their needs. Possession of vast oil reserves in fact reduced the incentive to rely upon the skills and quality of the people. The oil-rich Gulf states invested their monies in the metropolitan countries, and imported labour from elsewhere in Arabia and the Indian subcontinent, creating enclaves of second-class, disenfranchised non-citizens. The obvious solution should have been some form of regional economic integration, and for a while pan-Arab nationalism was a potent rallying force in the postwar settlement. But time and again the West, and more especially the US and its bridgehead client state Israel, managed to divide and break the incipient regional solidarities.

A *third* characteristic consequence of the dependent development strategies of the neo-colonial period was the process of urbanisation coupled with rapid population explosion. Dependent incorporation into the world capitalist economy implied a neglect for subsistence agriculture, rural–urban migration, and swelling numbers of unemployed and underemployed city-dwellers. This shift of the social location of Islamism engendered an important shift in the ideological realm as well. For today's masses who follow the Islamists are not 'traditionalists', writes Oliver Roy, instead:

> they live with the values of the modern city – consumerism and upward social mobility; they left behind the old forms of conviviality, respect for elders and for consensus, when they left their villages . . . they are fascinated by the values of consumerism imparted by the shop windows of the large metropolises; they live in a world of movie theatres, cafes, jeans, video and sports, but

they live precariously from menial jobs or remain unemployed in immigrant ghettos, with the frustration inherent in an unattainable consumerist world . . . Their militant actions exist in symbiosis with their urban environment: except in Afghanistan and Kurdistan, the guerillas of the contemporary Muslim world are city-dwellers.[35]

A *fourth* social structural characteristic of dependent development in the neo-colonial period is the emergence of a new category of educated individuals produced by the expansion in state-funded education established along western lines. Oliver Roy variously refers to this class of intellectuals as 'lumpen intelligentsia', or the 'Islamist new intellectuals' or 'neo-fundamentalists'. They are young people with school and even university education who cannot find positions or professions that correspond to their expectations or visions of themselves, either in the saturated state administrative sector or in industry because national capitalism is weak, or in the traditional network because of the devaluation of religious schools, or in modern universities which are also saturated and experiencing a loss of social status. Thus, the newly educated of the Muslim world find no social ratification, either real or symbolic, for what they perceive as their new status.[36]

In an unusual and provocative analysis of the Islamic world today, Oliver Roy dissects the ideological pretensions, the social basis and the political project, of this lumpen intelligentsia that forms the core of the contemporary neofundamentalist crescent. In doing so, he debunks as a myth the theory that it could consolidate into a new force in international relations or indeed posit a threat to the West.

According to Roy, the lumpen intelligentsia are differentiated from, and resent, the clerical scholars (the *ulema*, or scholars of high Islam) because unlike these scholars they have no state-legitimated and supported relationship to that corpus of knowledge.[37] At the same time they have smatterings of western education without, again, having an institutional connection to that body of knowledge.

Roy makes the important point that there is a direct relationship between the configuration of the new intellectual's 'conceptual' space and the social space that he occupies. As self-proclaimed mullah or as militant he preaches amongst the urban poor. He operates in meeting houses, sites of worship, educational centres, and new suburban settings not yet socialised by the state. He rejects, and is marginalised by, both the westernised professionals and governing class on the one hand, and the state-legitimated clerics (the *ulema*) on the other. His conceptual apparatus reflects how he operates on the fringes of both.

The western-style intellectuals and the clerical scholars have in common that both their social status and their methodology is guaranteed by processes of investiture and authorisation that distinguish them from the masses. Their claims to truth, each in their own way albeit in methodological opposition to each other, have an assured connection to their own procedures of acceptance and institutional validation, whether these are the rules of logic and objectivity and peer scrutiny as with western science and intellectual positions, or the norms of analogous reasoning and peer consensus within the clerical community of the *ulema*. They are both validated by examination and titles that accord social positions to them. But the neofundamentalist small-time mullahs operate outside of these approved networks of knowledge transmission. And thus, argues Roy, the neofundamentalist intellectual is quintessentially an *autodidact*. He is a tinkerer, creating a montage of fragments of knowledge combined from both these different conceptual universes, using a method of invocation and incantation as emblematic *display* of knowledge, rather than as object of systematic study. Fragmentary modern knowledge drawn from an immense variety of immediately accessible (through TV, newspapers and so on) fields of western knowledge, including economics, sociology, nuclear physics and biology, is immediately integrated within a Qu'ranic framework in which claims to truth drawn from the Qu'ran or the Tradition and cited as verses, are positioned as the equivalents of concepts drawn from modern science and ideologies.

There is nevertheless a unity in this montage of borrowed fragments. It is the mystical site of the divine *Tawhid*, the Oneness of God which extends to all his Creation, including, most importantly, the Perfect Man (*Insan Kamil*). According to the myth of the Perfect Man, it is the ethical disposition of one's soul that gives unity to one's knowledge and practice. Hence there is an emphasis on mental conversion, on devotion, on lifestyle and on purity. But there is no political programme of action, no model of a new civic society, no worked-out alternative system of economic and social organisation.

As the radical or 'political' Islam of the postindependence years slides into neofundamentalism, it assembles the outcasts of a failed modernism, mobilising them around the myth of a return to an Islamic authenticity that never existed. Such Islamism, Roy concludes, is not a geostrategic factor: it will neither unify the Muslim world nor change the balance of power in the Middle East. For it cannot withstand power. What today's Islamists advocate:

> is not the return to an incomparably rich classical age, but the establishment of an empty stage on which the believer strives to realize with each gesture the ethical model of the Prophet.[38]

The empty stage is that of civic society which is non-existent. The Islamisation of officially secular and moderate regimes targets personal law and penal law, leaving intact the existing economic formation and the political model inherited from previous regimes. Through processes of globalisation, the business élites and governing classes may continue to be picked off, divided against one another, corrupted and incorporated into the global system.

Thus, neofundamentalism, while originating as a sociocultural movement of protest and frustration of a generation of youth that has not been integrated socially, economically or politically, yet in a paradoxical way becomes an agent of accommodation of those social sectors at once produced by and excluded from the accelerated modernisation of Muslim societies.

10

The Developmental States of East Asia

The fast and sustained pace of growth of seven countries in East Asia, collectively sometimes referred to as the seven 'dragons', has forced a major rethink in development studies. The seven countries are: Singapore, Hong Kong, South Korea, Taiwan, Malaysia, Thailand, and Indonesia. Curiously, it has taken rather a long time for the rethink to occur. For, as a recent World Bank study has discovered, already since 1960 these high performing East Asian countries (HPEAs) have grown faster than any other group of countries in the world, including the rich countries (see Figure 10.1).

One reason for this lag between reality and our perception of it is owed to the statistical presentations of world order which are produced annually by international organisations in their 'state of the world' reports. For over 30 years it has been commonplace to rank the nations of the world *not* by growth rates or economic performance, but by economic groupings based on income. The ranking of the world's economies in ascending order of GNP per capita has yielded classifications of economic groupings by arbitrary cut-off points in the ascending order of GNP per capita.

Conventional World Bank rankings are: low-income, middle-income and high-income countries but, as the World Bank itself acknowledges in its 1993 report on *The East Asian Miracle*, classification by income does not necessarily reflect development status. Moreover, 'once the classification is fixed for any publication, all the historical data presented are based on the same economic grouping.'[1] Thus, presentation by economic income grouping can hide and prevent other possible classifications such as those based on

Figure 10.1 The economic growth of the world's regions
(average growth of GNP per capita, 1965–90)

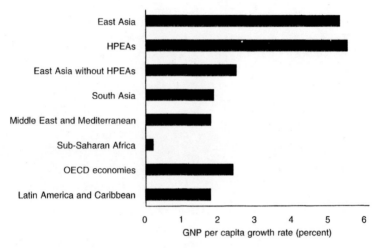

Source: World Bank, *The East Asian Miracle* (New York: Oxford University Press, 1993) p. 2. Reproduced with permission.

growth, changing composition of structure of production, distribution of income, and so on.

Classifications are the cornerstone in any theorising. For a long time development theory took as its starting point the income *gap* between rich and poor countries, between north and south, First and Third World. It was this gap that prompted the search for the 'sameness' within each group as well as the difference between them. The task which development theory set itself was to theorise, and explain, what made the former rich and what the latter had to do to become rich (modernisation theory), or what made the former rich and kept the latter poor (as in dependency theory). Modernisation theory was closely allied to neo-classical liberal economics which stressed the benefits to developing countries of participating in the international economy, on the basis of their comparative advantage arising from natural factor endowments. This theory advocated the pursuit of open-door policies towards trade and investment, emphasising the growth-related benefits of receiving technology and capital inputs from the advanced countries. Modernisation theory added to this the argument that because of the structural compatibility between economic institutions and practices on the one hand, and political, social and cultural institutions on the other, less-developed countries should model their social and political structures after the example of the West (see Chapter 2).

Dependency theorists argued exactly the opposite: they pointed to the debilitating limitations of the historically developed international division of labour, the resulting deterioration of the terms of trade for less-developed countries, and the distorted internal social structure dominated by transnational class alliances which prevented internal autonomous development and industrialisation. Their policy prescription was either a radical break with the world system or, in watered down more pragmatic versions, policies of self-reliance and selective de-linking. Thus they placed emphasis on import-substitutive industrialisation with all the price-distorting state intervention in the economy that this entails.

The Role of the State in Economic Development

Already by the mid-1970s, some East Asian states – South Korea, Hong Kong, Singapore and Taiwan, collectively known as the 'four Tigers' – had notched up a decade of near double-digit growth. In contrast to the Latin American newly-industrialising countries (NICs) of that period, this growth was export led, and at a superficial glance at first seemed to confirm the thesis of orthodox neo-classical writers that the fast pace of economic development in these countries owed to liberal, 'market conforming' regimes and 'open-door' policies towards inward investment and foreign trade. But the neo-classical tradition gradually had to come to terms with the incontrovertible evidence of extensive direct government intervention in the East Asian economies. In an effort to salvage the neo-classical tradition, the nature of state intervention was at first argued to be in line with the prevailing orthodoxy, rather than going against it. Thus Bela Balassa,[2] Chalmer Johnson,[3] E. K. Y. Chen,[4] and various World Bank documents of the period argued that government interventions were merely of the kind that aimed at creating macro-economic stability, and a suitable environment for entrepreneurs to perform their functions by providing certain public goods such as basic education. Where interventions in credit and fiscal policies did occur, these were said to be mainly in order to 'get the prices right' (in line with international prices and not as a distortion of international prices).

Eventually some writers within the neo-classical tradition, dubbed revisionists or institutionalists, came to admit that state interventions in East Asian economies were not merely 'market conforming' but rather 'market guiding', even deliberately 'market distorting'.[5] It was beginning to be appreciated that East Asian countries used very selective financial instruments (credit and tax policies), trade policies, inward investment screening policies, and industrial relations policies to channel investment decisions into directions that conformed with national priorities. These interventions did not just remain at the level of macro-economic policies but were sector and firm-specific.

This marked the beginning of an understanding of the nature of 'state-capitalism', in which the primary purpose of government intervention was to promote the interests of the business sector as a whole and to do so by creating the conditions for capital accumulation and productivity improvement, even if this meant extensive bureaucratic regulation and neglect (or repression) of the interests of specific sectors and groups.

For their part, neo-Marxist dependency writers for a time had dismissed the success of the East Asian Tigers as an *under*developing sidekick of the productive decentralisation of multinational corporations from the core of the world system. They had argued that the 'success' owed to a temporary comparative advantage entirely based on the super-exploitation of cheap labour in especially designated 'free export processing zones' with few linkages to the surrounding economy, and that it resulted in deepening inequalities and marginalisation. This position came to be known as the new international division of labour (NIDL) thesis (Folker Fröbel *et al.*[6]).

In applying the dependency paradigm to diminish the achievements of the observed process of industrialisation, NIDL theorists contended that the stimulus for the industrialisation of certain peripheral countries came from the deepening crisis in the core economies of the world system, and the associated problems of valorisation of capital. This pushed core capital out into the periphery in the search for large amounts of unskilled labour power. Technological advances in global communications and transport permitted the spatial dispersal of intermediate production processes, creating branch-plant industrialisation massively dependent on corporate decisions and technical inputs from the core economies. The originators of the NIDL thesis (F. Fröbel *et al.*) asserted that the 'world factory' had overtaken the world market. As to the question why some peripheral nations were selected in this way and not others or all, NIDL theorists merely pointed to the availability in these countries of vast armies of cheap unskilled labour helpfully offered to international capital by repressive regimes that restricted trade unionisation and offered tax incentives to boot.

In the course of the 1980s, as the economic success of these countries was consolidated in real, autonomous upgrading of productive capacity as well as in social and civic advance of the masses, the NIDL thesis looked increasingly threadbare. In the generalist versions of the world system and dependency theses, the states of the core countries had been regarded as 'strong', while those in the periphery were naturally assumed to be 'weak', that is a mere instrument of international capital. But in the more detailed, specific examinations of real cases, it was now admitted that while some developing states were 'weak', others were 'strong'. Writers standing in the neo-Marxist tradition began to take a closer look at the social origins and the functions of the state in these countries. Historical structuralist analysis showed that strong states were associated with a degree of autonomy of the state bureaucratic apparatus that owed to a specific class composition coupled with a specific geopolitical situation.[7]

Theories of the Developmental State

The two intellectual traditions converged somewhat in theories of the developmental state. This convergence broke the debilitating mould that had for so long dominated the agenda of development studies and that had up until then equated capitalism with democracy, and state bureaucracies with socialism. But this is not to say that the convergence ended up with only one theory of the developmental state. Rather there were different variations on the same theme: neo-classical and neo-Marxist traditions did not so easily relinquish their methodologies or their world views.

One way in which the neo-classical argument has tried to square the circle is by re-introducing Listian political economy into the debate.[8] Friedrich List was a nineteenth-century German political economist who was concerned with how Germany could fashion national policies to develop its manufacturing industry in the face of competition from the more advanced British manufacturing industry, in a world where the belief in free trade was enshrined in the canons of classical economics. List had argued that when societies at different levels of development come into contact with one another, the more highly-developed society and the more productive economy unleashes a process of 'displacement competition' within the less-developed and less-efficient society and economy. This results in peripheralisation and structural deformation unless it is counteracted by effective political steering (strong state intervention) aimed at temporarily 'dissassociating' the economy and society from the international competition.

Neo-Listian theory added to this the observation that delayed development has become increasingly more difficult, and in the process the salience of dissociative conditions for such development has become more pronounced. Development strategy has thereby become even more 'political'. That is to say the social agents of delayed development have changed, from private enterprise needing a bit of mercantilist state protection (as in List's days) to the strong nationalist state.

Neo-Listian theory explained the success of the East Asian countries with reference to the strategic role of the state in taming domestic and international forces and harnessing them to a national economic interest, coining the term 'the 'developmentalist state' for this purpose. It is pointed out that the developmentalist state has a role different from that of the Keynesian welfare state in the already advanced countries. The Keynesian welfare state serves to restrain market rationality by measures to protect groups vulnerable to the consequences of market rationality. By contrast, the developmentalist state restrains market rationality in order to pursue a policy for industrialisation *per se*.[9] The difference between the two forms is made evident in the difference in the sizes of the public sectors: in the advanced countries the public sectors are twice as large as those in the developmental statist countries. In the developmentalist state it is not the size of the public sector that counts but its use in subsidising certain strategic industries and sectors.

The neo-Listian approach to the developmentalist state was considerably strengthened by cross-referencing the experience in the NIEs to the postwar experience of Japan. Indeed, a concept of the 'developmental' state had originally been coined by Chalmer Johnson[10] to describe the manner in which the Japanese bureaucracy in the postwar period had fashioned government–industry relations and had directed the structural transformation of the Japanese economy. Japan's all-powerful Ministry of Industry and Trade (MITI) had encouraged companies to move capital and workers out of declining industries such as coal and textiles, into those with a high potential of growth such as steel, petrochemicals and cars, and later semi-conductors and biotechnology. Meanwhile, the Ministry of Finance (MoF) controlled all aspects of foreign economic relations, including imports of foreign goods and technology, access to foreign exchange, and direct and indirect investment.[11]

Recent departures within the neo-classical tradition now address the issue of the competitive success of nations in more general terms. An example is the 'new trade theory' developed by Paul Krugman and others.[12] This theory has become sufficiently influential and its arrival is sufficiently timely to put heart into various anti-free trade movements, including those in the US. What the theory says (taking its inspiration from the East Asian success) is that the real world is very different from that assumed in the liberal free trade theory. Domestic markets are not, after all, well-functioning, and domestic distortions do exist as do external economies. Shunning the traditional comparative-advantage explanations of trade, the new theory emphasises *non-comparative advantage trade*. In their thinking, countries do not necessarily specialise and trade solely in order to take advantage of their differences, they also trade because of increasing returns which makes specialisation advantageous, *per se*. This, coupled with the existence of market distortions, makes a case for government intervention to create and promote *dynamic* advantages through, for example, support for new technologies.

To credit the state with developmentally successful intervention in the economy still leaves a lot of questions to be answered. What are the conditions that give rise to a developmental state? Why did it emerge in East Asia and not, say, in Latin America or Africa? What is the nature of government–business relations and of state–civil society relations? Broadly speaking, the answers to these questions have drawn either on culturally or 'area' specific factors *or* on historical-structural and geo-political factors. I classify them as excursions into comparative political economy and international political economy respectively.

Comparative Political Economy

One school of thought now argues that East Asian capitalism is a model of capitalism quite different from the model of capitalist development originating in the West. Peter Berger,[13] for instance, says that East Asian capitalism presents a 'second' case. It is a case of successful industrialisation that (unlike the western case) combines growth with equity from the beginning of the modernisation process. East Asia is also 'exceptional' in so far as public authority and state intervention have led the modernisation process rather than individual enterprise, the free market and representational democracy.

In Berger's view, cultural norms and values derived from the Confucian ethic explain both the public spiritedness of officialdom (that of the developmentalist bureaucracy), and the obedience of the populace who are said to prefer social harmony to conflict. Berger notes that there is some irony in the way that Confucianism is now presented (including by himself) as a cultural factor explaining successful economic development, when previously, following Max Weber, theoretical analyses have always pointed to Confucianism as one of the *obstacles* to economic development of East Asia. Confucianism was dismissed by Weber for its conservatism and antagonism to economic activity. Today it is widely praised for its 'respect for superiors, its collective solidarity, and its emphasis on discipline'.[14]

Other scholars, notably Lucian Pye, have also elevated Confucianism to a key explanatory variable in contemporary East Asian capitalism. Pye, too, notes the Confucian paradox in its apparent transformation from being a drag to being an engine of economic development. But he argues that the paradox is resolved when we consider that in the postwar period the Confucian tradition became coupled with advances in economics as an intellectual discipline, and the new mandarins in East Asia became schooled in the wisdom of western economic theories. This fusion between Confucianism and practical economics is worked out in three main domains. First in the ethical-moral legitimation of government, where the traditional paternalistic concern of government for the people has become translated into an obligation to improve the economic condition of the people. Governments feel they have the right to intervene in people's lives so long as they fulfil their obligation to improve their people's economic lot. Second, the principle of 'virtuocracy' which underpinned traditional Confucian status and hierarchy has been transposed with the principle of meritocracy. Traditional values which directed people to defer to and obey status and hierarchy because of the virtue and noble spirit of the élites have become commuted to a deference for educated élites, and have served to legitimate technocrats in government. And, third, the Confucian stress on harmony, which in practical political terms amounts to a demand for conformity and consensus, restricts the actions of political critics, labour agitators, student rebels and other challengers to the status quo.[15]

It requires a considerable stretch of imagination to spread a hypothesis of post-Confucianism (that is modernised Confucianism) to include an entire region noted for its multiple and competing religions, and to maintain, in Peter Berger's words, that:

Confucian-derived values hold sway in the lives of ordinary people, many of whom have never read a Confucian classic and have little education.[16]

Nevertheless, other scholars too, and not least 'postcolonial Chinese intellectuals,[17] have asserted that in the melting pot of East Asian culture Confucianism has syncretically mixed with other religions and traditional value systems such as Buddhism, Taoism, Shintoism, folk religions and even Christianity, creating a unique system of ethics characterised by diligence, respect for authority, familism and a positive attitude to the affairs of the world.

This is the kind of unrigorous and simplistic social science theorising that, in the view of others, merely serves as an ideological prop to repressive regimes in their suppression of unpallatable facts. Such facts, for example, include the existence of martial law in Taiwan which was not lifted until 1987, after which Confucian values of 'obedience' spontaneously gave way to a storm of labour and environmental protests; the all-pervasive censorship in Singapore which gags the media, the churches and the public, and prompts many to vote with their feet and emigrate; or the fury of democratic movements in Korea which in the late-1980s successfully confronted the authorities with a forthright militancy that achieved some timid democratic reforms.[18] Indeed, it is testimony to organised union militancy in at least three of the four "Tiger" economies

(Korea, Taiwan and Hong Kong) that wages have been driven up to the point where capital (including not least domestic capital) has been forced to seek cheaper locations further afield, in Malaysia, Indonesia and Thailand. There the entire cycle of boot-camp managed export-industrialisation and the struggle for democratisation has only just begun.[19]

International Political Economy

Those standing in the Marxist tradition have predictably not paid so much attention to cultural explanations of the emergence of the developmental states in East Asia. Rather, they have tended to emphasise geo-political and historical-structural factors.

Many analysts argue that the legitimating basis for government authority in directing East Asian capitalism has rested not so much on Confucian values as on the geo-political reality of US Pacific dominance in the postwar period.[20] This Pacific dominance was articulated in strategic military and economic aid to the postwar regimes, the object of which was to develop Japan, South Korea and Taiwan as bullwarks against communism. For example, the US provided economic and military aid to South Korea totalling $13 billion or $600 per capita in the period 1945–79, and during the 1950s US aid accounted for five-sixths of Korean imports. The comparable figure for Taiwan was $5.6 billion.[21]

Admittedly, while American aid was a major contributor to the economies of South Korea and Taiwan during the 1950s, this was not the case with Hong Kong and Singapore whose economies had previously served as regional entrepots and who still retain entrepot functions to this day.[22] But both prospered as small enclaves at the cutting edge of the US containment policy of communism in the Far East. Hong Kong became the gateway for Communist China's clandestine commercial exchanges with the West, while Singapore's take-off in the mid-1960s was owed in no small measure to its profitable oil and ship repairing commerce with American forces in Vietnam.[23]

American geo-political interests in the region did more than contribute military and economic assistance and provide commercial opportunities. More important perhaps than the power of the

US to shape international security arrangements was that it understood with remarkable enlightened self-interest that security arrangments depended on shaping international economic arrangements. As Stephen Krasner has noted:

> Economic prosperity was thought to be a prophylactic against communism. American policy makers promoted European economic unification even though this was, in the long term, bound to place American products at some comparative disadvantage; and they tolerated explicit Japanese discrimination against American exports and direct investment. Their basic objective was to increase the level of absolute well-being in the western alliance.[24]

Other countries in the region benefitted in the same way from American security-inspired largesse. As benevolent hegemon the US was prepared to allow relative political autonomy in economic matters and tolerate the mercantilist policies of the regional states in an otherwise Bretton Woods-supervised free trade world. As Stephen Haggard writes:

> These strategic considerations dictated significant exceptions to the liberal, multilateral norm in East Asia just as they did in Europe. Trade, financial and aid links were self-consciously developed to serve three mutually supportive goals: economic reconstruction, strengthening the internal political position of pro-American political élites, and cementing strategic relations through economic interdependence.[25]

Under these circumstances, mercantilism, or state directed economic development, became for the externally politically supported regimes the legitimating basis for their intervention in the economy and the restructuring of government business relations. Over time their survival became dependent upon economic success. Instead of having to 'buy out' rent-seeking strong men as the fledgling national regimes in Africa had to do (see Chapter 8), they could at first command authority and resources to a degree sufficient to protect policy-makers from clients demanding payouts.

Freed from these political pressures, decision-makers and technocrats were better able to direct economic policy and state intervention in ways that were not only efficient but also profitable for the business class. In directing businesses to adapt to the opportunities available in export markets, former clients were forced out of rent-seeking and into productive activities. Over time this helped develop a business class who identified their own interests with those of the state as an autonomous organisation. Export success and economic expansion financed subsequent market interventions by government and helped further insulate bureaucrats from the temptations of corruption. Fast economic development, in turn, generated a broader 'growth coalition' supportive of policies geared towards promoting economic efficiency which sustained an institutional and political framework that enabled bureacuracies to follow through with successful policies.[26]

Thus, as Manuel Castells sums it up:

> for the developmental state economic development is not a *goal* but a *means*. It is a means *first* of survival and *next* to break away from dependency and to assert the national interest, even at the price of becoming unconditional military frontliners for the United States.[27] [Emphasis added]

And he adds:

> In a deliberate parallel with Marx's theory of social classes, I propose the idea that the developmental state effects the transition of a political subject 'in itself' to a political apparatus 'for itself' by affirming the only legitimacy principle that did not seem to be threatening for the international powers overseeing its destiny: economic development.[28]

To such geo-political analyses must be added the historical structural analysis of the development of capitalism on a world scale. While geo-political forces helped firm up the early regimes and motivate their interventions in directing their economies and fashioning state–business and state–society relations, equally there were confluent forces at work in the way global capitalism had reached a level of development of productive forces and relations of production which gave rise to 'peripheral Fordism'. In Chapter 3 we have described how peripheral Fordism came about and how it selectively honed in on *some* but not all developing countries depending on the availability of a docile labour force, authoritarian regimes sympathetic to international capital and supportive of a business class willing to seize the chance to participate on a subcontracting, junior-partner, basis to the accumulation of capital on a global scale.

Limits of the East Asia Developmental Model

The question of how far the developmental state phenomenon in East Asia was *historically* specific, rather than *culturally* specific, is important in determining both the limits of this model for the future of the developmental states themselves and the emulation of their model by other, second generation, industrialisers in the region. After all, a model, as Berger helpfully reminds us, is a term that has two connotations: 'on the one hand it means a specific pattern or type, on the other it means an example to be emulated.'[29]

The historical specificity of the 'model' relates to the external environment of the geo-politics of the cold war and its unique conjunction with a certain phase in the development of capitalism on a world scale. Critics, like Walden Bello and Stephanie Rosenfeld, argue that 'the old strategy of high-speed, export-oriented growth will not get the NICs through the 1990s', and that therefore a comprehensive, alternative vision of an alternative model of development is required.[30]

By the late-1980s the *Dragons [were] in Distress*, as in the pithy title of Bello and Rosenfeld's excellent study of three NICs – Korea, Taiwan and Singapore.[31] The external environment of these countries had radically changed, and in the attempt to redirect the developmental strategy their states came up against the limits of the internal environment as well.

Geo-politically, the US had ceased to be the guardian of the liberal trading order and in fact had become aggressively protectionist, blaming the NICs together with Japan for its huge trade deficit. The end of the cold war and the extinction of the Soviet threat undermined any last vestige of US strategic interest in maintaining the exceptionally favourable trading and currency status of the countries in the region, or in bolstering their authoritarian regimes. A battery of punitive US trade measures and currency manipulations, coupled with the deep recession in the mid-1980s, forced Korea, Taiwan and Singapore into rethinking their strategy away from export-oriented industrialisation for mass markets abroad and towards either seizing a commanding role in the new high-tech driven world economy (as in Singapore's strategy), and/or a deepening of the domestic market as in the more populous Taiwan and Korea.

However, according to Bello and Rosenfeld, these strategies now threaten to unravel because of the social and ecological consequences of the previous phase: repression has disenfranchised the middle classes, has alienated the poor from an 'economic miracle' built on their backs, and has caused a collapse of the agricultural sector and environmental degradation that chokes off further growth. A growing crisis of political legitimacy intertwines with a developing economic crisis.

It is true that, judging by conventional measures of quality of life, namely life expectancy, mortality rates and literacy rates, all seven dragons have scored undisputed successes, but the downside is recorded in appalling air and water pollution, deforestation and overcrowding.[32] Moreover, the record of social progress as measured by declining income inequality and poverty levels continues to be a matter of interpretation and dispute. The statistics are not robust: the World Bank makes a lot of the claim that all the high performing East Asian economies (HPEAs) have combined high-speed growth with equity, but in its trailblazing report published in 1993 it relies on figures that only cover the period 1970–80, where attributed, or does not attribute them at all.[33]

In relation to Korean data, Bello and Rosenfeld use statistics collected and analysed by various South Korean writers, in unpublished manuscripts,[34] which point to increasing income inequality over the same period 1970–81 which the World Bank claims recorded declining income inequality. Others, too, have doubted the reliability of the claim of reduction in income inequality in South Korea, arguing that the data having been 'derived from surveys that exclude wealthy households, single person households, nonfarm households in rural areas and small farmers'.[35] Singaporean claims of narrowing income inequalities have been questioned by Paul.[36]

It is of some irony that notwithstanding the fact that the World Bank has been thoroughly discredited in the eyes of most observers except itself, it yet maintains a near monopoly over the statistical presentation of our collective understanding of world order. It is very unusual to find, even in the works of critics, statistics that are *not* derived from World Bank data. But for its own data, the World Bank relies on the submissions of governments. Authoritarian governments, such as those under discussion here, are hardly likely to admit to shortcomings in social distribution and equity. Meanwhile, local critics are censured and cowed, making it very difficult to achieve a correct assessment of the situation.

But even if we accept the consensus which, for right or wrong, has developed in respect of the 'combined equity with growth' thesis of the East Asian model, it can hardly be disputed that the region as a whole still faces an uphill task in lifting the mass of the population above subsistence levels. And the question to ask in the context of a globalising economy is under what conditions can the developmental states complete the project of national developmentalism?

In the conclusion of their book, Bello and Rosenfeld argue:

> that it has become evident that economic models that pit efficiency against equity and economic growth against ecological equilibrium are obsolete.[37]

They discern the contours of a comprehensive alternative paradigm with features which are probably in anyone's good guide to development: democratic participation, the growth and consolidation of the domestic market, ecologically sustainable development, a selective export policy, and the development of equitable regional associations.

However, in the view of this author, pressures of globalisation frustrate the drive to maturity of the state-led capitalist development process, unless this drive is undertaken within a consciously pursued regional framework. In the context of a globalised world economy, it becomes increasingly difficult for the state to subordinate business interests to its own strategic concerns. As Nigel Harris has noted, the endeavour of building competitive capacity through state-assisted economic development has a contradictory result. To the extent that the private sector has been encouraged to survive as a means to accelerate growth, to that extent governments have been successful in creating a strong private capitalist class ultimately capable of challenging the priorities of state policy. Moreover the change in the social weight of the business class *at home* is not the only implication. Harris says:

As the world economy becomes increasingly integrated, the mark of maturity of a national capitalist class is that world competition drives it to operate internationally, to merge increasingly with global capital. This is only feasible with the liberation of capital from all that mass of restrictions which national governments seek to impose in order to capture a larger share of any surplus for the nation . . . National liberation freed the State; restructuring and liberalization now freed capital . . . Thus paradoxically, national economic development that was impelled by the rivalries within the State system now produces a new component in the market system that in part contradicts the independence of the State.[38]

The rising figures of regional and overseas direct investment by the Tiger economies is testimony to their deepening participation in the process of globalisation. Annual FDI flows from the Republic of Korea, Singapore and Taiwan were $5.7 billion during 1988–92 compared to $0.4 billion during 1983–7. And although most of this outward investment is located in the East Asian region, such investments have also increased in Europe and North America.[39]

Globalisation not only affects the developmental process in the increasing interwovenness of global and domestic capital. More important is the re-shaping of the world economy into high-value producers and routine, high-volume producers, as discussed in Chapter 8. Modern factories and state-of-the art machinery can be installed almost anywhere on the globe throwing 'routine' producers into competition with one another in capital's relentless search for the cheapest locations. Thus, competition from low-cost producers may frustrate the completion of the developmental project in the successful East Asian economies.

Regionalisation: The Next Lap?

The best hope for the multitudes in the East Asian region who are not yet benefiting from the economic growth that has taken place, is an accelerating process of regional economic integration. While the developmental possibilities of export-oriented industrialisation are limited, productive upgrading and internally-based growth are constrained by the limits of national markets and consumer demand. It is therefore important that the drive to maturity of East Asian capitalism becomes locked into a wider coherent territorial space in which the positive social dynamics of capitalist development may be played out. What are the chances of such regional integration?

A major problem is what is sometimes referred to as the 'variable geometry' of the region. What indeed is the region? Where does it begin, where does it end? And which countries belong to it? For reasons both of political history *and* of economic realities, there are today several competing, if loose, regional groupings (sometimes no more than *initiatives* for regional groupings) with part-different, part-overlapping membership. The fact that these intitiatives coexist despite conflicting conceptions of the region, and of the nature and extent of wished for economic cooperation, is testimony to the fluidity of the present time when globalising and regionalising forces take turns to wax and wane.

The hardiest of the groupings is the Association of South East Asian Nations (ASEAN), originally formed in 1967, and until quite recently more preoccupied with anti-communist security issues than with economic integration. ASEAN includes the Philippines, Malaysia, Thailand, Singapore, Indonesia, Brunei and, of late, Vietnam. Tellingly, it *ex*cludes three of the four Tigers: Hong Kong, Taiwan and South Korea. In 1989, the Prime Minister of Malaysia, Mahathir Mohammed, set up the East Asia Economic Grouping (soon to be watered down to a mere caucus, EAEC) with the specific aim to develop a trade bloc, dominated by the yen, as a counterweight to EU and NAFTA, and seeking to include besides ASEAN, South Korea, Hong Kong, Taiwan and eventually China. Japan was invited to lead the caucus, and although at first very cautious has since shown signs of warming to the concept. Meanwhile China, too, has become a leading actor within the variable geometry of the region by actively pursuing a concept of 'Greater China' or the 'China Circle' mapping within its subregional orbit southern China, Taiwan and Hong Kong–Macau as one viable growth triangle.[40]

Anxious not to be left out and to pre-empt protectionist moves, Australia, in 1992, with the wholehearted support of the US, proposed the Asia Pacific Cooperation Forum (APEC) striving to include all of the above countries minus Vietnam, but plus the US, Australia, New Zealand, and today even Mexico and Chile. APEC's expressed aims are to promote 'open regionalism', emphasising the neo-liberal creed of liberalisation, privatisation and open markets. ASEAN countries have reacted coolly to the APEC initiative, fearing marginalisation by the larger players, notably the US. In 1993 they responded by setting up the ASEAN Free Trade Area (AFTA), agreeing to reduce tariffs on intra-ASEAN trade goods over a 15 year period, with about 40 per cent of this trade being targeted for accelerated reductions.[41] This move was parried by APEC, in 1994, when it announced the formation of a (non-discriminatory) Asia–Pacific trade liberalisation scheme aimed to produce free trade by 2020. AFTA responded by extending its effective preferential list of trade goods and shortening the implementation period to ten years.[42]

Thus, competing conceptions of the 'region' dovetail with competing economic ideologies of discriminatory versus non-discriminatory trade, or regional trade integration versus global liberalisation of trade. But, importantly, issues of post-cold war geo-political strategy (notably the role of the US as a continuing hegemon keeping historic enemies in check) are also at play as are issues of cultural assertiveness. For example, 'shared Asian values' have been put forward as an explanatory source of Asian dynamism and as a legitimating basis for what in the West are often regarded as trade-restricting human-rights abuses. The EAEC is nicknamed in some regional capitals as 'East Asia without the Caucasians'.[43]

Meanwhile, there are changes in political economy happening on the ground that make these competing ideologically-driven configurations of regionalisation at once more compelling and yet, in some ways, less critically different. As Paul Bowles and Brian MacLean[44] argue in a persuasive review of emerging trading arrangements in the region, much of our present second-guessing of the evolution of trade blocs is based on *de facto* analyses of cross-border trade culled from statistical examinations of customs books. One such authoritative 'trade pattern' approach, for example, was undertaken by Frankel in 1991 and came to the conclusion that intra-ASEAN trade in the period 1985–90 was neither growing relative to world trade nor relative to ASEAN's share of world trade.[45] However, such analyses often fail to capture the extent and depth of intra-firm trade (trade occurring within multinational enterprises) spreadeagled across countries in one region.

Since the revaluation of the yen following the Louvre Accord of 1985, Japanese foreign direct investment in all of Asia has jumped from 50 per cent to 80 per cent of all Japanese FDI flows.[46] As William Tabb notes, East Asia has emerged as an increasingly

tightly coordinated manufacturing bloc, exhibiting a complex regional pattern of production and distribution, with Japanese multinationals cross-exporting and importing parts from and between
their facilities in the region, assigning to each a specific role within a
dynamically flexible but coherent strategic plan organised and
administered from Japan.[47] This 'flying geese' pattern of regional
trade has, according to one estimate, increased the index of intra-
industry trade by 91 per cent for the Philippines, 90 per cent for
Indonesia, 85 per cent for Thailand and 64 per cent for Malaysia
during 1979–88.[48] According to Lim, these intra-industry trade
patterns make the logic of regional trading arrangements (for
example as in AFTA's or EAEC's proposals) more compelling in
so far as the ASEAN countries 'as a group can offer investors . . . a
combination [of advantages] that no member individually pos-
sesses'.[49]

Thus, the fact that the division of labour within the region has
become more a *process* rather than a *product* division, makes the
case for regional trade integration of the AFTA and EAEC variety
more compelling; yet it is *also* a case, as Bowles and MacLean point
out, that is qualitatively different from past objectives of trade
integration. For, whereas in the past regional economic integration
initiatives were meant to maximise *inward looking trade creation* as
the reason for forming a trade bloc, today the objective is one of
outward looking investment creation.[50] In this sense, it seems to me,
there may not be much difference in outcome between APEC's and
AFTA's approaches to regionalisation: both are a step towards a
deepening integration within the global economy. The important
question is which of the two approaches is more likely to maximise
the chances that capitalist development in the region not only
exploits and alienates the working class, but also produces the
material base for its emancipation. It seems to me that the AFTA
and EAEC approaches, for all the dangers of Japanese imperialism,
have the advantage here because they offer greater scope for the
development of oppositional cross-national movements.

11

Democracy, Civil Society and Postdevelopment in Latin America

In this part of the book we illuminate, in separate chapters, the manner in which globalisation impacts upon and is responded to in different regions of what used to be called the Third World. Each time we select a dominant theme as a conduit for our inquiry. These themes are not arbitrarily chosen. Rather they reflect the preoccupation in the literature with what is happening in the various parts of the world. They are intended to convey a kind of summary statement of the intellectual consensus, a sound-bite characterisation. Africa is 'about' the disintegration of the state and the collapse of civil society; East Asia is 'about' the success of state-led development; the Middle East is 'about' the Islamic anti-developmentalist revolt. Likewise Latin America today is about the return to 'democracy' and the birth of 'civil society'. As Norbert Lechner has put it: 'If revolution was the articulating axis of the Latin American debate in the 1960s, in the 1980s the central theme is democracy.'[1]

This debate about the democratisation of Latin America is first and foremost a debate amongst Latin American intellectuals themselves, more especially the Latin American left. As such the debate cannot be divorced from the particular historical circumstance, post-cold war and postmodern, in which the Latin American left tries to accommodate and transcend the forces of globalisation and the legitimating mantle of neo-liberal ideology. As we shall see, this situation is not without irony, but neither is it without hope. For it signals that at the precise historical juncture when structural forces appear to be at their most imperative, agency may yet find its political moment.

The Latin American Intellectual Left

Why should we privilege the Latin American intellectuals in our understanding of Latin America today? And why the left? It is because, as Jorge Castañeda in his comprehensive book on the subject *Utopia Unarmed* tells us, they have always fulfilled a central and even disproportionate role in Latin American societies and politics. They are an entity unto themselves; they make up a separate estate.[2]

As to the reasons why this should be so, Castañeda points to two: the postcolonial domestic social structure, and the particular relationship of Latin American intellectuals with the outside world. The postcolonial domestic social structure has always been characterised by a strong state and a weak civil society, in which political parties were often unrepresentative, civil institutions (judges, courts, a free press and trade unions) weak or absent, and nation building incomplete. In this situation the intellectual stood out, Castañeda argues. But the term 'intellectual' encompasses a broad spectrum: 'almost any one who writes, paints, acts, teaches, and speaks out, even sings, becomes "an intellectual".'[3] They write, speak, advocate, or do what is accomplished elsewhere by more specialised institutions or groups. And, he continues, from the early part of the twentieth century most of the better known Latin American intellectuals were on the left of the political spectrum, even if they did not always dominate the region's thinking or politics.[4]

On the other hand, the prominence of these intellectuals stemmed from 'their role as a conduit between a region avid for ideas, experiences, and doctrines from abroad, and an outside world where these commodities were produced and generated'.[5]

I would add that this intellectual articulation with the West, sometimes confrontational, sometimes accommodating but often at the cutting edge of political theory, arises from a different postcolonial condition from that found in other regions of the world. For in Latin America, colonialism had succeeded more or less completely in wiping out native culture and society, and the present population, certainly those strata of the urban middle class from which intellectuals are chiefly drawn in any society, are of European descent. Thus, in the main they did not draw on native roots, culture or religion, in their search for national identity and self-expression.

This double positioning of the Latin American intellectual left at the seam between Latin America and the rest of the world, and between a strong state and a weak civil society, helps us to understand the tumultuous trajectory of the region's postwar transition from developmental aspirations through the long night of the generals and the debt debacle of the 1980s, to the contemporary accommodation with, and struggles to transcend, the neo-liberal challenges. For, while as a class or stratum the native intelligentsia served, as Castañeda has put it, as mediators or interlocutors between two sets of actors that often proved incapable of communicating directly with each other (that is state and society),[6] it has also to be recognised that *individuals* from these strata were frequently coopted by the political class and drafted into office, or were otherwise seduced into participating in the leadership of political parties, writing their platforms and giving direction to the policies that shaped the region. Thus they often had political power. Castañeda quotes the writer García Márquez:

> There is a curious relationship between intellectuals and political power in Latin America. The State and the powers-that-be both need us and fear us. They need us because we give them prestige they lack, they fear us because our sentiments and views can damage them. In the history of power in Latin America, there are only military dictatorships or intellectuals. No wonder then – and it is a fascinating thing – that there was so much coddling of the intellectuals by the State. Under these circumstances, one cannot be always completely independent.[7]

There is another reason for singling out the Latin American left. It is my view that the neo-liberal adjustment of Latin America to the world economy in fact has preceded and pre-charted the neo-liberal integration of the advanced countries as well. And much of the experience with the return to democracy, particularly the rise of new social movements and the changing role of civil society, is a foretaste of things to come in the 'old' democracies of the West as well. The Latin American left's reflection on the nature of the new political economy, therefore, becomes an invaluable inspiration to those who search for ideas about social reconstruction in the old democracies too.

Postwar Developmentalism and Dependency Theory

Before the Second World War, Latin America occupied a position in the world economy much the same as other colonial areas (hence Lenin's designation of Latin America as a 'semi-colony'[8]). It produced primary exports in exchange for manufactured goods from the West; its mines and plantations were either directly owned or controlled by foreign companies; its ruling landed oligarchies were a handmaiden to western interests; and national policies of exchange rates, tariffs and taxation favoured the export sector over the interests of the native urban industrialists and workers. However, the depression of the 1930s and the subsequent war years forced Latin American countries onto a path of import substitution as an emergency measure to produce goods which could no longer be obtained from abroad. The experience with this effective, if historically contingent, structural break with the world capitalist system was positive, and in the aftermath of the Second World War it grew into a fully fledged model of development.

The theoretical foundations for this model were laid by Raøúl Prebisch, an Argentinian economist and one-time director of the Economic Commission for Latin America (ECLA – or CEPAL to give it its Spanish acronym). In a seminal paper in 1950, Prebisch[9] argued that the classical Ricardian theory of international trade was not applicable in the context of the existing international division of labour, and instead contributed to trade-generated inequality and structural underdevelopment. Prebisch and his colleagues at ECLA favoured import substitution as a means to help the process of infant industrialisation of underdeveloped countries, and they assigned a leading role to the state in pursuing policies of inward-directed development combining state-protected industrialisation with import substitution under the aegis of foreign investment.

Elsewhere I have described how the 'structuralist' analysis of Prebisch and his colleagues in ECLA were not only influential in shaping early postwar policies in Latin America, but also became the crucible from which later neo-Marxist dependency theory was cast.[10] Indeed, dependency theory was principally a Latin American theory of development.

There were other influences, however, which *ab initio* reinforced the state-centric nature of the postwar policies. Duncan Green recalls how the Soviet industrialisation and the heavily state-led revival of the European economies after the Second World War further established the centrality of the state in successful economic planning. He sums up the comprehensive catalogue of state policies: investment in infrastructure required by industry; subsidising basic foods and imposing price controls to keep labour costs down in urban areas; protection of local industries against foreign competition; nationalisation of key industries, such as oil, utilities and steel, and establishing new ones; and supporting an overvalued exchange rate making Latin America's exports dear and imports cheap.[11]

The model of 'import substitutive industrialisation' (ISI) became the trademark of Latin America in the 1950s and 1960s, and although it was subsequently discredited and negatively compared with the ostensibly more successful export oriented strategy of industrialisation (EOI) of the East Asian economies, it was, as Green reminds us, successful within its own terms and it transformed the region's economies:

> By the early 1960s, domestic industry supplied 95 per cent of Mexico's and 98 per cent of Brazil's consumer goods. From 1950 to 1980 Latin America's industrial output went up six times keeping well ahead of population growth. Infant mortality fell from 107 per 1000 live births in 1960 to 69 per 1000 in 1980, life expectancy rose from 52 to 64 years. In the mid 1950s, Latin America's economies were growing faster than those of the industrialized West.[12]

The ECLA theorists, however, had failed to address the issue of class and income distribution. Indeed the political companion to the economic theory of ISI in those early days was populism: a concerted effort by the ruling élite to mobilise and unite industrialists, urban masses and peasants alike around the message of nationalism and national development, while conveniently blaming imperialism (more especially American imperialism) and unequal exchange for any policy failures. But in time the issues of class and income distribution would rebound on their policies with a vengeance.

By the mid- to late-1960s, the ISI model began to falter: balance-of-payments problems worsened; real wages did not rise sufficiently quickly to stimulate domestic demand; unemployment grew more acute and income inequalities ever more severe; and industrial production became increasingly concentrated in products typically consumed by élites.

It is at this point that dependency theory came into its own, injecting class into the analysis of underdevelopment. André Gunder Frank,[13] T. dos Santos,[14] Celseo Furtado,[15] Norman Girvan,[16] Osvaldo Sunkel[17] and many other left-of-centre intellectuals pointed out that the ISI model had in fact led to a deepening of dependence and to further underdevelopment because the existing, colonially-inherited class structure had rendered a highly unequal income distribution which limited internal domestic markets. This, in turn, they argued, had two correlate effects: on the one hand, it had skewed the industrialisation process towards meeting the needs of the élites, while such a pattern of production involved heavy reliance on imported producer goods, spare parts, technology and so on.

On the other hand, the increasingly severe balance-of-payments problems resulting from this pattern of industrialisation made for ever-greater dependency on foreign firms which were invited to set up their producer-goods plants and technology locally. The combination of a limited domestic market with foreign industrial subsidiaries encouraged a grotesquely inefficient system of production and a net outflow of resources. Latin American subsidiaries became the dumping ground for obsolete foreign plant and machinery, their capacity was grossly underutilised and their labour absorption rate became regressive. Over time, remitted returns on foreign investment came to exceed net inflows several times.[18]

Military Regimes, Internationalisation and US Imperialism

Industrialisation and social modernisation in the postwar era led to the emergence of new middle and working-class sectors which demanded the right to participate in the political life of their countries. Populist political parties, peasant and labour unions, and progressive sectors of the church all encouraged the mobilisation of the lower classes. Their demands for land and income redistribution, for higher wages and social programmes threatened the property rights and accumulation potential of the dominant coalitions. During the course of the 1960s the developing political crisis deepened with the emergence of guerilla warfare and urban terrorism, and the threat of Cuban-inspired subversion, even though, as Richard Gott has argued, Cuba's support for the guerrilla movements, especially in the early years, was more imagined than real.[19]

Meanwhile high inflation, serious balance-of-payments difficulties and economic stagnation further buffeted the populist regimes in countries like Brazil, Bolivia, Argentina, Ecuador, Uruguay and Chile. In these conditions a return to authoritarian rule by military dictatorships was seen by many élites, including the nascent middle classes, as a bulwark against the capture of the state by revolutionary forces. They thought it would help to restore the conditions of social and political stability that were requisites for capital accumulation and economic growth.[20]

By the middle of the 1970s, many Latin American countries and several of the Caribbean states were run by military governments (Venezuela, Colombia, Mexico and Costa Rica being exceptions). Between 1969 and 1978, it is estimated that imports of military equipment and arms of various types grew by more than 300 per cent in real terms, with Argentina, Brazil, Peru and Chile being the leading purchasers.[21]

Military coups, of course, were nothing new in Latin America. They had been a major theme of Latin American political life for more than 150 years. Even so the return to military rule came as something of a surprise to political observers because it had been assumed that economic modernisation would be accompanied by the consolidation of civilian government and the 'professionalisation' of the armed forces. Moreover, the military interventions that heralded the 'long night of the generals' of the 1970s were unusual in so far as they departed from the previous pattern in which the military had been content to merely take 'temporary custody' of the national constitution. The new wave of military regimes instead announced their intentions to stay in power as long as was 'necessary' to carry out social and economic reforms. Hence their designation as 'garrison' states, or even 'military developmental' states.[22]

The nature of these social and economic reforms, and the repressive severity with which they were imposed, cannot be understood without regard to the changing international context in which they took place. They coincided with the beginning of the world-wide economic recession, the collapse of the Bretton Woods system, the oil price hikes and the recycling of petrodollars in the 1970s, and the acceleration of the internationalisation of capital. To this potent cocktail must be added the renewed aggressive interest of American foreign policy in the region, whether exemplified by armed invasion as in the Dominican Republic in 1965, or covert interventions by the CIA in toppling, for example, Goulart in Brazil in 1964 and Allende in Chile in 1973,[23] or whether typified in countless instances of financial backing for dictators, the training of, and assistance to, their armies and police for rural 'pacification' programmes (Honduras, El Salvador, Nicaragua) and the higher education of the generals and officers class in neo-liberal economics.[24] In the words of Robert McNamara (US Defence Secretary in the 1960s, and President of the World Bank in the 1970s):

> They are the new leaders. I don't need to expiate on the value of having in leadership positions men who have previously become closely acquainted with how we Americans think and do things. Making friends with those men is beyond price.[25]

The Dance of the Millions

The oil price hikes and the petrodollar recycling in the 1970s dramatically changed the size and composition of foreign investments in Latin America. Along with other non-oil producing countries, most Latin American countries needed to borrow heavily to cover balance-of-trade deficits. For their part, international banks were falling over themselves to lend. Before the 1970s the bulk of Latin America's foreign capital had come from public sources (bilateral and multilateral aid) and direct foreign investment; by the end of the decade the proportions had reversed.[26] What is more, the bulk of new lending went to private companies and parastatal enterprises; relatively little ended up covering government deficits. Spectacular waste and corruption fed a spiral of inflation and a frenzy of capital flight in which 'much of the money being borrowed from abroad was funnelled straight out again' as the World Bank itself admitted.[27] Perverse Reaganomics[28] in the early 1980s, which increased dollar interest rates to dizzying heights, massively increased the debt burden and set the scene for the harrowing de-development of the debt decade.

In the chapter on Africa we introduced the reader to the general forces underlying the debt crisis and the principal features of IMF/ World Bank debt management policies of the 1980s. What it is necessary to point out here is that the renegade insertion of Latin American economies in the new world system of maniacal capital integration explains the support for the administrative terror of the generals by the global capitalist élites, and made them turn a blind eye to horrendous human rights abuses, including torture, killings and disappearances, as well as the systematic exclusion of large sectors of the population. James Petras recalls an interview with an international banker who said:

> We lend to Chile because whatever problems they have down there [those little things like torture] we're the first on the list to get paid before anyone else.[29]

Thus, wrote Petras, the social sectors on which the junta depended – the financiers, the multinationals, the banks – were the very ones who were the main beneficiaries of the junta. They were also the instruments of inflation:

> By increasing profits, through price gougings, not through in-creases in production; through speculation, not through innova-tion, and through loans, not through investments, they generated the inflationary spiral.[30]

Even a cursory examination of the region's political economy in the run up to the debt crisis and the imposed structural adjustment policies of the 1980s cannot fail to notice variations in political style, economic policies and performance. Some regimes (for example Brazil, Venezuela) have been labelled 'bureaucratic authoritarian'[31] because they continued with state-centric development programmes, while others (Pinochet's Chile, or Argentina after 1976) were ultra monetarist, combining export-oriented accumulation with a strident form of privatisation. Some regimes were less repressive than others, giving encouragement to the 'voluntarist' theories of development and dependency which we noted in Chapter 3.[32] While some regimes had no economic record to boast of, not even in terms of the paper exercise of national account statistics, others recorded very high rates of economic growth (for example Brazil, Mexico [up to 1979] and Chile) even though deep reversals during the adjustment years that followed exposed these achievements as superficial.

The New Democracy: State, Civil Society and Market Reforms

Nonetheless, all these variations were nothing compared to the outcome when, in the 1980s, the austerity programmes imposed by the IMF and World Bank led to economic contraction, de-industrialisation, savage reduction in wages and declining living standards, and popular revolt *everywhere*; and when *all* governments had to withdraw or reduce subsidies and funding for the social sectors, including health, housing and education, laying bare a wasteland from which new shoots of democracy and civil society would spring.

Duncan Green, in his lucid and commanding study of the economics and politics of the neo-liberal reforms in Latin America, observes the 'cruel twist of history that made the debt crisis and structural adjustment coincide with Latin America's return to (more-or-less) democratic rule . . .'.[33] The nature of that democratic rule and the forms of civil society that have emerged, or are emerging, is what today captures the attention of the Latin American left.

However it is wrong to speak of 'coincidence'. The word 'coincidence' carries a notion of accident and chance happening. This prevents one from making generalisations to other situations and parts of the globe. Yet this is precisely what we must do. For the neo-liberal adjustment in Latin America is a precursor of the neo-liberal integration of other parts of the world, particularly the advanced countries themselves. By understanding the dynamics of the relationship between economic and political forces in Latin America, much may be learnt about the new forms of democracy that could be, and are, emerging there too. In this sense, Latin America is today 'ahead' in the game, as it were, and this is why the reflexivity of the left of the emerging Latin American political economy should engage the attention of the people in the West, the traditional core of the world capitalist system.

The neo-liberal agenda that was imposed by the joint IMF stabilisation programmes and the World Bank structural adjustment programmes, and which was backed by the US (dubbed 'the Washington Consensus') forged new relations between state, society and the market. In the interstices of these three, new forms of political mobilisation occurred, new democratic rights were prioritised and new demarcations between public and private domains were drawn. To capture the democratisation process in Latin America in the past decade we will make a distinction that some writers[34] have made between political democratisation and social democratisation. Whereas the former refers to the establishment of a principle of automony in a constitution with a bill of rights and the reform of state power to maximise accountability to elected representatives and ultimately the citizen body, the latter refers to an experimentation with different democratic mechanisms and procedures in civil society.[35]

Civilian Rule and Political Democracy

The apparent paradox of the return to civilian rule at the very time that structural adjustment programmes came into operation dissolves if we consider that structural adjustment policies by their nature require a measure of popular legitimation which the dictatorships who had contracted the debt burden had not needed. After all, contracting debt is a highly private, invisible and unaccountable affair, but paying the monies back would bear down directly on every section of society, through devaluations, hyperinflation, wage reductions, public sector cutbacks and so on. The debts had to be socialised or 'nationalised'.[36] This was made crystal clear in the very first round of debt rescheduling negotiations in the early 1980s: fresh loans (if only to repay old debts) were made conditional upon an acceptance on the part of the debtor countries of national, that is government, responsibility for all outstanding loans, including private sector loans.[37] The international gulag of World Bank, IMF and US bankers were shrewdly aware of the political implications, which is why already by the turn of the decade 'human rights' suddenly appeared on the US Administration's agenda. Where Jimmy Carter led, Ronald Reagan followed with the establishment of the National Endowment for Democracy.[38] The World Bank, too, spent much energy during the 1980s driving home the virtues of electoral democracy.

International 'concern' was confluent with mounting internal opposition to the regimes from all walks of life. The once broad support for the juntas among the middle classes disintegrated as the arbitrariness of the human rights abuses affected many of their class as well as those of the lower strata,[39] and the economic depression of the early-1980s dragged down all but the very few who had been able to avail themselves of pseudo-legal channels to transport their (and their country's) wealth abroad.

Much has been made in the literature of the fact that the struggle against the dictatorships took place outside previously existing left-wing party and organisational structures, and that instead multiple new forms of grassroots and human rights movements were sweeping across Latin America. There was a difference between what Salvador Samoya has called 'the party left' and the 'movement left',[40] and ever since the dying days of the military regimes and their return to the barracks, the 'movement' left has been the fulcrum of the region's redemocratisation. In some respects this is not surprising since the juntas had either obliterated or crippled the traditional left's party organisations, and the foreign, capital-intensive, export-oriented industrialisation of the junta years had stripped the trade unions of much of their membership. But it is certainly interesting that intellectuals from the traditional Marxist–Leninist (party) left joined the grassroots movements in a struggle for electoral democracy, in what appears to have been a lasting reversal of traditional priorities.

In the past, left-wing parties in Latin America had often been led by communists or had proto-socialist leanings in which electoral democracy had been subordinated to demands for social justice and national independence. And although in the revolutionary days of the 1950s and 1960s many communist parties had been anti-soviet, this had not prevented them from adopting the Marxist–Leninist conceptions of a 'vanguard' party with the overriding aim of capturing the state-apparatus. However, the arbitrary jailings and killings, the gagging of the media and the all-pervasive censorship exercised during the junta years awakened the intellectual left to the virtues and significance of bourgeois-democratic values. It quickly began to acquire notoriety for its advocacy of democracy, and as Castañeda suggests, they played a key role in the grassroots explosion: 'conceptualizing it, narrating it, and socializing it and . . . channelling it into political expression and structured political parties'.[41]

The intellectual left's support for, even coalition with, democratically elected governments who *nolens volens* had to preside over a brutal reversal of economic fortunes, a staggering widening of inequalities, and a deepening misery of the masses,[42] has perforce led them into a rethink of the relationship between state and market as well. It is a rethink that is proving particularly challenging because of the collapse of the socialist world and the absence of alternative existing models to the neo-liberal agenda. They have to do their rethinking all on their own!

Thus far the results of this rethinking are confusion and disarray. Steve Ellner, in an introduction to an edited volume on *The Latin American Left*, observes that its response to neo-liberalism and perestroika has been far from uniform. While nearly all leftist spokespersons are opposed to the elimination of social welfare programmes and many favour lengthy moratoria on payment of foreign debt, there is no consensus on privatisation or the role of the state in promoting economic development.[43] Indeed, some of yesterday's radical populists have transformed into neo-liberal protagonists, while others continue to make clarion calls for a 'popular economic alternative'[44] even though the 'big idea' remains elusive.

Duncan Green has classified the left's responses to the neo-liberal realities of Latin America today using a simple and useful, but theoretically not very sophisticated, dichotomy: short-term tinkerers and long-term utopists,

> there are those concerned with short term improvements within the existing global and national economic frameworks, and those who think in the longer-term, and believe the existing order must be swept away and a new society built from scratch in order to achieve any lasting improvement in the lives of ordinary Latin Americans.[45]

The former, not surprisingly, are those who are either in power or hoping to achieve it in the next elections. Their concept of democracy is one of a 'democratic pact' in which the various parties commit themselves to an overriding allegiance to the procedural norms of democracy, and the rule of law, in order to rebuff threats from the old military regime. The democratic pact may lead to a further social pact (*concertación*) intended to bring the state together with capital and labour in a bid to regulate wages and profits.[46]

Paradoxically – and this is the truly arresting difference with yesteryears – the utopists, those who take a longer view, are to be found amongst the proponents of grassroots, local alternatives. They are suspicious of state power of any kind and look instead to a strategy of local organisation and mobilisation. The practice of these grassroots movements, and the theories of civil society and democracy that they have spawned is what we turn to next.

The New Social Movements and Civil Society

The extraordinary increase in the organisational capacity of civil society in the Latin American region in the last two decades is both a source of hope and a key point of departure in much theorising about a postmodern social reconstruction. What is civil society? The philosopher Hegel once defined it as everything 'beyond the family but short of the state'.[47] Civil society encompasses all voluntary associations, organisations and networks engaged in some form of collective action. In Latin America today the terms voluntary organisations, grassroots movements, new social movements, popular movements, and non-governmental organisations (NGOs) are all used interchangeably with civil society.

How do we explain this growth, and what pointers for the future does it hold? And more crucially what are the connections between it and the still fragile process of political democracy?

The movements vary in origin and in collective purpose, and hence in the form of politicisation and empowerment that may be ascribed to them. Nevertheless, they have a number of shared characteristics: they are issue rather than class-oriented; they have formed at local, grassroots level; they operate largely outside the prevailing state structures; and they originate mostly in the experience of poverty and exclusion. Castañeda identifies four broad categories: the ecclesiastical base communities; the neighbourhood and urban dwellers' movements and 'self-help' associations; the women's movement; and environmental associations, Indian groups and human-rights organisations.[48]

The CEBs (ecclesiastical base communities – from the Spanish *comunidades eclesiásticos-de base*) are probably the earliest and best known grassroots movements. They emerged in the mid-1960s, and grew in strength and number until their heyday in the early 1980s when it has been estimated that as many as three to four million people were active in many tens of thousands of such groups located in rural areas or on the outskirts of the region's larger urban centres.[49] They had their origins in pastoral work when priests and nuns began to break out of the traditional mould 'to go to the people'.[50] They divided parishes into local units and got to know the people through house visits, learning their vocabulary, views and popular culture. They organised discussion meetings in which the Bible served as a guide to re-interpret the experience of people's everyday lives and as a methodology for raising people's social and political consciousness. The emphasis was on dialogue; equally as much on the priests being 'evangelised' by the people as *vice versa*. Paulo Freire's early invention of this methodology of *Conscientization and Evangelization* took a full political turn in the liberation theology of Camilo Torres, Leonardo Boff and many other Church intellectual leaders who argued as a matter of theological principle that there could be no reform without taking power.[51]

The CEBs, however, were diverse: many remained devotional groups without overt political, let alone revolutionary aspirations. Others blended with, or inspired, urban dwellers' groups and neighbourhood associations with more modest social goals: housing, public transportation and other urban services, clean water, land, electricity, health and education. These urban movements sprang up precisely because the exclusionary politics of the military regimes, and of the structural adjustment democracies that followed, withdrew state-support and subsidies for such services. They combined self-help programmes with active campaigning at the local, municipal level. The tremendous growth of large cities in the region has given such movements an added political importance. It is estimated that the percentage of large-city inhabitants living in shanty towns varies from 30 per cent in Bogota to 70 per cent in Caracas.[52] Moreover, well over 70 per cent of the population of Latin America now lives in cities.

The movements have led to leftist coalitions taking power at municipal level in contrast to the rightist coalitions that rule the national state. In some countries, they have placed the effective decentralisation of the state on the agenda.[53] More importantly, some of the larger such movements have grown into financially viable and accountable non-governmental organisations (NGOs). Their financial backing from international NGOs,[54] (and – by a truly perverse twist – sometimes the World Bank itself[55]) have made it attractive for municipal governments, beset by austerity, to enter into 'negotiated interactions' and collaborative arrangements with such NGOs over the provision of services.[56] The consensual, participative or 'consociational' democracy[57] characteristic of the grassroots days has, however, many times been subverted through political clientelism, corruption and cooptation at the local level.

The women's movement in Latin America deserves a place all on its own in the annals of the resurrection of civil society. It is a unique collection of diverse groups with quite different goals. They came together during the years of struggle against the military and have continued to cooperate though less successfully since.[58] There were women's human-rights groups organised by the mothers and grandmothers of the 'disappeared';[59] and neighbourhood-based groups of poor women (housewives' committees)[60] who had to band together to ensure daily survival for their families. In coming together with feminist groups, often drawn from teacher and student movements, their political consciousness was raised in societies characterised by centuries of male domination and church-supported gender exclusion.

A final category of grassroots movements includes environmental groups, Indian-rights groups and native peasant movements. The coalition of such movements is especially interesting partly because they are of more recent origin, and they are therefore still on the ascendancy, and partly because it is these movements in particular which those who have tried to theorise a postmodern, postdevelopmental path seem to have in mind as examples.

Imagining Postdevelopment

Social movements have become a privileged arena for Latin American social enquiry today. The most comprehensive study of recent social movements is a ten-country study carried out by the Latin America Social Science Council under the general direction of Fernando Calderón.[61] The study examines the relationships between crisis, movements and democracy and explores to what extent they are 'constructing new social orders, propitiating new models of development and promising the emergence of new utopias'. It seeks in the movements 'evidence of a profound transformation of the social logic . . . a new form of doing politics and a new form of sociality . . . a new form of relating the political and the social, the public and the private'.[62]

Sadly, there is not much evidence of such profound transformation just yet. In his own survey of the Latin American social movements, Abby Peterson concludes that:

> at the end of the day, the social changes generated by the social movements are functional to the continued existence of present-day society – their explosive or transcendental power is nonexistent.[63]

But if Utopia has not yet arrived, there is no denying the intellectual enthusiasm for trying to imagine its birth in the spaces that have been vacated by the withdrawal of capitalism and modernity from much of the periphery. As Arturo Escobar puts it, in a riposte to Jürgen Habermas:

> In the Third World, modernity is not 'an unfinished project of Enlightenment'. Development is the last and failed attempt to complete the Enlightenment in Asia, Africa and Latin America.[64]

Many Latin American utopists stand in a postmodern tradition, using Foucauldian discourse analysis to 'deconstruct' all of the development discourse of the last four decades. They critique it as a system of knowledge produced by the First World about the 'underdevelopment' of the Third World, not only as an instrument of economic control and management, but also as a knowledge 'discipline' which marginalises and precludes other ways of seeing and doing. This deconstruction, or 'context smashing', as Roberto Unger[65] prefers to call it, is a necessary first task in order to free our imagination and make it ready for a 'reverse discourse'. It is a bit like paint-stripping walls before putting fresh paint on. It is also a task which many of these writers carry through with remarkable persuasion. I especially recommend Arturo Escobar's wonderful critique of developmentalism in *Encountering Development: the Making and Unmaking of the Third World*.

Escobar concludes that rather than searching for development alternatives, we need to speak of 'alternatives *to* development', that is a rejection of the entire paradigm. This radical move away from development and towards postdevelopment is seen as an historical possibility already underway in innovative grassroots movements and experiments.[66]

But what, exactly, is there to see? What *are* these alternatives? Anyone asking this question and reading this literature will be disappointed by the paucity of the examples. What utopian alternative is there in, say, the 'hybrid experience' of the popular resistance of the Kayapo Indians who use video cameras and planes to defend their culture and ancestral lands in the Brazilian rain forest?[67] Or in the inventive nature of 'coping strategies' in slums, or in the use of local native knowledge of healing practices, or the new political culture in which:

> identity construction is more flexible, modest and mobile, relying on tactical articulations arising out of the conditions and practices of daily life.[68]

But we are asking the wrong question. The future is not here yet and remains open-ended. The real strength in the postmodernist turn in Latin American development discourse is precisely that it wants it to remain so in order to give the social movements a chance to speak. Their advocacy of ethnographic methodology, and 'nomad' science is genuinely meant to be subservient to the marginalised and oppressed. Rather than summoning the power of a conceptual apparatus or a pre-established form of intervention nomad science stays close to the everyday life experiences of the people, seeking not to extract constants but to follow social life according to changing variables.[69]

As David Slater sagely comments, 'Perhaps, after all the words, all one can say is that the movements *are* there, and they *move*.'[70]

Conclusion

In this book I have tried to do two things. First, to navigate students of 'development' through today's currents of literature, and, second, to reorganise the field in a manner that I believe to be consistent with new emerging agendas reflecting a variety of development situations and options. What are these new agendas, situations and options?

Let us revisit the argument briefly.

In the first part of the book I have used Robert Cox's concept of Historical Structures to look back on the development of world capitalist relations between rich and poor countries, and the manner in which these relations have been understood and theorised in the past. For a long time, until about the 1970s, the material conditions and social forces of this relationship shaped a view of world order as one of a geographic core–periphery hierarchy, pyramidal in shape.

While radically opposed theories and ideologies argued over the rights or wrongs of this pyramid, projected diverging historical trajectories, and came up with different policy prescriptions, they still shared some fundamental premises. *First*, theirs was a universalist and inclusive credo: all human beings on the planet had a right to partake in the fruits of technological and economic advancement. *Second*, the world pyramid was envisaged as an overall structure of nation-states, and the state was accorded a central role as arbiter of human affairs and as agent of development. *Third*, world-wide social progress was assumed possible because the 'logic' of the capitalist system was thought to have an inherent drive to expansion and incorporation.

Globalisation (discussed in Part II) has rearranged the architecture of world order. Economic, social and power relations have been recast to resemble *not* a pyramid but a three-tier structure of concentric circles. All three circles cut across national and regional boundaries. In the core circle we find the élites of all continents and nations, albeit in different proportions in relation to their respective geographic hinterlands. We may count in this core some 20 per cent

239

of the world population who are 'bankable'. They are encircled by a fluid, larger social layer of between 20 and 30 per cent of the world population (workers and their families) who labour in insecure forms of employment, thrown into cut-thoat competition in the global market. State-of-the-art technology, frenzied capital mobility and neo-liberal policies together ensure both a relentless elimination of jobs by machines, and a driving down of wages and social conditions to the lowest global denominator.

On the first point, a UNDP report in 1993 projected the gap between world output and jobs to grow twice as fast in the 1990s as in the 1980s. On the second point, the distinguished historian Paul Kennedy recently has warned of the 'global gales ahead'.[1] Quoting research by Harvard Business School researchers, Jensen and Fagen, he argues that the move to market-oriented production in South America, Indonesia, India, parts of China and the rest of south east Asia which is taking place today, is likely to put 1.2 billion Third World workers into world-wide product and labour markets over the next generation. The vast majority of them earn less than \$3 per day. As a consequence, wages in the traditional advanced countries are set to fall by as much as 50 per cent. This is entirely consistent with our discussion of the global divison of labour in Chapter 7.

The third, and largest, concentric circle comprises those who are already effectively excluded from the global system. Performing neither a productive function, nor presenting a potential consumer market in the present stage of high-tech information-driven capitalism, there is, for the moment, neither theory, world view nor moral injunction, let alone a programme of action, to include them in universal progress. Developmentalism is dead, containment and exclusion rule OK!

In the third part of the book, I described a variety of situations and options that are present in different parts of the postcolonial world. I used the term 'postcolonial' to capture the notion that the distinct social formations which have emerged are a result of the way in which the aftermath of colonialism interacts with the forces of globalisation and responds to it. I identified four such postcolonial conditions or situations.

A first condition, that of 'exclusion and anarchy', is exemplified in subSaharan Africa, where all too frequently the patrimonial state form emerging after independence proved too weak to weld a viable political unity or civil society out of the mosaic of ethnic fragments bequeathed by colonial administrations. The failure to progress from a juridical state to an empirical state derailed the state-led developmental project. It made countries in Africa especially vulnerable to the deepening dependency characteristic of the neo-colonial period. Globalisation, including structural adjustments imposed since the 1980s, has overwhelmed the fragile social and political orders while further peripheralising their economies. The combined outcome of these external and internal forces manifests itself in a zone of civil collapse, anarchy and instability on the edge of the global system. And, while today there *are* forms of constructive contestations, for example in innovative coping strategies at the micro-level,[2] my own view is that these are not indicative of what is going to happen in the foreseeable future. Rather, *other* forms of contestations, frequently expressed in resource wars, fragmentation into warlordism, banditry and large-scale population displacements are more likely to characterise the region for some time to come. In emerging international practices of conditionality, aid and humanitarian relief, we discern policies of management and containment rather than of incorporation of the region in the global economy.

I sketched a second postcolonial condition in the anti-developmentalism of fundamental Islam. Here the failure of the developmentalist project, coupled with the exclusionary effect of contemporary processes of globalisation, has interacted with the spirit of renewal ever-present within Islam *and* with its long history of cultural confrontation with the West, to render a quite different social formation. It is one in which the politics of religious identity and lifestyle has gained pre-eminence in the private sphere without, however, yielding a political project to (re)create civil society and rearrange state–society relations. As long as the state élites continue to be co-opted into the global élite system there is neither much hope for constructive rebellion nor any threat to established geopolitical relations.

In East Asia, the state-led developmentalist project has succeeded in catapulting the economies of a small number of NICs into the heartland of the reconstructed global capitalist sytem. A unique postwar configuration of geostrategic forces has assisted the emergence of a state apparatus relatively autonomous from civil relations, and hence relatively free to steer an export-oriented path to industrialisation at a precise historical juncture when the world capitalist system of production underwent transformative change.

However, today the gales of globalisation threaten the drive to maturity of the developmentalist project (and the social emancipation of the masses) unless this drive becomes anchored in a regional division of labour. There are signs that a resurgent Asianisation may provide the glue to just such regionalisation.

We encountered a fourth and final postcolonial condition in Latin America. For reasons peculiar to its own colonial history, the continent has a long intellectual tradition of absorption, experimentation and revolt against western models of modernity and progress. This intellectual commitment has helped to politicise the process of impoverishment and exclusion as the counterpart of Latin America's dependent insertion in the world economy. In recent decades, as Latin America has become a testing ground for neo-liberal policies of globalisation and privatisation, democracy and the strengthening of civil society have become the arena for intellectual and political renewal.

Reconstructing Universalism, Regional Mercantilism or Postdevelopment?

What, finally, may we ask, are the options for the future? Can we construct a new political project of engagement in today's polarised world?

The circular structure of inclusion and exclusion of the new global order has given a devilish twist to the structure/agency dilemma which has always been at the heart of social theory. The twist is that while structural forces and hence structuralist theory and politics continue to imprison those in the inner circles of the global system, agency is thriving outside it, in the circle of exclusion. After all, multinationals *must* follow the logic of the market. Likewise, millions of well-meaning individuals with cash and sympathy to spare who turn their minds to, for example, 'ethical investments', find that their pockets, their mortgages and/or their pension funds, are dictated by economic interests that they cannot control and cannot disengage from. Even the leading Latin American *dependista* writer, Fernando Enrico Cardoso (who at one time wrote so persuasively about the 'passion for the possible'[3]) discovered that when he became President of Brazil, in 1994, market rationality overruled his commitment to social reform.

Where is human agency in all this? Forms of voluntary exclusion, such as the present wave of 'downshifting' taking hold of American middle classes, may be a subversive response, but it hardly amounts to a thought-through political project. On the other hand, socialist and social-democratic arguments for emancipation and universalist provision *perforce* do so on the basis of an a priori determining position of the economy. They take the formal market economy as a given, and they attempt to squeeze the excluded back into it. They start from the premise that it is possible to involve the whole population in 'economically viable' activity, preferably through investment in human capital, skilling ever more people to chase after dwindling numbers of global jobs. Such a political project implies a return to a Keynesian welfare state form that ignores the historical realities of globalisation. Alternatively, appeals from the internationalist left to transnational collective solidarity of anti-systemic movements rely, equally naively, on some magic wand that waves away the fragmentation of class, gender, ethnic and nationalist loyalties and single issue politics which constitute the very counterpart of globalisation.

Regional capitalist alliances, such as those emerging in East Asia, may extend the progressive drive to maturity and social emancipation of capitalist relations of production, but only if they are not overrun by the integrationist imperative of global capital. This, as I have argued elsewhere,[4] will only happen if the regionalisation impulses there are matched and strengthened by regional competitive bloc formations in other parts of the world. Such a neo-mercantilist scenario would see the world disintegrate into regional competitive blocs each with their own periphery. Trade wars could be expected to spill over into investment wars, while the existence of divisive and mutually-exclusive currency areas would rein-in the present untrammelled growth of speculative global finance.

The neo-mercantilist competitive agenda of each bloc would set up political pressures for a regaining of control by the public domain over regional markets and money flows and set up systemic pressures to re-absorb these flows back into production and trade within each of the respective regions including their peripheries. The advantage of such a scenario and political strategy would be that it buys time for the progressive promise of capitalism to be fulfilled. The downside is that such a political project is likely to feed the most destructive of inter-capitalist rivalries on a diet of nationalist and racist loyalties which the history of the twentieth century can hardly be expected to recommend.

All of the above political strategies remain entrapped in structuralist thinking, in so far as they take for granted the determining logic of market competition and capitalist accumulation. By contrast, as in Latin America, those intellectual activists engaged with the excluded sphere have the advantage of poststructuralist 'imagination'. They can play with the tasks of articulating alternative productive strategies and rationalities – autonomous, culturally grounded, democratic and ecologically friendly – without having to worry overmuch about overthrowing or taming the global capitalist system, for the capitalist system is not anywhere near where they are playing.

The only thing they have to worry about, but it is a serious worry, is in how far their efforts 'to stop being what we have not been, what we will never be, and what we do not have to be . . . namely (strictly) modern',[5] dovetails with the containment policies of the global capitalist system and leaves the excluded zone 'free' of undoubted advantages of technological and economic progress. The quip attributed to Fidel Castro many years ago, that there is only one thing worse than being exploited by the multinationals, namely *not* being exploited by the multinationals, is as true today as it was then.

Yet, I believe, there are merits in these postdevelopment experiments. First and foremost, they free up our imagination. They dare to experiment with community exchange systems, establishing working links between unmet wants and needs and unused resources. In the excluded zones we can think imaginatively about money and the function of money. An essential first step is to develop 'twin' or 'parallel' economies in which circulation money is divorced from interest-bearing money, and where the leakages between the formal and the informal economy are strictly controlled. Geoff Mulgan reminds us of the long, if largely forgotten, history of imaginative thinking about money, from Silvio Gesell in the 1930s to Claus Offe's work on alternative monies and Robin Murray's work on municipal money today. Keynes sagely predicted that the future will learn more from Gesell than from Marx.[6]

In the past, experiments with local monies, and with local efforts to revitalise local communities, came to naught because the national state, acting on behalf of national capitalist interests, suppressed them. Today the national state, being more interested in assisting the internationalisation of domestic capital, may be pressured to leave well alone. This offers a window of opportunity that coincides with the new division, described in Chapter 6, between real time (global) economic activities and material (local) economic activities. It is an opportunity that must not be missed!

Notes and References

Preface

1. Dudley Seers, 'Introduction', in D. Seers (ed.), *Dependency Theory, A Critical Assessment* (London: Francis Pinter, 1979).
2. Wolfgang Sachs, 'Development: A Guide to the Ruins', in *The New Internationalist*, June 1992, p. 5.
3. Already in 1991, the United Nations Development Programme (UNDP) estimated that about 100 million people in the rich industrialised countries and another 100 million living in the erstwhile socialist countries of Eastern Europe had joined the ranks of the poorest in the world. UNDP, *Human Development Report, 1991* (Oxford: Oxford University Press, 1991), pp. 23–6.
4. Cf. UNDP, *Human Development Report, 1992* (Oxford: Oxford University Press, 1992) p. 36.

Part 1 Introduction

1. B. Horvat, 'Political Economy', in *Encyclopaedia of the Social Sciences* (New York: Collier Macmillan, 1968) p. 611.
2. T. Mun, *Englands Treasure by Forraign Trade* (1664) (Oxford: reprinted for The Economic History Society by Basil Blackwell, 1928) p. 5.
3. I. Wallerstein, *The Capitalist World Economy* (Cambridge: Cambridge University Press, 1979).
4. A. Smith, *Wealth of Nations*, Book IV, quoted in B. Horvat (1968), *op. cit.*, p. 611.
5. A. Smith, *The Wealth of Nations* (New York: Random House, 1937) p. 423, quoted in T. Sowell, 'Adam Smith in Theory and Practice', in Gerald P. O'Driscoll, Jr. (ed.), *Adam Smith and Modern Political Economy: Bicentennial Essays on The Wealth of Nations* (Amnes, Iowa: Iowa State University Press, 1979).
6. On Marx's concept of mode of production and its historical evolution, see Hobsbawm's edition of Marx and Engels' *Pre-capitalist Economic Formations* (London: Lawrence & Wishart, 1964); see also Barry Hindess and Paul Q. Hirst, *Pre-capitalist Modes of Production* (London: Routledge & Kegan Paul, 1975) and Umberto Melotti, *Marx and the Third World* (London: Macmillan, 1977).
7. R. Gilpin, *The Political Economy of International Relations* (New Jersey: Princeton University Press, 1987) p. 15.

246

8. K. Waltz, *Man, the State and War* (New York: Columbia University Press, 1959) and *Theory of World Politics* (Reading, Mass.: Addison Wesley, 1979). Among the principal early prophets of these realist perspectives are H. Morgenthau, *Politics Among Nations* (New York: Knopf, 1948); K. Thompson, *Political Realism and the Crisis of World Politics* (Princeton, NJ: Princeton University Press, 1960); and E. H. Carr, *The Twenty-Years' Crisis, 1919–1939: An Introduction to the Study of International Relations* (London: Macmillan, 1939).
9. R. O. Keohane, *After Hegemony: Cooperation and Discord in the World Political Economy* (Princeeton, NJ: Princeton University Press, 1984).
10. S. Amin, *Class and Nation, Historically and in the Current Crisis* (New York: Monthly Review Press, 1980).
11. C. Chase-Dunn, *Global Formation, Structures of the World Economy* (Oxford: Basil Blackwell, 1989).
12. For a schematic comparison of the three conceptions of political economy, see Robert Gilpin, *US Power and the Multinational Corporation: The Political Economy of Foreign Direct Investment* (London: Macmillan, 1976) Table 6, p. 27.
13. See J. George and D. Cambell, 'Patterns of Dissent and the Celebration of Difference: Critical Social Theory and International Relations', *International Studies Quarterly*, 34 (1990) pp. 269–93.
14. For example, the relatively recent journal *Review of International Political Economy* claims to represent this 'new' international political economy; see the editors' statement, 1, issue 1.
15. In a seminal paper in 1981, Robert Cox set out the brush strokes of the new theory. The discussion that is presented here is based on this article: R. Cox, 'Social Forces, States and World Orders: Beyond International Relations Theory', *Millenium: Journal of International Studies*, 10 (2) (1981) pp. 126–55. See also his 'Multilateralism and World Order', *Review of International Studies*, 18 (1992) pp. 161–80, and his book *Production, Power and World Order: Social Forces in the Making of History* (New York: Columbia University Press, 1987).
16. A. Gramsci, *Selections from Prison Notebooks* (originally written 1929–1935) (London: Lawrence & Wishart, 1971).
17. R. Cox, *Social Forces*, see note 15, p. 135.
18. *Ibid.*, p. 135.

1 The History of Capitalist Expansion

1. S. Kuznets, 'Quantitative Aspects of the Economic Growth of Nations: X-levels and Structure of Foreign Trade: Long-term Trends', *Economic Development and Cultural Change*, 15 (2) Part II (January 1967) pp. 1–45.
2. In 1993. Source: Tables 5 and 6 in World Bank, *Global Economic Prospects and the Developing Countries* (Washington: World Bank, 1995).

3. I. Wallerstein, *The Capitalist-World Economy* (Cambridge: Cambridge University Press, 1979) p. 15.

4. I. Wallerstein, *ibid.* For an excellent discussion on Wallerstein's additions to Marx's model, see Christopher Chase-Dunn, *Global Formation, Structures of the World-Economy* (Oxford: Basil Blackwell, 1991) especially Part 1, Chapter 1.

5. S. Amin, *Imperialism and Unequal Exchange* (New York: Monthly Review Press, 1977).

6. A. G. Frank, *Dependent Accumulation and Underdevelopment* (New York: Monthly Review Press, 1979).

7. E. Mandel, *Late Capitalism* (London: New Left Books, 1976).

8. A. Szymanski, *The Logic of Imperialism* (New York: Praeger, 1981).

9. H. Magdoff, *Imperialism: From the Colonial Age to the Present* (New York: Monthly Review Press, 1978).

10. For a discussion of these periodisations, see C. Chase-Dunn, *op. cit.*, note 4, Chapter 3.

11. P. Baran, *The Political Economy of Growth* (New York: Monthly Review Press, 1967) (originally published in Spanish in 1957).

12. Cf. W. Rodney, *How Europe Underdeveloped Africa* (Dar es Salaam: Tanzania Publishing House; and London: Bogle L'Ouverture, 1972). See also my own book, A. M. M. Hoogvelt, *The Sociology of Developing Societies* (London: Macmillan, 1976) Chapter 4.

13. See A. M. M. Hoogvelt, *ibid.* Chapter 4 for a more extensive discussion.

14. H. Magdoff, *op. cit.*, note 9, p. 102.

15. H. Magdoff, *ibid.*, pp. 29–35.

16. See B. Thomas, 'The Historical Record of Capital Movements to 1913', in J. H. Adler (ed.), *Capital Movements and Economic Development* (London: Macmillan, 1967) pp. 3–32, reprinted in John H. Dunning, *International Investment* (Harmondsworth: Penguin Books, 1972) pp. 27–58.

17. A. K. Cairncross, *Home and Foreign Investment* (New York: Harvester Press, 1975) p. 3 – first published Cambridge University Press, 1957.

18. Quoted in A. P. Thornton, *The Imperial Idea and its Enemies* (London: Macmillan, 1985) p. 76.

19. Cf. H. Wesselinck, *Verdeel en Heers, De Deling van Afrika 1880–1914* (Amsterdam: Bert Bakker, 1991) opening citation.

20. B. Kidd, *The Control of the Tropics* (1989), quoted in A. P. Thornton, *Doctrines of Imperialism* (New York: John Wiley, 1965) p. 85.

21. A. P. Thornton, *The Imperial Idea and its Enemies*, *op. cit.*, note 18, p. 76.

22. See Fieldhouse on the difference and complementarity of peripheral or core explanations of colonial imperialism, in D. K. Fieldhouse, *Economics and Empire 1830–1914* (London: Macmillan, 1973) especially Chapter 4.

23. See V. I. Lenin, *Imperialism, the Highest Stage of Capitalism* (Moscow: Progress Publishers, 1978; first published 1916); N. Bukharin,

Imperialism and World Economy (New York: International Publishers, 1929; first published in 1917); and R. Hilferding, *Finance Capital, a Study in the Latest Phase of Capitalist Development* (London: Routledge & Kegan Paul, 1981; first published in 1910).

24. J. A. Hobson, *Imperialism, a Study* (London: Unwin Hyman, 1988 3rd edn; first published in 1905).

25. 'Necessity' as being a necessary policy of finance capital, not, however, in the sense of 'not being able to be overcome'. Bukharin condemned this meaning of 'necessity' as a limit to action, as semi-imperialism. Imperialism was the policy of finance capitalism which was itself a highly-developed capitalism implying the ripeness of the objective conditions for a new socio-economic form. And although finance capital cannot pursue any other policy (this is the meaning of necessity) it is not necessary in terms of not being able to overcome it. Bukharin, *op. cit.*, note 23, pp. 141–3.

26. N. Bukharin, *ibid.*, p. 28.

27. V. G. Kiernan, *Marxism and Imperialism* (London: Edward Arnold, 1974).

28. Fieldhouse, *Economics and Empire, op. cit.*, note 22, p. 66.

29. For example France after the the Franco-Prussian war – see H. Daalder, 'Imperialism' in *Encyclopedia of the Social Sciences* (New York: Collier Macmillan, 1968).

30. *Ibid.*, pp. 103–4.

31. For a critique of the alleged refutations of economic theories of imperialism, see P. Baran and P. M. Sweezy, 'Notes on the Theory of Imperialism', *Monthly Review*, 17 (March 1966) pp. 15–31. The authors argue that there is a fatal methodological error in comparing costs and rewards for nations as a whole, because the relevant actors on the imperalist stage are classes and their subdivisions down to and including their individual members.

32. B. Warren, *Imperialism, Pioneer of Capitalism* (London: Verso, 1980).

33. J. A. Schumpeter, *Imperialism and Social Classes* (New York: Kelley, 1951).

34. B. Warren, *op. cit.*, note 32, p. 65. Note, however, Anthony Brewer's observation that this line of criticism in part owes to a semantic confusion caused by different uses of the term 'imperialism'. For Lenin in particular, imperialism did not specifically refer to the possession of colonies. He explicitly recognised that earlier stages of capitalism also involved colonial expansion – just as he recognized that the 'semi-colonies' of S. America were really victims of imperialist control and domination. cf A. Brewer, *Marxist Theories of Imperialism* (London: Routledge & Kegan Paul, 1980) p. 117.

35. A. Lipietz, 'New Tendencies in the International Division of Labour: Regimes of Accumulation and Modes of Regulation', in A. Scott, M. Storpor and contributors, *Production, Work, Territory: The Geographical Anatomy of Industrial Capitalism* (Winchester, Mass.: Unwin Hyman, 1988) p. 21.

2 Neo-colonialism, Modernisation and Dependency

1. J. O'Connor, 'The Meaning of Economic Imperialism', in R. Rhodes, *Imperialism and Underdevelopment* (New York: Monthly Review Press, 1970). See especially p. 117, which lists the chief manifestations of neo-colonialism as identified by the African leaders at the conference.

2. For confirmation of both the long-term downward trend, and the fluctuations, of all non-oil commodity prices since 1950, see World Bank, *World Development Report* (Oxford: Oxford University Press, 1987) Figure 2.3, p. 17, and the Appendix on the terms of trade, p. 176.

3. Ernest Mandel first coined this term. He defined 'technological' rents as 'surplus profits derived from the monopolization of technical progress, from discoveries and inventions which lower the cost price of commodities but cannot (at least in the medium run) become generalised throughout a given branch of production and applied by all competitors, because of the structure of monopoly capital itself: difficulties of entry, size of minimum investment, control of patents, cartel arrangements and so on'. cf E. Mandel, *Late Capitalism* (London: New Left Books, 1978) p. 192.

4. P. Worseley, *The Third World* (London: Weidenfeld & Nicolson, 1964) p. 52.

5. F. Fanon, *The Wretched of the Earth* (Harmondsworth: Penguin, 1963) Chapter 3.

6. N. Chomsky, 'Foreword' to Y. Fitt, A. Faire and J.P. Vigier, *The World Economic Crisis* (London: Zed Press, 1972) p. 4.

7. Quoted in Jenny Pearce, *Under the Eagle: US Intervention in Central America and the Caribbean* (London: Latin America Bureau, 1981) p. 27.

8. D. Harrison, *The Sociology of Modernization and Development* (London: Unwin Hyman, 1988).

9. Cf. W.W. Rostow, *The Stages of Economic Growth* – somewhat superfluously subtitled 'A non-Communist Manifesto' (Cambridge: Cambridge University Press, 1960). This work has no doubt been the most influential. Other important economists who have brought in social and even psychological variables into their economic development theories were: A. Lewis, *The Theory of Economic Growth* (London: Allen & Unwin, 1955), and E. E. Hagen, *On the Theory of Social Change* (Homewood, Ill: Dorsey, 1962). By far the most comprehensive of all these approaches was Gunnar Myrdal *et al.*, *Asian Drama*, Vols I–III (New York: Pantheon, 1968).

10. See, N. J. Smelser, 'Towards a Theory of Modernization', in A. Etzioni and E. Etzioni, *Social Change* (New York: Basic Books, 1964) pp. 258–74. This is probably the most widely quoted theoretical text on modernisation. Another early work of great influence was B. F. Hoselitz and W. E. Moore (eds), *Industrialisation and Society* (The Hague: Mouton, 1963). For an extensive discussion on modernisation theories, see A. M. M. Hoogvelt, *The Sociology of Developing Societies* (London: Macmillan, 1976) Chapter 3.

11. For an excellent discussion on the historical specificity of the idea of development as a form of western imposed administrative reform of the Third World, see P. W. Preston, *Theories of Development* (London: Routledge, 1982) Chapter 2 (the idea of development).

12. L. Trotsky, *The Permanent Revolution* (1928) (New York: Merit Publishers, 1969). See also M Lowy, *The Politics of Combined and Uneven Development* (London: Verso, 1981) Chapter 2.

13. P. Baran, *The Political Economy of Growth* (New York: Monthly Review Press, 1967) (first published in Spanish in 1957).

14. A. G. Frank, *Capitalism and Underdevelopment in Latin America* (New York: Monthly Review Press, 1967).

15. T. dos Santos, 'The Structure of Dependence', in C. K. Wilber (ed.), *The Political Economy of Development and Underdevelopment* (New York: Random House, 1970).

16. L. Pearson *et al.*, *Partners in Development* (London: Pall Mall, 1970) p. 81.

17. R. Jenkins, *Exploitation* (London: Paladin, 1971).

18. For a further discussion, see Chapter 11 of this book.

19. For a discussion on autocentric versus peripheral development, see S. Amin, *Unequal Development* (New York: Monthly Review Press, 1976).

20. R. Prebisch, *The Economic Development of Latin America and the Principal Problems* (New York: UN Economic Commission for Latin America, 1950); and H. Singer, 'The Distribution of Gains between Investing and Borrowing Countries', *American Economic Review*, Supplement, May 1950.

21. A. Emmanuel, *Unequal Exchange. A Study of the Imperialism of Trade* (London: New Left Books, 1971).

22. For an extensive discussion on the programmatic achievements of the Third World in putting its case on the agenda of the international community see A. M. M. Hoogvelt, *The Third World in Global Development* (London: Macmillan, 1982) Chapter 2. See also P. Willets, *The Non-aligned Movement: The Origins of a Third World Alliance* (London: Frances Pinter, 1978); and M. Ul Haq, 'Intellectual Self-Reliance', opening speech at the establishment of Third World Forum, January 1975 at Karachi; printed in *International Development Review*, no. 1 (1975) pp. 8–13. About 100 leading Third World scholars and officials of international organisations attended this conference.

3 Crisis and Restructuring: The New International Divisional of Labour

1. Cf. S. Amin, *The Law of Value and Historical Materialism* (New York: Monthly Review Press, 1978) Chapter 6.

2. D. Becker, 'Development, Democracy and Dependency in Latin America: A Postimperialist View', *Third World Quarterly*, 6 (2) (April 1984) pp. 411–31.

3. S. Amin, 'Towards a New Structural Crisis of the Capitalist System'; paper submitted to the Third World Forum at its meeting in Karachi,

Pakistan 5–10 January 1975; and *The Law of Value and Historical Materialism, op. cit.*, note 1.

4. We will return to the definition and the description of 'Fordism' extensively in Chapter 5.

5. D. Harvey, *The Condition of Postmodernity* (Oxford: Basil Blackwell, 1989) p. 135.

6. Cf. A. Lipietz, 'How Monetarism has Choked Third World Industrialization', *New Left Review*, no. 145 (1984) pp. 71–88, 73.

7. UNCTAD, *Trade and Development Report* (1981) p. 102.

8. P. R. Odell, *Oil and World Power* (Harmondsworth: Penguin, 1983, 7th edition) Figure on p. 138.

9. For a discussion of the relative price movements between primary products and manufactures over the colonial and neo-colonial periods, see M. Barratt Brown, *The Economics of Imperialism* (Harmondsworth: Penguin, 1974) Chapter 10.

10. On the concept of social wage, I. Gough, *The Political Economy of the Welfare State* (London: Macmillan, 1979) pp. 108ff and Appendix D. On the link between the social wage and imperialist profits, see R. Sutcliffe, *Hard Times* (London: Pluto Press, 1983).

11. An oft-quoted study by Vaitsos in 1970 propelled 'technological rents' to the forefront of the dependency debate. Vaitsos discovered that in the pharmaceutical industry in Colombia, for example, as little as 3.4 per cent of effective returns to the parent company consisted of 'declared' profits. Another 14 per cent was accounted for by royalty payments, while 82.6 per cent was contributed by the parent company's overpricing of its sales to the affiliates. cf. C. V. Vaitsos, 'Bargaining and the Distribution of Returns in the Purchase of Technology by Developing Countries', *Bulletin of the Institute of Development Studies*, 3 (1) (1970) pp. 16–23.

12. S. Amin, *The Law of Value and Historical Materialism, op. cit.*, note 1, p. 77.

13. See for example the argument developed by J. Toye in 'Development Policy in the Shadow of Keynes,' Chapter 2 of his book *Dilemmas of Development* (Oxford: Basil Blackwell, 1987).

14. This calculation is based on the statistical tables in Annexes of the 1970 and 1982 issues of *Development Cooperation: Review of the OECD Development Assistance Committee* (Paris: OECD, 1970 and 1982).

15. S. George, *A Fate Worse than Debt* (Harmondsworth: Penguin, 1988) especially Chapter 1.

16. The term 'world market factory' was first coined by F. Fröbel, J. Heinrich and O. Kreye, *The New International Division of Labour* (Cambridge: Cambridge University Press, 1980) p. 6.

17. P. Jalée, *Imperialism in the Seventies* (New York: The Third Press, 1972), p. 83.

18. See G. Arrighi, 'A Crisis of Hegemony', in S. Amin, G. Arrighi, A. G. Frank and I. Wallerstein, *Dynamics of Global Crisis* (New York: Monthly Review Press, 1982) pp. 55–108.

19. F. Halliday, *Cold War, Third World* (London: Hutchinson Radius, 1989) p. 33.

20. P. Evans, 'Transnational Linkages and the Economic Role of the State: An Analysis of Developing and Industrialised Nations in the Post-World War II Period', in P. Evans and D. Rueschemeyer *et al.*, *Bringing the State Back In* (Cambridge, Mass.: Cambridge University Press, 1985).

21. A good example is the regional volumes of the 'Sociology of Developing Societies' series, edited by T. Shanin, published by Macmillan and Monthly Review Press in various years in the 1980s.

22. A pathbreaking essay on the new approaches to development theory in this period was D. Booth, 'Marxism and Development Sociology: Interpreting the Impasse', *World Development* 13 (7) (1985). See also his contribution to F. J. Schuurman (ed.), *Beyond the Impasse, New Directions in Development Theory* (London: Zed Books, 1993).

23. For examples of this bottom-up 'empowerment approach', see R. Chalmers, *Rural Development, Putting the Last First* (London: Longman, 1983); and P. Oakley and D. Marsden, *Approaches to Participation in Rural Development* (Geneva: ILO, 1984).

24. E. Boserup is widely credited with having been the first writer to systematically explore the role of women in economic development. While her work was a *tour de force* in its novelty, it was theoretically underdeveloped. Nevertheless, it alerted donor agencies to the exclusion of women from the benefits of progress and is said to have inspired the UN Decade for Women that was to follow. E. Boserup, *Woman's Role in Economic Development* (London: Earthscan, 1970).

25. M. Mies, *Patriarchy and Accumulation on a World Scale, Women in the International Division of Labour* (London: Zed Books, 1986) pp. 122ff. See also B. Mass, *The Political Economy of Population Control in Latin America* (Montreal: Women's Press, 1975); and N. Kardam, 'Bringing Women In' in *Women's Issues in International Development Programs* (Boulder: Lynne Rienner Publishers, 1991). While most literature is confident about the 'double' burden of women in the Third World, the concept of 'triple' exploitation has been developed by D. Gills in 'The Forgotten Workers: Rural Women in Korean Development' (Sheffield: University of Sheffield PhD thesis, 1994).

26. M. Mies, *Patriarchy and Accumulation on a World Scale, Women in the International Division of Labour* (London: Zed Books, 1986); see also V. Bennholdt-Thompson, 'Investment in the Poor: Analysis of World Bank Policy', *Social Scientist*, 8 (7) (February 1980, Part I), and 8(8) (March 1980, Part II); C. von Werlhof, 'The Proletarian is Dead. Long Live the Housewife?' in I. Wallerstein *et al.* (eds), *Households and the World Economy* (New York: Sage, 1984); and K. Young *et al.* (eds), *Of Marriage and the Market: Women's Subordination in International Perspective*, 2nd edn (London: Routledge, 1984).

27. M. Mies, *op. cit.*, note 25, p. 127.

28. For a good coverage of the issue of women versus gender in development, see G. Waylen, *Gender in Third World Politics* (Buckingham:

Open University Press, 1996); a good introduction is also R. Pearson, 'Gender Matters in Development', in T. Allen and A. Thomas (eds), *Poverty and Development in the 1990s* (Oxford: Oxford University Press and Open University Press, 1990).

29. M. Mitra, 'Women in Dairying in Andhra Pradesh', term paper, mimeo, Institute of Social Studies, The Hague, 1984, cited in Mies, *op. cit.*, note 25, p. 131.

30. C. Mohanty, Introduction, in C. Mohanty, A. Russo and L. Torres (eds), *Third World Women and The Politics of Feminism* (Bloomington and Indianapolis: Indiana University Press, 1991) p. 11.

31. J. H. Momsen and J. Townsend, *Geography of Gender in the Third World* (New York: SUNY Press, 1987).

32. C. Mohanty, 'Under Western Eyes', in C. Mohanty, A. Russo and L. Torres (eds), *op. cit.*, note 30, pp. 51–80.

33. A. Ong, 'Colonialism and Modernity: Feminist Re-presentations of Women in Non-western Societies', *Inscriptions*, 3–4 (1988) pp. 79–93; cited in J. Townsend, 'Gender Studies: Whose Agenda?', in F. Schuurman (ed.), *Beyond the Impasse, New Directions in Development Theory* (London: Zed Books, 1993) pp. 169–86, 183.

34. The Brazilian sociologist and politician (today President of Brazil) Fernando Henrique Cardoso was one of the key contributors to the 'dependency associated development' vision. See F. H. Cardoso, 'Associated-dependent Development: Theoretical and Practical Implication', in A. Stepan (ed.), *Authoritarian Brazil: Origins, Policies, and Future* (New Haven: Yale University Press, 1973). Together with Enzo Faletto he wrote the classic text *Dependency and Development in Latin America* (Berkeley: University of California Press, 1979; translation, with new introduction and post-scriptum of their orginal Spanish volume published in 1969).

35. D. Becker (1984) *op. cit.*, note 2.

36. I. Wallerstein, *The Capitalist World Economy* (Cambridge: Cambridge University Press, 1980) p. 5.

37. This section is a summary of Wallerstein's arguments in Chapters 4 and 5 of *The Capitalist World Economy, ibid.*

Part II   Introduction

1. A. M. M. Hoogvelt, *The Third World in Global Development* (London: Macmillan, 1982) p. 208.

2. R. Cox, 'Social Forces, States and World Orders: Beyond International Relations Theory', *Millenium: Journal of International Studies*, 10 (2) (1981) pp. 126–55.

3. Cf. B. Warren, *Imperialism, Pioneer of Capitalism*, (London: New Left Books, 1980); and F. H. Cardoso and E. Faletto, *Dependency and Development in Latin America* (Berkeley: University of California Press, 1979), especially the preface to the American edition.

4. See for an example of the re-statement of this view, even after the collapse of the socialist experience, S. Amin, 'The Future of Socialism', in *Monthly Review*, July–August 1990, and also S. Amin, G. Arrighi, A. G. Frank and I. Wallerstein, *Transforming the Revolution, Social Movements and the World System* (New York: Monthly Review Press, 1990).

5. For a repeat of this ingrained view, see S. Amin, G. Arrighi, A. G. Frank and I. Wallerstein, *Transforming the Revolution* (New York: Monthly Review Press, 1990).

6. P. Sweezy, 'Globalisation – To What End?', *Monthly Review*, 42 (9) (February 1992) p. 1.

7. R. Boyer, 'Technical Change and the Theory of "Regulation"', in G. Dosi and C. Freeman *et al.*, (eds), *Technical Change and Economic Theory* (London: Pinter Publishers, 1988).

4 From Expansion to Implosion

1. I am indebted to my PhD student Mrs Rongyan Qi for helping with the tables in this chapter.

2. P. Dicken, *Global Shift, The Internationalisation of Economic Activity* (London: Paul Chapman, 1992) p. 16.

3. S. Kuznets, 'Quantitative Aspects of the Economic Growth of Nations: X-level and Structure of Foreign Trade: Long-Term Trends', *Economic Development and Cultural Change*, 15 (2), Part II (Jan 1967).

4. S. Kuznets, *ibid.*, pp. 7–8.

5. S. Kuznets, *ibid.*, p. 10.

6. In 1988, see The Economist Intelligence Unit, *China, Japan & the NICs* (London: December, 1989) p. 7 and table on p. 199. The figure of 5.7 per cent of world trade, or 25 per cent of developing country trade, is arrived at after stripping out the re-exports of Hong Kong and Singapore.

7. S. Kuznets, *op. cit.*, note 3, p. 28.

8. Note that the reference to 'all other areas' in the narrative and in the accompanying Table 4.4 embraces Eastern Europe and the Soviet Union.

9. Note that Paul Hirst and Grahame Thompson in their book *Globalization in Question* (London: Polity Press, 1995) come to the same conclusion. Using gross figures of ratios of trade relative to output 'confirms unequivocally that "openness" was greater during the Gold Standard period than even in 1980s', p. 28.

10. UNCTC, *Transnational Corporations in World Development, Trends and Prospects* (New York: UN, 1988) p. 16.

11. C. Tugendhat, *The Multinationals* (London: Eyre & Spottiswoode, 1971) p. 24.

12. UNECOSOC, *Multinational Corporations in World Development* (New York: UN, 1973) pp. 13–14.

13. For a discussion of the methodology used, see the footnote on p. 135 of the sequel to the report, *Transnational Corporations in World Development, a Re-Examination* (New York: UN, 1978).

14. UN Department of Economic and Social Affairs, *Economic Report 1947* (Lake Erie, NJ: United Nations, 1948).

15. J. H. Dunning, *Studies in International Investment* (London: Allen & Unwin, 1970) cf. p. 23 and p. 19 respectively. See also, *The Problem of International Investments, A Report by the Study Group of members of the Royal Institute of International Affairs* (Oxford: Oxford University Press, 1947).

16. For the 1960 figure, see M. Barratt Brown, *The Economics of Imperialism* (London: Penguin, 1974) pp. 206–7. For 1966, see L. B. Pearson, *Partners in Development* (London: Pall Mall Press, 1970) p. 100. For 1974, see *Transnational Corporations in World Development* (note 13), Table III, p. 242. For 1989 see UNCTC, *World Investment Report* (New York: UN, 1991) Table 4, p. 11.

17. See UNCTC, *World Investment Report* (1991) *ibid.*, Table 4, p. 11.

18. P. Hirst and G. Thompson, *Globalization in Question, op. cit.*, note 9, p. 68.

19. *Ibid.*, p. 68.

20. B. Thomas, 'The Historical Record of Capital Movements to 1913', in J. H. Adler (ed.), *Capital Movements and Economic Development* (London: Macmillan, 1967) pp. 3–32, reprinted in J. H. Dunning, *International Investment* (Harmondsworth: Penguin, 1972) pp. 27–58, Table I, p. 34.

21. C. Crook, 'Fear of Finance', *The Economist*, 19 September 1992.

22. Crook reports on the central-bank estimate that in April 1989 turnover in the foreign exchange markets (which included the derivative markets) stood at roughly $900 billion each day. *Ibid.*, p. 9.

23. UNCTC, *World Investment Report* (New York: UN, 1994) p. 129.

24. International Monetary Fund, *Determinants and Systematic Consequences of International Capital Flows*, IMF Occasional paper 7, 1991, p. 7.

25. UNCTAD, *Trade and Development Report*, 1990, p. 110.

26. F. F. Clairmont, *The Rise and Fall of Economic Liberalism* (Penang: Southbound/Third World Network, 1996).

27. On the orthodox economics distinction between 'real' and 'monetary' economy, see H. Magdoff and P. M. Sweezy, 'Production and Finance', *Monthly Review*, May 1983, reprinted in H. Magdoff and P. M. Sweezy, *Stagnation and the Financial Explosion* (New York: Monthly Review Press, 1987) pp. 93–105. See also S. Strange, *Casino Capitalism* (Oxford: Basil Blackwell, 1986) p. 118, where she says the consequences for the real economy, for production, trade and employment can 'only be guessed at'.

28. P. Volcker, Chairman of the US Federal Reserve Board during much of the 1980s, is quoted in an interview with Anthony Sampson as saying: 'it seems to be easier to make money in some sense, with paper chasing paper, than in investing in real goods and services. If you're

doing some research and the pay-off is coming in fifteen years or twenty years at today's interest rates, it's hard to envisage a big enough pay-out to justify the investment that you make today', quoted in A. Sampson, *The Midas Touch: Money, People and Power from West to East* (London: Hodder & Stoughton, 1989) p. 13.

29. For a simple explanation of securitisation, see A. Hamilton, *The Financial Revolution* (Harmondsworth: Penguin, 1986) especially pp. 71–2. See also Barclays Bank, *Briefing* (January 1992), number 87, and *The Economist*, 'Corporate Finance' (June 1986) pp. 7–13.

30. Longmans, *Dictionary of English*.

31. *The Economist*, 'Corporate Finance', Survey 7 June 1986 p. 23.

32. *The Economist*, 19 September 1992, p. 30.

33. Quoted in A. Sampson, *The Midas Touch, op. cit.*, note 28, p. 179.

34. A. Sampson, *ibid.*, p. 179.

35. UNCTAD, *Trade and Development Report* (1989) p. 35 Table 17.

36. Cited in IMF occasional paper 7, *Determinants and Systemic Consequences of International Capital Flows* (March 1991) p. 11.

37. UNDP, *Human Development Report 1992* (Oxford: Oxford University Press, 1992) p. 36. Note that the UNDP in this report includes the countries of eastern Europe and the Soviet Union in the industrialised group. For confirmation of the widening gap in incomes between the traditional core and periphery countries, see also: P. Sweezy, 'Globalisation to What End', Part II, *Monthly Review*, 43 (10) (March 1992), Table IX, p. 10; and G. Arrighi, 'World Income Inequalities and the Future of Socialism', *New Left Review*, no. 189 (1991).

38. P. Bairoch, *The Economic Development of the Third World since 1900* (London: Methuen, 1975), p. 193.

39. UNDP, *Human Development Report 1991* (Oxford: Oxford University Press, 1991) p. 23.

40. UNDP, *Human Development Report 1992* (Oxford: Oxford University Press, 1992), p. 35.

41. An econometric study by Frank R. Gunther of Lehigh University in Bethlehem, Pennsylvania, which was carried out with support from both the UN and China's Ministry of Foreign Relations, estimates capital flight from China in the year 1990 at between US$ 15–25 billion, rising to between US$ 13–28 billion in 1991 and further still in 1992: reported in *Far Eastern Economic Review*, 15 July 1993, p. 73. This level of outflows exceeds the level of inflows into China. *Time Magazine* (12 July 1993) reports sums of similar magnitude fleeing to Hong Kong, and adds that at least half of these flows are capital flows that the Beijing Government cannot account for.

42. B. Riley, 'Funds Pour into New Growth Regions', *The Economist*, 7 February 1994.

43. Cf. B. Riley, *The Economist, ibid.*, and 'Africa: a Flicker of Light', *The Economist*, 5 March 1994.

44. J. P. Womack, D. T. Jones and D. Roose, *The Machine that Changed the World* (New York: Harper Perennial, 1990) p. 13.

45. M. Castells, 'The Informational Economy and the New International Division of Labor', in M. Carnoy, M. Castells, S. S. Cohen and F. H. Cardoso, *The New Global Economy in the Information Age* (New York: The Pennsylvania State University Press and London: Macmillan Press, 1993) p. 37.

5   From Fordist to Flexible Production

1.   K. Mannheim, *Man and Society in an Age of Reconstruction* (London: Routledge & Kegan Paul, 1940) p. 174 (first published in German in 1935).
2.   J. P. Womack, D. T. Jones and D. Roos, *The Machine that Changed the World* (New York: Rawson Associates, 1990) p. 27.
3.   J. P. Womack *et al.*, *ibid.*, p. 37 and p. 23.
4.   D. Harvey, *The Condition of Postmodernity* (Oxford: Basil Blackwell, 1989) p. 142.
5.   See D. Harvey, *The Condition of Postmodernity*, *ibid.* The summary of 'Fordism' in this chapter owes much to Harvey's excellent discussion in Chapter 9 of his book.
6.   For a discussion of these concepts and the role of technical change in economic theory, see G. Dosi *et al.*, *Technical Change and Economic Theory* (London & New York: Pinter, 1988) especially the contribution by C. Freeman and C. Perez, 'Structural Crises of Adjustment, Business Cycles and Investment Behaviour', pp. 38–66.
7.   C. Freeman, Preface to Part II of G. Dosi *et al.*, *ibid.*, p. 10.
8.   K. Dohse *et al.*, 'From "Fordism" to "Toyotism"? The Social Organisation of the Labour Process in the Japanese Automobile Industry', *Politics and Society*, 14 (2) (1985) pp. 115–46.
9.   A. Toffler, *Powershift, Knowledge, Wealth and Violence at the Edge of the 21st Century* (New York: Bantam Books, 1992) p. 102 and p. 239.
10. J. P. Womack *et al.*, *op. cit.*, note 2, p. 62. Note Womack *et al.*'s use of the word 'machine' here. Quite a mistaken analogy.
11. W. C. Kester, *Japanese Takeovers, the Global Contest for Corporate Control* (Boston, Mass.: Harvard Business School Press, 1991) especially Chapter 3, 'Japanese Corporate Governance'.
12. Note, however, the discussion by other writers on the subject of Japanese assembler–supplier relationships in the automobile industry. Womack *et al.* seem to describe a rather stylised picture of market price minus system. See for example B. Asanuma, 'The Organization of Parts Purchases in the Japanese Automotive Industry', in *Japanese Economic Studies* (Summer 1985) pp. 32–53.
13. A good example of such advocacy is J. MacDonald and J. Piggot, *Global Quality, The New Management Culture* (London: Mercury, 1990).
14. Cf. C. Lorenz, 'Power to the People', *Financial Times*, 30 March 1992; T. Stewart, 'A User's Guide to Power', *Fortune*, Spring 1991; A. Toffler, *Power Shift*, *op. cit.*, note 9, p. 210.

15. For an example of such a critique, see R. Delbridge, P. Thurnbull and B. Wilkinson, 'Pushing Back the Frontiers: Management Control and Work Intensification under JIT/TQM Factory Regimes', *New Technology, Work and Employment* (Autumn 1992) pp. 97–107.

16. For a discussion and critique, see P. N. Dale, *The Myth of Japanese Uniqueness* (London: Routledge, 1988) pp. 105–6; see also K. van Wolferen, *The Enigma of Japanese Power, People and Politics in a Stateless Nation* (New York: Vintage Books, 1990) pp. 165–7.

17. For a deeper analysis of cultural and psychological factors in Japanese industrial organisation, see A. Hoogvelt and M. Yuasa, 'Going Lean or Going Native? The Social Regulation of "Lean" Production Systems', *Review of International Political Economy* 1(2) (1994) pp. 281–303.

18. UNCTC, *Transnational Corporations*, fourth report, 'Trends and Prospects' (New York: UN, 1988) p. 42.

19. My discussion on the emulation of Japanese practices in Britain owes much to the thorough PhD thesis of one of my PhD students, Masae Yuasa, 'Autonomy or Dependency? The Reality and Discourse of Social Relations of Japanese Production Systems in UK Manufacturing Industry during the 1980s' (University of Sheffield, January 1995).

20. UNCTC, *op. cit.*, note 18, p. 42.

21. J. Tidd, *Flexible Manufacturing Technologies and International Competitiveness* (London: Pinter, 1991).

22. J. Tidd, *ibid.*, p. 92.

23. *Ibid.*, p. 96.

24. N. Oliver and B. Wilkinson, *The Japanization of British Industry, New Developments in the 1990s* (Oxford: Blackwells, 1992).

25. Commision of the European Communities, Directorate General Science, Research and Development, *What are Anthropocentric Production Systems? Why are they a Strategic Issue for Europe?* (Brussels: Report EUR 13968 EN), 1992.

26. *Ibid.*, p. 3.

27. *Ibid.*, p. 2.

28. Labour Research Department, *Human Resource Management Survey, Bargaining Report* (London: February 1995).

29. T. Elger and C. Smith (eds), *Global Japanization: The Transnational Transformation of the Labour Process* (London: Routledge, 1994) p. 32.

30. For a *concise* summary of the Regulation School's main conceptual apparatus, see R. Boyer, 'Technical Change and the Theory of "Regulation"', in G. Dosi *et al.* (eds), *Technical Change and Economic Theory* (London & New York: Pinter, 1988). For a *comprehensive* review of the diverse approaches loosely federated under the label Regulation School, see R. Jessop, 'Regulation Theories in Retrospect and Prospect', *Economy and Society*, 19 (2) (May 1990) pp. 153–216. For a *critical* review of regulation theories in comparison with other contemporary crisis and transformation theories, see P. Hirst and J. Zeitlin, 'Flexible Specialization versus post-Fordism: Theory, Evidence and Policy Implications', *Economy and Society*, 20 (1) (February 1991)

pp. 1–55. Finally, a thorough *critique* of the substantive theses of the Regulation School has been written by R. Brenner and M. Glick, 'The Regulation Approach: Theory and History', *New Left Review*, 188, pp. 45–99.

31. A. Lipietz, 'New Tendencies in the International Division of Labor: Regimes of Accumulation and Modes of Regulation', in A. Scott and M. Storper *et al.*, *Production, Work, Territory* (London: Allen & Unwin, 1986) pp. 16–39, p. 19.

32. P. Hirst and J. Zeitlin, *op. cit.*, note 30, p. 3.

33. M. Aglietta, *A Theory of Capitalist Regulation: The US Experience* (London: Verso, 1979); and A. Lipietz, *Mirages and Miracles* (London: Verso, 1987).

34. M. Aglietta, *ibid.*, p. 32.

35. For a very informative array of case studies of these new flexible systems across the western world, see T. Elger and C. Smith, *Global Japanization?, op. cit.*, note 29 (1995).

36. S. Gill, 'Theorizing the Interregnum: The Double Movement and Global Politics in the 1990s', in R. Cox *et al.*, *The International Political Economy of the Future* (London: Zed Press, 1995) pp. 51–77.

37. K. Ohmae, *Triad Power, the Coming Shape of Global Competition* (New York: The Free Press and Collier Macmillan, 1985) pp. xvi–xvii.

38. J. P. Womack *et al.*, *op. cit.*, note 2, pp. 218–22.

39. M. Hergert and D. Morris, 'Trends in International Collaborative Agreements', in F. Contractor and P. Lorange (eds), *Cooperative Strategies in International Business* (Lexington, Mass.: Lexington Books, 1988) pp. 99–110. Cited in P. Lorange and J. Roos, *Strategic Alliances, Formation, Implementation, and Evolution* (Oxford: Blackwell, 1992), pp. 13–14.

40. C. Freidheim, 'The Global Corporations – Obsolete so Soon?', quoted in *The Economist*, 'The Global firm R.I.P.', 6 February 1993.

41. R. Jaikumar and D. M. Upton, 'The Coordination of Global Manufacturing', in S. P. Bradley, J. A. Hausman, and R. L. Nolan (eds), *Globalization, Technology, Competition: The Fusion of Computers and Telecommunications in the 1990s* (Boston, Mass.: Harvard Business School, 1994) pp. 169–84.

42. M. J. Piore and C. F. Sabel, *The Second Industrial Divide* (New York: Basic Books, 1984).

43. P. Hirst and J. Zeitlin, 'Flexible Specialisation versus post-Fordism: Theory, Evidence and Policy Implications', *Economy and Society*, 20, no. 1 (February 1991) pp. 1–55.

44. See, for example, B. Jessop, 'Regulation Theories in Retrospect and Prospect', *Economy and Society*, 19, no. 2 (May 1990) pp. 153–216. Also R. Boyer, 'Technical Change and the Theory of "Regulation" in G. Dosi, C. Freeman *et al.* (eds), *Technical Change and Economic Theory* (London & New York: Pinter, 1988).

45   F. C. Clairmont and J. Cavanagh, 'The World's Top 200 Mega Corporations: Foundations of the Economic Gulag', *Economic and Political Weekly*, 5 February 1994.

6 Globalisation

1. P. Hirst and G. Thompson, *Globalization in Question?* (London: Polity Press, 1996) p. 195.
2. Cf. S. Kuznets, 'Quantitative Aspects of the Economic Growth of Nations: X-level and Structure of Foreign Trade: Long-Term Trends', *Economic Development and Cultural Change*, 15 (2) Part II (January 1967) pp. 7–8. Kuznets gave the historical figure. Today's figure is based on statistical tables in World Bank, *World Development Report* (Oxford: Oxford University Press, 1994). See also Table 4.1, p. 71 in Chapter 4 of this book. Note, however, that World Bank sources stress the tremendous growth in world trade relative to world income since 1990. See S. Otsubo, *Globalization: Accelerated Integration through World Trade* (Washington: World Bank International Economics Department, 1995) discussion paper.
3. United Nations, Conference on Trade and Development, *World Investment Report 1994: Transnational Corporations, Employment and the Workplace* (New York: United Nations, 1994) pp. 133–5.
4. P. Hirst and G. Thompson, *op. cit.*, note 1, pp. 95–7.
5. For example, A. Glyn and R. Sutcliffe, 'Global but Leaderless? The New Capitalist Order', in *Socialist Register* (London: Merlin Press, 1992), pp. 76–95; and D. M. Gordon, 'The Global Economy: New Edifice or Crumbling Foundations?', *New Left Review*, no. 168 (1988) pp. 24–64.
6. See Chapter 4 of this book, p. 77.
7. For a compact review of sociological theories of globalisation, see M. Waters, *Globalization* (London: Routledge, 1995).
8. T. Parsons, *Societies* (Englewood Cliffs: Prentice Hall, 1966); and *The System of Modern Societies* (Englewood Cliffs: Prentice Hall, 1971).
9. R. Robertson, *Globalization* (London: Sage, 1992).
10. M. Waters, *Globalization, op. cit.*, note 7, *passim*, pp. 39–46.
11. J. Nettl and R. Robertson, *International Systems and the Modernization of Societies* (London: Faber, 1968).
12. D. Harvey, *The Condition of Postmodernity* (Oxford: Basil Blackwell, 1989). The summary here is based on Chapters 14, 15 and 17 of his book.
13. R. Delbridge, P. Turnbull and B. Wilkinson, 'Pushing Back the Frontiers: Management Control and Work Intensification under JIT/TQM Factory Regimes', *New Technology, Work and Employment* (Autumn, 1992) pp. 97–107, p. 104.
14. D. Harvey, *op. cit.*, note 12, p. 241.
15. A. Giddens, *The Consequences of Modernity* (Cambridge: Polity Press, 1990), p. 64.
16. UNECOSOC, *Multinational Corporations in World Development* (New York: UN, 1973).
17. UNCTAD, *World Investment Report, 1993* (New York & Geneva: UN, 1994) p. 143.
18. P. Drucker, *The New Realities* (London: Heinemann, 1989) pp. 123–5. See also K. Ohmae, *Triad Power, the Coming Shape of Global*

Competition (New York: Free Press, 1985); and *The Borderless World: Power and Strategy in the Interlinked Economy* (London: Collins, 1990).

19. S. S. Cohen, 'Geo-economics and America's Mistakes', in M. Carnoy *et al.*, *The New Global Economy in the Information Age* (London: Macmillan, 1993) p. 98.

20. For the figure for 1990, see P. Dicken, *Global Shift, The Internationalization of Economic Activity* (Manchester: Paul Chapman, 1992) 2nd edition, Table 2.5, p. 30.

21. M. Aglietta, *The Theory of Capitalist Regulation* (London: Verso, 1976), p. 122.

22. P. Boccara, 'Qu'est-ce-que l'anthroponomie?', in *Cahiers du l'IRM, Individues et Société*, 1, and cited in R. Jessop, 'Regulation Theories in Retrospect and Propect', in *Economy and Society*, 19 (2) (May 1990) pp. 153–216, p. 168.

23. A. Lipietz, *Mirages and Miracles* (London: Verso, 1987) p. 15.

24. R. Jessop, *State Theory* (Oxford: Blackwell, 1990) pp. 317–18.

25. C. Sabel, 'Experimental Regionalism and the Dilemmas of Regional Economic Policy', paper presented to the conference on 'Socio-Economic Systems of Japan, the United States, the United Kingdom, Germany, and France', Institute of Fiscal and Monetary Policy, Tokyo, Japan, 16 February 1996.

26. R. Reich, *The Work of Nations* (London: Simon & Schuster, 1991) p. 211.

27. S. A. Bradley, J. Hausman and A. Nolan, *Globalization, Technology and Competition: The Fusion of Computers and Telecommunications in the 1990s* (Cambridge, Mass.: Harvard Business School Press, 1994) p. 111.

28. R. Jaikumar and D. M. Upton in S. A. Bradley *et al.*, pp. 173–4.

29. UNCTAD, *World Investment Report, 1994, op. cit.*, note 3, p. 194.

30. Based on C. Crook, 'Global Finance', *The Economist*, 19 September 1992.

31. P. Drucker, *op. cit.*, note 18, p. 121.

32. F. F. Clairmont, *The Rise and Fall of Economic Liberalism: The Making of the Economic Gulag* (Penang: Southbound and Third World Network, 1996) p. 29.

33. *The Economist*, 27 November 1993.

7 Global Regulation

1. M. J. Piore and C. Sabel, *The Second Industrial Divide* (New York: Basic Books, 1984) Chapter 10.

2. R. Cox, 'Social Forces, States and World Orders: Beyond International Relations Theory', *Millennium*, 10 (2) (1981) pp. 126–55, p. 139.

3. R. Cox, 'Structural Issues of Global Governance: Implications for Europe', in S. Gill (ed.), *Gramsci, Historical Materialism and International Relations* (Cambridge: Cambridge University Press, 1993) p. 261.

4. S. Strange, 'The Name of the Game', in N. X. Rizopoulos (ed.), *Seachanges: American Foreign Policy in a World Transformed* (Washington: Council on Foreign Relations, 1990) p. 260.
5. Cf. S. Gill, 'Hegemony, Consensus and Trilaterialism', *Review of International Studies*, 12, pp. 205–21, and K. v.d. Pijl, *The Making of an Atlantic Ruling Class* (London: New Left Books, 1984). See also H. Sklar (ed.), *Trilaterialism, the Trilateral Commission and Elite Planning for World Management* (Boston: South End Press, 1980).
6. S. Gill and D. Law, 'Global Hegemony and the Structural Power of Capital', *International Studies Quarterly*, 33 (1989) pp. 475–99.
7. J. G Ruggie, 'International Regimes, Transactions and Change – Embedded Liberalism in the Post War Order', *International Organisation*, 36, pp. 379–414.
8. K. Watkins, *Fixing the Rules, North–South Issues in International Trade and the GATT Uruguay Round* (London: Catholic Institute for International Relations, 1992).
9. GATT, Uruguay, Final Protocol, quoted in L. Walker, 'Gatt: the Uruguay Round and the Developing Countries', PhD thesis, University of Sheffield (1996) Chapter 7, section 4.
10. K. Watkins, *op. cit.*, note 8, p. 95.
11. UNCTAD (1992), *Strengthening National and International Action and Multilateral Cooperation for a Healthy, Secure and Equitable World Economy*, eighth session, Cartegena de Indias, 8 February 1992, UNCTAD/TD/L339, 24, pp. 62–3; quoted *passim* in J. van Wijk and G. Junne, *Intellectual Property Protection of Advanced Technology, Changes in the Global Technology System: Implications and Options for Developing Countries*, Report prepared for the United Nations University's Institute for New Technologies, INTECH, contract no. 91/026, Maastricht, The Netherlands, October 1992.
12. J. van Wijk and G. Junne, *ibid.*, p. 61.
13. H. Hyman, 'Privatization; the Facts', in C. Veljanovski, *Privatisation and Competition: a Market Prospectus* (London: Hobart Paperbacks, 1989). See also J. Vickers and G. Yarrow, *Privatization, an Economic Analysis* (Cambridge: MIT Press, 1988). Note, however, that the 1990s have seen further swingeing privatisations (eg. railways) not here included in the total.
14. B. Hugill, 'A Civil Service on its Last Legs', *The Observer* (29 May 1994) p. 22.
15. *Labour Research*, December 1990.
16. D. Sandberg, 'The Pirate Privateers', *New Internationalist*, September 1994; see also R. T. Naylor, *Hot Money and the Politics of Debt* (Toronto: McClelland & Stewart, 1989).
17. For examples of this, see A. Showstack-Sassoon (ed.), *Women and the State* (London: Hutchinson, 1987).
18. L. Dominelli and A. Hoogvelt, 'Globalisation, the Privatisation of Welfare and the Changing Role of Professional Academics in Britain', *Critical Perspectives on Accounting*, no. 7 (1996) pp. 191–212; and L. Dominelli and A. Hoogvelt, 'Globalisation, Contract Government and

the Taylorisation of Intellectual Labour in Academia', *Studies in Political Economy*, no. 49, Spring 1996.

19. International Labour Office, *World Labour Report*, 1994.
20. Organisation of Economic Cooperation and Development, *Employment/Unemployment Study: Interim Report by the Secretary General* (Paris: OECD, 1993).
21. J. Rifkin, *The End of Work, the Decline of the Global Labor Force and the Dawn of the Post-Market Era* (New York: G. P. Putnam's Sons, 1995). See especially his Chapter 12, 'Requiem for the Working Class'.
22. UNCTAD, *World Investment Report* 1994, p. 188. The report refers here to the much publicised report by a special committeee of the Parliament of France under direction of Senator Jean Arthuis which gave a very pessimistic assessment of the link between relocation and unemployment.
23. P. Dicken, *Global Shift* (London: Paul Chapman, 1992) p. 67.
24. P. Dicken, *ibid.*, p. 36.
25. *Business Week* (19 December 1994) pp. 28–30.
26. R. Reich, *The Work of Nations* (New York: Simon & Schuster, 1993) p. 95.
27. M. Castells, *The Information Age, vol. I*: The Rise of the Network Society (Cambridge, Mass. & Oxford: Blackwell, 1996) p. 266.
28. A. Touraine, *The Post-industrial Society, Tomorrow's Social History – Classes, Conflicts and Culture in the Programmed Society* (New York: Random House, 1971), original in French (1969); D. Bell, *The Coming of Post-industrial Society, a Venture in Social Forecasting* (New York: Basic Books, 1973); P. Drucker, *The Post-Capitalist Society* (London: Butterworth–Heinemann, 1993); A. Toffler, *Powershift* (New York: Bantam Books, 1992).
29. Cf. S. Bradley, J. Hausman and R. Nolan, *Globalization, Technology, Competition* (Cambridge, Mass.: Harvard University Press, 1994) p. 47.
30. R. Moss Kanter, 'The Future of Bureaucracy and Hierarchy', in P. Bourdieu and J. S. Coleman, *Social Theory for a Changing Society* (Boulder, Col.: Westview Press, 1991).
31. R. Moss Kanter, *ibid.*, p. 77.
32. G. Bannock, *Small Business Perspective* (London: Graham Bannock & Partners, 1992).
33. C. Sabel, 'Learning by Monitoring: the Insitutions of Economic Development', in N. Smelser and R. Swedberg (eds), *Handbook of Economic Sociology* (Princeton, NJ: Princeton-Sage, 1994) pp. 137–65.
34. P. Krugman, 'Growing World Trade: Causes and Consequences', in *Brookings Papers on Economic Activity*, 1 (1995) pp. 327–77, p. 337.
35. See my discussion in A. M. M. Hoogvelt, *The Third World in Global Development* (London: Macmillan, 1982) pp. 192–3.
36. W. Hutton, *The State We're In* (London: Jonathan Cape, 1995) p. 105 *et seq.*
37. For a discussion of the restructuring of the welfare state in the post-Fordist period, see R. Burrows and B. Loader (eds), *Towards a Post-*

Fordist Welfare State? (London: Routledge, 1994), especially P. Bagguley, Chapter 5, 'Prisoners of the Beveridge Dream, the Political Mobilisation of the Poor Against Contemporary Welfare Regimes'.

38. This emphasis on global markets as providing the integration of the supply-side and the demand-side of a global flexible regime of accumulation is frequently overlooked or indeed not supported by others whose analysis in other respects bears a resemblance to the present one. For example, Mike Geddis, in his contribution to Burrows and Loader's volume (*ibid.*) on the post-Fordist welfare state, argues that the regime of post-Fordist flexibility has so far meant an emphasis on so-called lean production, and the restriction of new consumption norms to the have-lots. Lean production means lean consumption. See M. Geddis, 'Public Services and Local Economic Regeneration in a Post-Fordist Economy', Chapter 9, in R. Burrows and B. Loader, *ibid.*

39. Comment in an interview in the *Horizon* BBC TV documentary programme, 'The Battle for Aids', 4 December 1995.

40. For an overview of, and theoretical distinction between, these various types of community-oriented economic organisations, see A. A. McArthur, 'Community Business and Urban Regeneration', *Urban Studies*, 30 (4/5) (1993) pp. 849–73.

41. R. E. Goodin, 'Self-reliance versus the Welfare State', *Journal of Social Policy*, 14 (1985) pp. 25–47.

42. A. A. McArthur, *op. cit.*, note 40, p. 867.

Part III Introduction

1. For example, F. Jameson, 'Actually Existing Marxism', *Polygraph: an International Journal of Culture and Politics*, 6/7 (1993) pp. 171–95. In his earlier, best-known, work, Jameson focused on postmodern culture as the logic of late capitalism. Today, Jameson appears to equate a subsequent development in late capitalism, 'late, late' capitalism with postmodern capitalism. F. Jameson, *Postmodernism, or, the Cultural Logic of Late Capitalism* (Durham: Durham University Press, 1990).

2. 'Institutional endorsement' is particularly noticeable in the US where courses in 'post-colonial studies' and 'post-colonial' literature abound. See E. Shohat, 'Notes on the "Post-Colonial"', *Social Text*, 31/32 (1993) pp. 99–113, p. 99. In the UK too the term 'postcolonial' is beginning to work its way onto curricula of university courses.

3. For an excellent argument, see N. Fraser, 'From Redistribution to Recognition? Dilemmas of Justice in a "Post-socialist Age"', *New Left Review*, no. 212 (1995) pp. 68–93.

4. A. Portes and D. Kincaid, 'Sociology and Development in the 1990s: Critical Challenges and Empirical Trends', *Sociological Forum*, 4 (1989) pp. 479–503; quoted in M. J. Watts, 'Development I: Power, Knowledge, Discursive Practice', *Progress in Human Geography*, 17 (2) (1993) pp. 257–72, p. 262.

5. C. Wright Mills, *The Sociological Imagination* (Oxford & New York: Oxford University Press, 1959) pp. 165–7.

6. E. Meiksins Wood, 'What is the "Postmodern" Agenda? An Introduction', *Monthly Review* (July/August 1995), special issue 'In Defense of History', pp. 1–12.
7. A. Dirlik, 'The Postcolonial Aura: Third World Criticism in the Age of Global Capitalism', *Critical Inquiry*, 20 (2) (1994) pp. 328–56.
8. E. Shohat, *op. cit.*, note 2, p. 101.
9. *Ibid.*, p. 103.
10. A. Dirlik, *op cit.*, note 7, p. 329.
11. A. Dirlik, *ibid.*, pp. 330–1. Dirlik notes, however, these exceptions: A. Appadurai, 'Global Ethnoscapes: Notes and Queries for a Transnational Anthropology', in R. G. Fox (ed.), *Recapturing Anthropology: Working in the Present* (Santa Fe, N. Mexico: 1991); and A. Ahmad who, like Dirlik himself, relates postcoloniality to contemporary capitalism, see A. Ahmad, *In Theory: Classes, Nations, Literatures* (London: Verso, 1992).
12. E. Shohat, *op. cit.*, note 2, p. 110. Also, A. McClintock, 'The Angel of Progress: Pitfalls of the Term "Post-Colonialism"', *Social Text*, 31/32 (1993) pp. 84–97.
13. B. Ashcroft, G. Griffiths and H. Tiffin, *The Empire Writes Back: Theory and Practice in Post-colonial Literatures* (London: Routledge, 1989).
14. P. Williams and L. Chrisman (eds), *Colonial Discourse and Postcolonial Theory* (New York: Harvester Wheatsheaf, 1993).
15. Thiongo'o Ngugi wa, *Decolonising the Mind: The Politics of Language in African Literature* (London: James Currey/Heinemann, 1986).
16. J. Nederveen Pieterse and Bhikhu Parekh, 'Shifting Imaginaries: Decolonization, Internal Decolonization, Postcoloniality', in J. Nederveen Pieterse and Bhikhu Parekh (eds), *Decolonization of Imagination, Culture, Knowledge and Power* (London: Zed Books, 1995).
17. Quoted in F. Mulhern, 'The Politics of Cultural Studies', *Monthly Review* (July/August 1995) pp. 31–40, p. 32.
18. H. Bhabha has been especially important in the discussion of hybridity, see his 'The Commitment to Theory', *New Formations*, no. 5 (1988) pp. 5–25.
19. G. Prakash, 'Postcolonial Criticism and Indian Historiography', *Social Text*, no. 31/32 (1992) p. 8.
20. H. Bhabha, *passim*, in R. J. C. Young, *Colonial Desire: Hybridity in Theory, Culture and Race* (London: Routledge, 1995) p. 175.
21. H. Bhabha, 'Commitment to Theory', *op. cit.*, note 18, p. 21.
22. A. Escobar, *Encountering Development, the Making and Unmaking of the Third World* (Princeton: Princeton University Press, 1995) p. 219.

8 Africa: Exclusion and the Containment of Anarchy

1. P. Drucker, *The New Realities* (London: Heinemann, 1989) p. 120.
2. S. George, *The Debt Boomerang* (London: Pluto Press and the Transnational Institute, 1992) pp. 84–5. Note that Susan George's

figures are based on OECD data published in OECD, *Financing and External Debt of Developing Countries, 1989 Survey* (Paris: OECD, 1990).

3. The first five sections of this chapter are a reworked and shortened version of an earlier paper published in ROAPE, see A. Hoogvelt, 'Debt and Indebtedness: The Dynamics of Third World Poverty', *Review of African Political Economy*, no. 47 (Spring 1990) pp. 117–27.

4. This calculation is based on the statistical tables in Annexes of the 1970 and 1982 issues of *Development Cooperation, Review of the OECD Development Assistance Committee* (Paris: OECD, 1970 and 1982).

5. R. T. Naylor, *Hot Money and the Politics of Debt* (Toronto: McClelland & Stewart, 1987).

6. Bank for International Settlements, *59th Annual Report 1989* (Basle: BIS, 1989) p. 135–6.

7. R. T. Naylor, *op cit.*, note 5, p. 59.

8. Up until the end of the decade, in the combined total of international assets of banks of industrial nations the US dollar still reigned supreme with just under 50 per cent of reported holdings, while the Japanese yen despite growing in importance was second (14 per cent). The Deutsch Mark came third (13 per cent). See Bank for International Settlements, *59th Annual Report, op cit.*, note 6, p. 116.

9. UNCTAD, *Trade and Development Report, 1989* (New York: United Nations, 1989) Table 19, p. 38.

10. *The Guardian*, 9 January 1987.

11. Quoted in S. Bransford and B. Kucinski, *The Debt Squads* (London: Zed Books, 1988) p. 18.

12. In 1989 the IMF announced a change in policy. It now no longer insists that countries be current on their debt to private creditors before drawing on its resources. However, the guidelines for the implementation of this new policy are strict and include the Fund's satisfaction with the concerned country's medium-term adjustment strategies. And even where the commercial credits have been resumed independent of such packages, the international banks and other financial institutions have wished to reassure themselves that IMF supervision of the recipient economy is firmly in place.

13. A. Leftwich, 'Governance, Democracy and Development in the Third World', *Third World Quarterly*, 14 (3) (1993) p. 607.

14. *Ibid.*, p. 608.

15. For references, see J. Toye in *Dilemmas of Development* (Oxford: Blackwell, 1987) Chapter 5. Toye gives an overview of the 'counter revolution' in development theory in the 1980s and he describes its resonance with the orthodox Marxist left.

16. UNCTAD, *Trade and Development Report, 1989*, p. 106. On the virtues of debt conversion schemes, see also International Monetary Fund, *Annual Report, 1988* (Washington: IMF, 1988) p. 46.

17. Reported in *The Economist*, 5 March 1994.

18. World Bank, *Adjustment in Africa: Reform, Results, and the Road Ahead, a World Bank Policy Research Report* (New York: Oxford

University Press, 1994). Note that the World Bank has commissioned many reports and reviews of its structural adjustment lending. For a good discussion and comprehensive bibliography, see S. Ponte, 'The World Bank and "Adjustment in Africa" ', *Review of African Political Economy*, no. 66 (1994) pp. 539–58.

19. D. Ghai and C. Hewitt de Alcantara, 'The Crisis of the 1980s in Africa, Latin America and the Caribbean: An Overview', in D. Ghai (ed.), *The IMF and the South* (London: Zed Books on behalf of United Nations Research Institute for Social Development, 1991) paras pp. 14–17.

20. *Ibid.*, p. 16.

21. African NGOs have produced a common declaration to UNCTAD IX, held in Midrand, South Africa between 24–8 April 1996 in which they condemn the imposition of the neo-liberal paradigm through SAPs as a form of recolonisation of the continent.

22. K. Watkins, 'Debt Relief for Africa', *Review of African Political Economy*, no. 62 (1994) pp. 117–27, p. 126. For further reading on the evolution of poverty, social conditions and income inequality under structural adjustment, see also G. Cornia, S. Jolly and F. Stewart (eds), *Adjustment with a Human Face: Protecting the Vulnerable and Promoting Growth* (Oxford: Clarendon Press, 1987); and P. Gibbon, 'The World Bank and African Poverty 1973–91', *Journal of Modern African Studies*, 30 (2) (1992) pp. 193–220.

23. D. Avramovic, 'Depression of Export Commodity Prices', *Third World Quarterly*, July 1986.

24. R. Weil, 'Somalia in Perspective: When the Saints go Marching In', *Monthly Review*, 44 (10) (March 1993).

25. B. Martin, 'Gains without Frontiers', *New Statesman and Society* (9 December 1994) pp. 22–3. The senior manager whom Martin quotes is Davison Budhoo. See also B. Martin, *In the Public Interest? Privatisation and Public Sector Reform* (London: Zed Books, 1994).

26. B. Martin, *ibid.*, p. 23.

27. See B. Riley, 'Funds Pour Into New Growth Regions', *The Economist*, 7 February 1994.

28. A. Leftwich, 'Governance, Democracy and Development in the Third World', *Third World Quarterly*, 14 (3) (1993) pp. 605–24, p. 610. For further reading on the pressures towards democratisation in Africa, see other contributions to the same issue of *Third World Quarterly*, including the literature review by E. Reinierse, pp. 647–64.

29. C. Bayliss, 'Political Conditionality and Democratisation', *Review of African Political Economy*, no. 65 (1995) pp. 321–37.

30. A. Leftwich, *op cit.*, note 28, p. 606.

31. For an excellent review of the literature on the links between political and economic reform in Africa, see C. Bayliss, *op. cit.*, note 29.

32. B. Gills, J. Rocamora and R. Wilson (eds), *Low Intensity Democracy, Political Power in the New World Order* (London: Pluto Press, 1993).

33. A. Sawyer, 'The Politics of Adjustment Policies', ECLA Document ECA/ICHD/88/29, quoted in C. Hewitt de Alcantara and D. Ghai, *op. cit.*, note 19, p. 27. See also J.-J. Barya, 'The New Political Con-

ditionalities of Aid: An Independent View from Africa', *IDS Bulletin*, 24 (1) (1993) pp. 16–23.

34. For example, R. Sandbrook, *The Politics of Africa's Economic Recovery* (London: Cambridge University Press, 1993); C. Bayliss, *op. cit.*, note 29, *passim*, p. 333.

35. J. Walton and D. Seddon, *Free Markets and Food Riots: The Politics of Global Adjustment* (Oxford: Blackwell, 1994). See also M. Chossudovsky who holds the World Bank team in Rwanda directly responsible for the political and social repercussions of shock therapy that brought the country to civil war, in 'IMF/World Bank Policies and the Rwandan Holocaust', *Third World Resurgence*, no. 52 (1994).

36. W. Reno, 'Markets, War, and the Reconfiguration of Political Authority in Sierra Leone', *Canadian Journal of African Studies*, 29 (2) (1995). See also his book *Corruption and State Politics in Sierra Leone* (Cambridge: Cambridge University Press, 1995).

37. *Ibid.*, p. 217.

38. S. P. Huntington, *Political Order in Changing Societies* (New Haven & London: Yale University Press, 1968).

39. J. C. Scott, *Comparative Political Corruption* (Englewood Cliffs, NJ: Prentice-Hall, 1972) p. 35.

40. M. Duffield, *The Symphony of the Damned: Racial Discourse, Complex Political Emergencies and Humanitarian Aid* (Birmingham: School of Public Policy, University of Birmingham, occasional paper, 2 March 1996).

41. Cf. M. Barrett, *The Politics of Truth* (Oxford: Polity Press, 1991) p. 130 *passim*.

42. Examples of this 'discourse analysis' approach to the new aid agenda, are A. Leftwich, 'Goverance, the State and the Politics of Development', *Development and Change*, no. 25 (1994) pp. 363–86; and M. Robinson, 'Aid, Democracy and Political Conditionality in Sub-Saharan Africa', in G. Sorensen (ed.), *Political Conditionality* (London: Frank Cass, 1993) pp. 85–99; and 'Strengthening Civil Society in Africa: The Role of Foreign Political Aid', *IDS Bulletin*, 26 (2) (1995) pp. 70–80.

43. ODI, *NGOs and Official Donors* (London Overseas Development Institute Briefing Paper 1–4, August 1995), quoted in M. Duffield, *op. cit.*, note 40, p. 8. For a comprehensive review and detailed advocacy of the NGO approach to 'development' see M. Edwards and D. Hulme (eds), *Making a Difference, NGOs and Development in a Changing World* (London: Earthscan, 1992). See also J. Clark, *Democratising Development: The Role of Voluntary Organisation* (London: Earthscan, 1991). Clark notes that there are today some 4000 development NGOs working in OECD member countries, dispersing almost $3 billion dollars worth of assistance every year and that they work with between 10 000–20 000 southern NGOs. For a critical assessment on the role of NGOs in development, see Alan Fowler, 'Distant Obligations: Speculations on NGO Funding and the Global Market', *Review of African Political Economy*, no. 55 (1992) pp. 9–29.

44. M. Duffield, *op. cit.*, note 40. Much of this section of the chapter is based on Duffield's thesis as developed in this work. Note, however, that Duffield has also elaborated his thesis in connection with other zones of insecurity on the edge of the global economy, notably the Balkan. In an outstanding report for UNICEF, in 1994, Duffield first developed his theory of 'complex political emergencies' with reference to both Angola and Bosnia. See M. Duffield, 'Complex Political Emergencies', an exploratory report for UNICEF (Birmingham: University of Birmingham, School of Public Policy, 1994).
45. M. Barker, *The New Racism* (London: Junction Books, 1992).
46. R. Kaplan, 'The Coming Anarchy: How Scarcity, Crime, Overpopulation and Disease are Rapidly Destroying the Social Fabric of Our Planet', *Atlantic Monthly* (February 1994) pp. 44–76. This article formed the basis of the BBC's dramatic documentary, *Pulp Futures*, in 1995.
47. P. Richards, mimeo, 'Fighting for the Rain Forest: Youth, Insurgency and Environment in Sierra Leone' (University College London: Department of Anthropology, 1995); and M. Duffield, *op. cit.*, note 40, p. 10 and *passim*.
48. M. Duffield, *ibid.*, p. 12.
49. *Ibid.*, pp. 42–3.

9   Islamic Revolt

1.   *The Economist*, Editorial, 'Living with Islam', 18 March 1995.
2.   S. Huntington, 'The Clash of Civilizations?', *Foreign Affairs* (Summer 1993) pp. 22–49.
3.   F. Fukuyama, *The End of History and the Last Man* (London: Hamish Hamilton, 1992).
4.   S. Huntington, *op. cit.*, note 1, p. 26.
5.   See our discussion of this in Chapter 6.
6.   S. Huntington, *op. cit.*, note 2, p. 24.
7.   G. H. Jansen, *Militant Islam* (London: Penguin, 1978) p. 1, quoting K. Ahmad, 'Islam, its Meaning and Message'.
8.   Cf. W. M. Patton, 'Shi'ahs', in J. Hastings (ed.), *Encyclopaedia of Religion and Ethics* (Edinburgh: T. & T. Clark, 1908) pp. 453–8.
9.   E. Gellner, *Postmodernism, Reason and Religion* (London: Routledge, 1992).
10. E. Gellner, *ibid.*, p. 7.
11. G. H. Jansen, *op. cit.*, note 7, p. 29.
12. S. Bromley, 'The Prospects for Democracy in the Middle East', in D. Held (ed.), *Prospects for Democracy* (Oxford: Polity Press, 1993) pp. 380–412, p. 383. See also S. Bromley, *Rethinking Middle East Politics, State Formation and Development* (Oxford: Polity Press, 1994).
13. E. Gellner, *op. cit.*, note 9, p. 9.
14. E. Gellner, *ibid.*, p. 10.
15. E. W. Said, *Orientalism* (London: Routledge & Kegan Paul, 1978).

16. M. Rodinson, 'The Western Image and Western Studies of Islam', in J. Schacht with C. E. Bosworth (eds), *The Legacy of Islam* (Oxford, Clarendon Press, 1974) pp. 9–62, p. 11.
17. M. Rodinson, *ibid.*, p. 37.
18. M. Rodinson, *ibid.*, pp. 49–50.
19. E. Said, *Orientalism* (London: Penguin Books, 1985) p. 259.
20. M. Rodinson *op. cit.*, note 16, p. 48.
21. M. Rutven, *Islam in the World* (London: Penguin, 1991) p. 292.
22. E. Said, *Orientalism, op. cit.*, note 19, p. 240 quoting T. E. Lawrence.
23. See Chapter 2 of this book on the roots of neo-colonialism.
24. G. H. Jansen, *op. cit.*, note 7, p. 14.
25. G. H. Jansen, *ibid.*, p. 62
26. E. Said, *Culture and Imperialism* (New York: Vintage Press, 1994).
27. E. Said, *Orientalism, op. cit.*, note 19, p. 3.
28. G. H. Jansen, *op. cit.*, note 7, p. 68.
29. G. H. Jansen, *ibid.*, p. 75.
30. O. Roy, *The Failure of Political Islam* (London: I.B. Tauris, 1995) p. 3.
31. O. Roy, *ibid.*, p. 83. For similar classifications, see also G. H. Jansen, *op. cit.*, note 7, p. 134.
32. P. Aarts, quoting N. Chomsky, in 'Democracy, Oil and the Gulf War', *Third World Quarterly*, 13 (3) (1992) p. 527.
33. S. Bromley, *American Hegemony and World Oil: The Industry, the State System and the World Economy* (Oxford: Polity Press, 1991) p. 250.
34. S. Bromley, 'The Prospects for Democracy in the Middle East', in D. Held (ed.), *Prospects for Democracy* (Oxford: Polity Press, 1993) pp. 380–406.
35. O. Roy, *op. cit.*, note 30, p. 4.
36. *Ibid.*, p. 93.
37. *Ibid.*, pp. 98–9.
38. *Ibid.*, p. 196.

10 The Developmental States of East Asia

1. World Bank, *The East Asian Miracle* (New York: Oxford University Press, 1993) p. xv.
2. B. Balassa, 'Trade Policies in Developing Countries', *American Economic Review*, 61 (May 1971); *Policy Reform in Developing Countries* (New York: Pergamon, 1977); and *The Newly Industrializing Countries in the World Economy* (New York: Pergamon, 1981).
3. C. Johnson, *MITI and the Japanese Miracle* (Stanford, CA: Stanford University Press, 1982). See also 'Political Institutions and Economic Performance: The Government-Business Relationship in Japan, South Korea and Taiwan', in F. C. Deyo (ed.), *The Political Economy of the New Asian Industrialism* (Ithaca, NY: Cornell University Press, 1987) pp. 136–64.

4. E. K. Y. Chen, *Hyper-growth in Asian Economies: A Comparative Study of Hong Kong, Japan, Korea, Singapore and Taiwan* (New York: Holmes & Meier Publishers, 1979).

5. A. Amsden, 'The State and Taiwan's Economic Development', in P. Evans, D. Rueschemeyer and T. Skocpol (eds), *Bringing the State Back In* (New York: Cambridge University Press, 1985) pp. 78–106. See also A. Amsden, *Asia's Next Giant: South Korea and Late Industrializiation* (New York: Oxford University Press, 1989).

6. F. Frobel, J. Heinrichs and O. Kreye, *The New International Division of Labour: Structural Unemployment in Industrialized Countries and Industrialization in Developing Countries* (Cambridge: Cambridge University Press, 1980).

7. Cf. M. Castells, 'Four Asian Tigers With a Dragon Head: A Comparative Analysis of the State, Economy, and Society in the Asian Pacific Rim', in R. P. Appelbaum and J. Henderson, *States and Development in the Asian Pacific Rim* (California: Sage Publications, 1992) pp. 33–70.

8. One of the first such attempts was D. Senghaas, *The European Experience: A Historical Critique of Development Theory* (Leamington Spa: Berg, 1985). The neo-Listian position is fully developed by G. White and R. Wade in their introduction to G. White (ed.), *Developmental States in East Asia* (London: Macmillan, 1988).

9. See R. Wade, 'State Intervention in "Outward-looking" Development: Neoclassical Theory and Taiwanese Practice', in G. White (ed.), *ibid.*, pp. 30–67.

10. C. Johnson, *MITI and the Japanese Miracle: the Growth of Industrial Policy, 1925–1975* (Stanford: Stanford University Press, 1982).

11. See G. W. Noble, 'The Japanese Industrial Policy Debate', in S. Haggard and Chung-in Moon, *Pacific Dynamics* (Boulder, Col.: CIS Inha University and Westview Press, 1989) pp. 53–96, p. 55 for a list of major 'developmental state' writers on postwar Japan.

12. P. Krugman, *Strategic Trade Policy and the New International Economics* (Cambridge, Mass.: MIT Press, 1986).

13. P. L. Berger, *The Capitalist Revolution, Fifty Propositions about Prosperity, Equality and Liberty* (Aldershot: Wildwood House, 1987).

14. P. L. Berger, *ibid.*, p. 163.

15. L. Pye, 'The New Asian Capitalism: A Political Portrait', in P. L. Berger and Hsin-Huang M. Hsiao (eds), *In Search of an East Asian Development Model* (New Brunswick: Transaction Publishers, 1988) pp. 86–7.

16. P. L. Berger, 'An East Asian Development Model?' Chapter 1, in P. L. Berger and Hsin-Huang M. Hsiao (eds), *In Search of An East Asian Development Model* (New Brunswick: Transaction Publishers, 1988, second printing, 1990) p. 7.

17. See R. MacFarquhar, 'The Post-Confucian Challenge', *The Economist*, 8 February 1980; M. Morishima, *Why has Japan Succeeded? Western Technology and the Japanese Ethos* (Cambridge: Cambridge University Press, 1982); G. Rozman (ed.), *The East Asia Region: Confucian*

Heritage and its Modern Adaptation (Princeton: Princeton University Press, 1991); Wong Siu-lun, 'Modernization and Chinese Culture in Hong Kong', *The China Quarterly*, no. 106 (1986) pp. 306–25; and J. P. L. Jiang (ed.), *Confucianism and Modernization: A Symposium* (Taipei: 1987).

18. See W. Bello and S. Rosenfeld, *Dragons in Distress: Asia's Miracle Economies in Crisis* (London: Penguin, 1990). In Taiwan, over 2900 labour disputes were registered in 1987 and 1988 alone, and over 4540 disputes went into arbitration in the district courts (pp. 227, 223). Emigration from Singapore, negligible in the 1960s, rose to 2000 families a year in the mid-1980s and to 4700 in 1989 (p. 333); and in South Korea, between 1987 and 1989 more than 7100 labour disputes erupted, while the number of unions more than doubled from 2725 to 7358 (p. 41).

19. Cf. *New Internationalist*, January 1995; and W. Bello and S. Rosenfeld, *Dragons in Distress: Asia's Miracle Economies in Crisis* (Harmondsworth: Penguin, 1990).

20. This section on the geo-political factors affecting East Asian development draws on an interesting essay by an MA student on our graduate programme in international studies, Anne Holgate Lowe, 'Geopolitical and Historical Factors in the East Asian Development Model' (University of Sheffield, Department of Politics, 1995).

21. CIA figures cited by B. Cummings, 'The Origins and Development of the North East Asian Political Economy: Industrial Sectors, Product Cycles and Political Consequences', in F. Deyo (ed.), *The Political Economy of the New Asian Industrialism* (Ithaca: Cornell University Press, 1987) pp. 44–83.

22. S. Haggard and Tun-jen Cheng, *Newly Industrializing Asia in Transition, Policy Reform and American Response* (Berkeley: Institute of International Studies, University of California Press, 1987).

23. M. Castells, *ibid*, note 7, p. 53.

24. S. Krasner, 'Trade Conflicts and the Common Defense: The United States and Japan', in S. Haggard and Chung-in Moon (eds), *Pacific Dynamics: The International Politics of Industrial Change* (Boulder, Col.: Westview Press, 1989) pp. 251–74, p. 252.

25. S. Haggard, 'Introduction', in S. Haggard and Chung-in Moon (eds), *Pacific Dynamics, ibid.*, pp. 1–21, p. 8.

26. S. Haggard, *Pathways from the Periphery* (Ithaca: Cornell University Press, 1990).

27. M. Castells, in R. P. Appelbaum and J. Henderson, *op. cit.*, note 7, p. 57.

28. M. Castells, *ibid.*, pp. 57–8.

29. P. Berger, *The Capitalist Revolution* (Aldershot: Wildwood House, 1987) p. 142.

30. W. Bello and S. Rosenfeld, *op. cit.*, note 19, p. 337.

31. W. Bello and S. Rosenfeld, *ibid.*

32. *New Internationalist*, 'Unmasking the Miracle', January 1995, pp. 18–19.

33. See World Bank, *The East Asian Miracle, op. cit.*, note 1, Figure 1.3 p. 31, and Table 1.1. p. 33.
34. W. Bello and S. Rosenfeld, *op. cit.*, note 19, pp. 37, 38. Here they cite Choi Jang-Jip, 'Interest Control and Political Control in South Korea: A Study of the Labor Unions in Manufacturing Industries', 1961–1980', PhD dissertation (Chicago: Department of Political Science, University of Chicago, August 1983) pp. 270–1; and Song Byung-Nak, 'The Korean Economy' (unpublished manuscript, Seoul, 1989) p. 27.
35. Kim Dae Jung, *Mass-participatory Economy* (Lanham, MD: University Press of America, 1985) p. 37, quoted in M. Hart-Landsberg, 'South Korea, The Fraudulent Miracle', *Monthly Review*, December 1987.
36. E. Paul, 'Prospects for Liberalization in Singapore', *Journal of Contemporary Asia*, 23 (3) (1993) pp. 291–305, 1993 p. 294.
37. W. Bello and S. Rosenfeld, *op. cit.*, note 19, p. 337.
38. N. Harris, 'States, Economic Development, and the Asian Pacific Rim', in R. P. Appelbaum and J. Henderson (eds), *States and Development in the Asian Pacific Rim* (California and London: Sage Publications, 1992) p. 78.
39. UNCTAD, *World Investment Report, 1994* (New York: United Nations, 1994) p. 76.
40. Ngai-Ling Sum, 'The NICs and Competing Strategies of East Asian Regionalism', in A. Gamble and A. Payne, *Regionalism and World Order* (London: Macmillan, 1996) pp. 207–46.
41. P. Bowles and B. MacLean, 'Understanding Trade Bloc Formation: The Case of the ASEAN Free Trade Area', *Review of International Political Economy*, 3 (2), pp. 319–48.
42. *Ibid.*, p. 343.
43. R. Higgott and R. Stubbs, 'Competing Conceptions of Economic Regionalism: APEC versus EAEC in the Asia Pacific', *Review of International Political Economy*, 2 (3) (1995) pp. 516–35, p. 523.
44. P. Bowles and B. MacLean, *op. cit.*, note 41, p. 326.
45. J. Frankel, 'Is Japan creating a yen bloc in East Asia and the Pacific?', paper presented to the NBER conference 'Japan and the US in Pacific Asia', 3–5 April, Del Mar, California, 1991; and 'Is a Yen Bloc Forming in Pacific Asia?' in R. Obrien (ed.), *Finance and the International Economy* (Oxford: Oxford University Press, 1991, Vol. 5). Both quoted in P. Bowles and B. MacLean, *op. cit.*, note 41, pp. 326–7.
46. P. Bowles and B. MacLean, *op. cit.*, note 41, p. 333, quoting J. Reidel, 'Intra-Asian Trade and Foreign Direct Investment', *Asian Development Review*, 8 (1) (1991) pp. 111–46.
47. W. K. Tabb, 'Japanese Capitalism and The Asian Geese', *Monthly Review*, 45 (10) (March 1994) pp. 29–40, p. 32.
48. K. Fukasaku, *Economic Regionalization and Intra-industry Trade: Pacific Asian Perspectives* (Paris: OECD Development Centre, Technical Papers, no. 53, 1992); quoted in P. Bowles and B. MacLean, *op. cit.*, note 41, p. 336.
49. P. Bowles and B. MacLean, *op. cit.*, note 41, pp. 336–7, quoting L. Lim, 'ASEAN: A New Mode of Economic Cooperation', paper

presented to the conference 'The Political Economy of Foreign Policy in Southeast Asia in the New World Order', September 1992, University of Windsor, Canada.
50. P. Bowles and B. MacLean, *op. cit.*, note 41, p. 341.

11 Democracy, Civil Society and Postdevelopment in Latin America

1. N. Lechner, 'De la Revolución a la Democracia', *La Ciudad Futura*, no. 2 (1986) p. 33, quoted by R. Munck, 'Political Programmes and Development: The Transformative Potential of Social Democracy', in F.J. Schuurman, *Beyond the Impasse: New Directions in Development Theory* (London: Zed Books, 1993) pp. 113–21, p. 115.
2. J.G. Castañeda, *Utopia Unarmed* (New York: Vintage Books, 1994) p. 177.
3. *Ibid.*, p. 177.
4. *Ibid.*, p. 183.
5. *Ibid.*, p. 183.
6. *Ibid.*, p. 179.
7. *Ibid.*, p. 196.
8. V.I. Lenin, *Imperialism, the Highest Stage of Capitalism* (New York and London: International Publishers, 1939 – first published in 1916) p. 85.
9. R. Prebisch, *The Economic Development of Latin America and its Principal Problems* (New York: Economic Commission for Latin America, 1950). This paper was later reworked and served as the founding document for the United Nations Conference on Trade and Development (UNCTAD) of which Prebisch became the first Secretary General. See R. Prebisch, 'Towards a New Trade Policy for Development', Vol. II of *Proceedings of the United Nations Conference on Trade and Development* (Geneva: UNCTAD, 1964).
10. A.M.M. Hoogvelt, *The Third World in Global Development* (London: Macmillan, 1982) pp. 167–8.
11. D. Green, *Silent Revolution, the Rise of Market Economics in Latin America* (London: Cassell & Latin America Bureau, 1995) p. 16.
12. *Ibid.*, p. 17.
13. A.G. Frank, *Capitalism and Underdevelopment in Latin America* (New York: Monthly Review Press, 1967) (originally published in Spanish in 1957).
14. T. dos Santos, 'The Structure of Dependence', in C.K. Wilber (ed.), *The Political Economy of Development and Underdevelopment* (New York: Random House, 1970).
15. C. Furtado, *Diagnosis of the Brazilian Crisis* (Berkeley: University of California Press, 1965).
16. N. Girvan, 'The Development of Dependency Economics in Latin America', *Social and Economic Studies*, 22 (1) (1973).
17. O. Sunkel, 'National Development Policy and External Dependency in Latin America', *Journal of Development Studies*, 6 (1) (1969).

18. For a review of these arguments, see A. M. M. Hoogvelt, *op. cit.*, note 10, Chapter 5.
19. R. Gott, *Rural Guerillas in Latin America* (Harmondsworth: Penguin, 1973) Introduction, pp. 51–2.
20. K. Roberts, 'Democracy and the Dependent Capitalist State in Latin America', *Monthly Review* (October 1985) pp. 12–26.
21. J. Schatan, *World Debt: Who is to Pay?* (London: Zed Books, 1987) p. 74.
22. P. Calvert, 'Demilitarisation in Latin America', *Third World Quarterly*, 7(1) (January 1985) pp. 31–43.
23. See E. Galeano, *Open Veins of Latin America*, especially his introduction to the new edition (New York: Monthly Review Press, 1978), reprinted in *Monthly Review*, 30 (7) (December 1978). On the American backing for the coup that toppled Allende in Chile, see also A. Sampson, *Sovereign State, the Secret History of ITT* (London: Hodder & Stoughton, 1973).
24. N. Chomsky and E. S. Sherman, *The Washington Connection* (Nottingham: Spokesman, 1978). Note in particular the illuminating picture of 'the Sun and its Planets' on the inside cover of the book. This gives statistics on US financial backing and army training for countries using 'torture on an administrative basis in the 1970s'. In Chile, a group of economists which came to power with Pinochet were dubbed 'the Chicago Boys' because many of them had studied at Chicago University under Milton Friedman, guru of neo-liberal economics (see S. Branford and B. Kucinsky, *The Debt Squads, the US, the Banks and Latin America* (London: Zed Books, 1988) p. 85.
25. E. Galeano, *op. cit.*, note 23, p. 21.
26. Jackie Roddick presents figures for the respective shares of public and private net inflows into the region between 1961–78. In the period 1961–5, banks contributed but 2.1 per cent of a total of US$1.6 billion, while public flows (bilateral and multilateral lending) contributed 60.2 per cent. In 1978, of a total of US$21.8 billion, public flows contributed a mere 7.3 per cent while banks contributed the lion share of 56.6 per cent. See J. Roddick, *The Dance of the Millions, Latin America and the Debt Crisis* (London: Latin America Bureau, 1988) pp. 27–8.
27. Quoted in J. Roddick, *ibid.*, p. 65.
28. See Branford and Kucinski, *op. cit.*, note 24, especially Chapter 9, 'Reaganomics against Latin America'.
29. J. Petras, 'Chile and Latin America', *Monthly Review*, 28 (9) (February 1977) pp. 13–24, p. 17.
30. *Ibid.*, p. 18.
31. A term originally coined by G. O'Donnell in *Modernization and Bureaucratic-Authoritarianism. Studies in South American Politics* (Berkeley: University of California Press, 1973).
32. See in particular F. Cardoso and E. Faletto, *Dependency and Development in Latin America* (Berkeley: University of California Press, 1979), especially their introduction to the American edition.
33. D. Green, *Silent Revolution, op. cit.*, note 11, p. 164.

34. See especially N. Bobbio, *Democracy and Dictatorship* (Minneapolis: University of Minesota Press, 1989), and D. Held, 'Democracy, the Nation-state and the Global System', in D. Held (ed.), *Political Theory Today* (Oxford: Polity Press, 1991). Both are referred to in D. Slater's excellent review of the region's new social movements, D. Slater, 'Power and Social Movements in the Other Occident', *Latin American Perspectives*, issue 81, 21(2) (Spring 1994) pp. 11–37.
35. D. Held, *ibid.,* p. 231.
36. R. T. Naylor, *Hot Money and the Politics of Debt* (Toronto: McClelland & Stewart, 1987) Chapter 22.
37. J. Roddick, *op. cit.*, note 26, p. 109.
38. In 1982, Ronald Reagan launched a new project 'exporting democracy world wide', setting up a special organisation for the purpose. The function of the National Endowment for Democracy (NED) was to distribute government money to citizens, organisations and unions fighting for the 'restoration of democracy in totalitarian countries' or in countries where democracy is still precarious', see *International Labour Reports*, issue 13 (January/February 1986) p. 7.
39. Eduardo Galeano gives a vivid description of this in the new edition of *Open Veins of Latin America*:

> *To operate effectively, the repression must appear arbitrary.* Apart from breathing, any human activity can constitute a crime. In Uruguay torture is applied as a routine system of interrogation: anyone may be its victim, not only those suspected or guilty of acts of opposition. *In this way panic fear of torture is spread through the whole population, like a paralyzing gas that invades every home and implants itself in every citizen's soul. . . Each crime builds horrible uncertainty in persons close to the victim and is also a warning for everyone else. State terrorism aims to paralyze the population with fear.*
>
> Galeano, *op. cit.*, note 23, p. 32. [Emphasis in original]

40. Cited in J. G. Castañeda, *op. cit.*, note 2, p. 202.
41. J. G. Castañeda, *ibid.,* p. 197.
42. There is a plethora of statistics on the region's economic decline and increased poverty over the whole of the period from 1970–95. Here, I mention just a few salient facts of the critical period in the 1980s when structural adjustments were imposed:

- In the period 1980–8, the combined GDP for Latin America and the Caribbean declined by 6.6 per cent. Add to this the losses incurred as a result of a deterioration of the terms of trade (−3.0 per cent) and those due to resource transfers out of the region (−6.0 per cent), and the fall in per capita income was 16 per cent over the period. Meanwhile the rate of inflation rose from 46.0 per cent in 1978–9 to 336.0 per cent in 1987–8. Breaking down the decline in per capita income by two sectors: owners of capital and workers, their

- Absolute Poverty: Between 1980–9 the estimated number of the
absolute poor in Latin America increased from 136 million to 183
million. See C. Reilly, *New Paths to Democratic Development in
Latin America* (Boulder, Col.: Lynne Rienner) p. 5. By 1993 the
figure had risen to over 200 million or 46 per cent of the total
population (D. Green, *op. cit.*, note 11, p. 202).

43. S. Ellner, 'Introduction', in B. Carr and S. Ellner (eds), *The Latin
American Left: From the Fall of Allende to Perestroika* (Boulder, Col.:
Westview Press, 1993).
44. Cf. D. Green, *Silent Revolution, op. cit.*, note 11, p. 188.
45. *Ibid.*, p. 192.
46. R. Munck, *Politics and Dependency in Latin America* (London: Zed
Books, 1985) p. 117.
47. Cited by C. Reilly (ed.) in his Introduction to, *New Paths to Democratic Development in Latin America, the Rise of NGO–Municipal
Collaboration* (Boulder, Col.: Lynne Rienner Publishers, 1995) p. 1.
48. J. G. Castañeda, *op. cit.*, note 2, Chapter 7, 'The Grass Roots Explosion'.
49. J. Daudelin and W. E. Hewitt, 'Churches and Politics in Latin America: Catholicism at the Crossroads', *Third World Quarterly*, 16 (2)
(1995) pp. 221–36, p. 224. Note the decline of these groups in recent
years which these authors blame in part on the Vatican's response
(stimulated also by the contemporary Protestant Evangelical invasion)
and partly by the general failure of the Catholic left to firmly set the
social agenda of the Church. They argue that today there is developing
something more akin to a throwback to traditional state–church
relations.
50. P. Berryman, 'Basic Christian Communities and the Future of Latin
America', *Monthly Review*, 36 (3) (July–August 1984) pp. 27–40, p. 28.
51. *Ibid.*, pp. 29–30.
52. J. G. Castañeda, *op. cit.*, note 2, p. 223.
53. H. Oporto, *La Revolución democrática: una nueva manera de pensar
Bolivia* (La Paz: Los Amigos del Libro, 1991), cited in D. Slater, *op.
cit.*, note 34, p. 23.
54. C. Reilly, *op. cit.*, note 42, p. 13.
55. Food rioting and the deterioration of the urban poor led the World
Bank in 1990 to initiate a series of social emergency programmes in
some Latin American countries to cushion the worst effects of the
structural adjustment programmes. As Reilly observes, 'these emergency funds occasioned the Bank to begin dealing directly with
subnational political actors and NGOs – perhaps initiating new

patterns for a multilayered presence for the development bank in the region', C. Reilly, *ibid.,* p. 14.

56. A recently published Guide to Directories of NGOs by the Inter-American Foundation refers to over 11 000 Latin American NGOs. Various contributors in C. Reilly's edited volume trace the interactions between NGOs and their financial backers with the municipal authorities.

57. Cf. C. Reilly, *op. cit.,* note 42, p. 263.

58. J. S. Jacquette, 'Conclusion', in J. S. Jaquette (ed.), *The Women's Movement in Latin America* (Boston: Unwin Hyman, 1989).

59. The best-known example was the 'Madres de la Plaza de Mayo' in Argentina, the mothers of the disappeared who rallied for years in downtown Buenos Aires. They became a symbol not only of the 'need to know' but of the necessity for Argentine society to come to terms with the dirty war. There were other such groups in other countries, for example the 'Confederation of Widows' of Guatemala, see J. G. Castañeda, *op. cit.,* note 2, p. 227.

60. The emancipatory story of Domitla Barrios de Chugara, leader of the Housewives Committee of the Siglo XX Mines in Bolivia, became world famous, partly also as an example of the power of the ethnographic methodology in which Latin American scholar intellectuals went out of their way to record the authentic voice of the people; cf. D. Barrios de Chungara (with M. Viezzier), 'Let Me Speak' (New York: *Monthly Review,* 1979) (see also 'Excerpts', in *Monthly Review,* 30 (9) (February 1979).

61. F. Calderon (ed.), *Los Movimientos Sociales ante la Crisis* (Buenos Aires: CLASCO, 1986). Cited in A. Escobar, 'Imagining a Post-Development Era? Critical Thought, Development and Social Movements', *Social Text,* 31/32 (1992) pp. 20–55, p. 32.

62. A. Escobar, *ibid.,* p. 33.

63. A. Peterson, 'Social Movement Theory', *Acta Sociologica,* 32 (4) (1989) pp. 419–26, cited in D. Slater, *op. cit.,* note 34, p. 29.

64. A. Escobar, *Encountering Development: the Making and Unmaking of the Third World* (Princeton: Princeton University Press, 1995) p. 221.

65. R. Mangabeira Unger, *False Necessity, Anti-necessitarian Social Theory in the Service of Radical Democracy* (Cambridge, MIT: Cambridge University Press, 1987) p. 362. See also his *Social Theory: Its Situation and its Task* (Cambridge: Cambridge University Press, 1987). Although Unger acknowledges no debt to Foucault, the message and the effort of his anti-enlightenment project is much the same as that of other postmodernists. Where he differs, however, is in the illusion of revolutionary reformism in which the development of new partipatory democracy can be a path of cumulative institutional innovation which can reconcile objectives of economic growth with the overcoming of the present brutal inequalities.

66. A. Escobar, 'Imagining a Postdevelopment Era', *op. cit.,* note 61, p. 27.

67. A. Escobar, *Encountering Development, op. cit*, note 64, p. 219.
68. *Ibid.*, p. 216.
69. A. Escobar, 'Imagining a Postdevelopment Era', *op. cit.*, note 61, p. 44.
70. D. Slater, *op. cit.*, note 34, p. 29.

Conclusion

1. P. Kennedy, 'The Global Gales Ahead', *New Statesman/Society* (3 May 1996) pp. 28–9.
2. Many of such positive grassroots strategies are documented in M. Barratt Brown, *Africa's Choices* (London: Penguin, 1995); and W. Rau, *From Feast to Famine, Official Cures and Grassroots Remedies to Africa's Food Crisis* (London: Zed Books, 1991).
3. F. Cardoso, 'The Consumption of Dependency Theory', *Latin American Research Review*, 12 (1977) p. 20.
4. A. Hoogvelt, 'Prospects in the Periphery for National Accumulation in the Wake of the Cold War and Debt Crisis', in B. Gills and S. Qadir (eds), *Regimes in Crisis* (London: Zed Books, 1995) pp. 72–81. See also C. Hines and T. Lang, *The New Protectionism* (London: Earthscan, 1993).
5. A. Quijano, *Estética de la Utopía, David y Goliath* (Lima: Sociedad y Política Ediciones, 1990) p. 37; quoted *passim* in A. Escobar, *Encountering Development, The Making and Unmaking of the Third World* (Princeton: Princeton University Press, 1995) p. 221.
6. Cited *passim*, in G. Mulgan, 'Creating a Twin Economy', *Demos*, no. 2, 1994.

Index

Printed in the United States
20516LVS00007B/32